Self-Esteem: A Family Affair

by Jean Illsley Clarke

Harper & Row, Publishers, San Francisco

New York, Grand Rapids, Philadelphia, St. Louis
London, Singapore, Sydney, Tokyo, Toronto

1817

Library of Congress Catalog Card Number: 78-50385
ISBN 0-86683-615-2 (previously ISBN-0-03-043916-7)
Printed in the United States of America

Illustrators:
Amy Salganik—Chapter pages
Terry Boles—Worksheet pages

Harvey Finkle—Cover photo

90 91 92 BANTA

To my family and yours

Preface

I wrote this book because I needed it myself when my children were little. Now they are big, and I still need it. My neighbor, Ryan, is little, and maybe his parents need it too. Ryan was born three years ago in October. All winter long as I drove past his house, I thought about his mother. She had worked full time before he was born, and she knew only a few neighbors.

I remembered when I first moved into this neighborhood, years earlier during a December snowstorm that seemed to last until May. My daughter went to nursery school and brought home mumps, chicken pox, German measles, and colds. She gave them to the baby. He had mumps, chicken pox, German measles, and colds, and I had the blues. Their father was out of town most of the time. Early in March, I bought a pot of red tulips. Survival tulips I called them. "If only spring would come," I thought. It did, and with it came friendly neighbors and good health. I looked forward to the days once again.

"What was it like for Ryan's mother?" I asked myself. When I stopped to see her, we talked about how great Ryan was—active, smiling, busy Ryan. In September she went back to work. Maybe that year was fine for her.

For me, those years could have been better. I needed better ways to take care of my children and myself, to build positive self-esteem in my family. I began to meet with groups of people who also wanted better ways to build self-esteem in their families. During the three years since the first group met, many people have contributed ideas and methods. Mothers, fathers, grandparents, foster and adoptive parents contributed as did part-time parents—sitters, nursery school teachers, people who care for children in their homes, nurses, ministers, social workers, and other people who care about children's and their own self-esteem. The experiences of many of these people are included in the family stories in this book.

The ideas and tools that were most helpful to these people include ways to practice alternative methods of parenting, some Transactional Analysis tools, affirmations for positive emotional development, and recycling (the theory that we have developmental cycles with recurring chances to resolve old as well as new problems).

The people I have met care about their families but often wish they had better ways or more options for dealing with individual family members and family situations. This book encourages people to claim their own strengths and to make their own decisions about appropriate child care, and it provides some tools for adults to get their own needs met. Based on the belief that people whose needs are met give better child care than people who are needy, this book will provide tools and options rather than one more round of "shoulds" about child care.

The book is based on the following assumptions:
1. Parenting is important.
2. The birth or adoption of a child is a major event in family life.
3. Some parts of our culture discount—do not take into account—the impact of the addition of a child and the importance of child rearing.
4. When we gave up extended families, we gave up one kind of support system and most parents are not assured of a support system (especially when their babies are little or when they move). We need to build a replacement.
5. All people who care for children—parents, day-care people, teachers, relatives, sitters, bus drivers—can offer self-esteem building messages to children.
6. Positive self-esteem is important for children, for adults, and for our culture.

How to Use This Book

The suggestions in this book are offered as a buffet table of options. You can trust your own judgment to know which tools will be helpful for you to use.

The people with whom I have been meeting wanted some information on emotional developmental tasks, some ideas and theories about what people need, some optional ways of saying and doing things, and lots of chances to practice. The book is built around these topics.

Ways of offering positive self-esteem for different ages and information about emotional developmental tasks are included in the stories and reviewed in the Parenting Tips information sheet at the end of each chapter. The family stories include sections on theory and the Glossary offers a ready reference for a short review of theories. Optional ways of saying and doing things are reported in the stories and expanded in the reference sheets at the end of each chapter. You can use these sheets to think through how to use the ideas in each chapter in your own family. Practicing alternative ways of doing and saying things in the exercises gives you a chance to try on ideas, to think how they fit for you.

Male and female children are equally important, so the theory sections of this book use male pronouns in half the chapters and female pronouns in the other half.

I hope that you will not choose to hear the ideas in this book as one more list of parenting "musts" but that you will dialogue with them. All parenting is based on beliefs and values that have helped us make sense out of our lives. Our lives differ and our beliefs and values will differ and we do not all have to agree. Let us say, for example, that you have decided to improve your ability to give constructive criticism. When you practice one of the Four Ways of Parenting exercises at the end of a chapter and you read an example of teaching morals or providing structure that does not agree with your value system, you can change the example! You can put in your own value system and still use the exercise to increase your skill.

The information in the Parenting Tips information sheets is taken from Pam Levin's *Becoming the Way We Are*, Dorothy Babcock and Terry Keepers' *Raising Kids OK*, all of the readings in the Bibliography, and the personal experience of living with three children and their friends. The tips are offered not as a recipe for raising children but as a composite of the best information, ideas, and experiences of the participants in the parenting groups where the tips were tested and revised. I invite you to examine them, think about them, try them out, enjoy them, improve upon them and use them to increase your happiness and your children's happiness.

I want you to use this book as a source of support for yourself. Please do not use it as a source of "shoulds" to demand of or blame on other people. I know that I can show my children positive self-esteem in myself and that I can affirm and invite them to feel positive about themselves. No one can "make" another person feel positive self-esteem. No one can force a spouse to change. We can only change ourselves and invite others to do so also.

I assume that you are interested in building positive self-esteem or you would not be reading this book. If you have not previously tried affirming or visualizing, and you want to use these methods, find time and ways to use them that will fit into your life. If you have to do some rearranging in order to carve out time for yourself, go ahead—it will benefit you and the people you live with. Claim the good things you are already doing; affirm your ability to love and to grow; make your own decisions about the ideas in this book; and become the kind of caring person you know you are. Read and enjoy!

People who want to facilitate a group learning experience based on this book will find help in the leader guide written by Jean Illsley Clarke. Available from Winston Press, Self Esteem: A Family Affair Leader Guide *includes detailed instructions for eight sessions.*

Self-Esteem: A Family Affair—Beliefs

List your beliefs about families.

Compare your beliefs with those on which this book is based. These beliefs are listed below.

Families are important.

The addition of a person (by birth, adoption, foster care, or remarriage) is a major event in family life. So is the leaving of any person.

Some parts of our culture are discounting the impact of the addition or loss of a child and of child rearing. (Example: Articles that imply that women working outside the home have more fulfillment than women who are rearing children full time. Or, the boss who expects a man to travel out of town the week his baby is due.)

When we gave up extended families, we gave up one kind of support system, and parents in nuclear families are not assured of a support system. We need to build new systems.

Parents are important people and so are all of the other people who care for children!

Children are important people, and children deserve caring adults whose needs are met.

Effective parenting can be learned by adults of any age.

Positive self-esteem is important for children and adults.

Table of Contents

1

Families Come in Different Sizes,
and Any One of Them
Is the Place to Build Positive Self-Esteem

Families come in different sizes and ages and varieties and colors. What families have in common the world around is that they are the place where people learn who they are and how to be that way. Families don't have to look any certain way or do any certain things. They just have to be.

I don't believe that there is such a thing as an ideal family, a broken family, or even a good family. I believe that there are different families and that they offer people different things. The family members decide whether the families are good or bad or whole or broken. And nobody can foretell what individuals will decide about their families. Religious leaders can't foretell, and the National Health, Education and Welfare Department can't foretell, and social workers can't foretell, and the Greater Metropolitan Family Education Association and the Extended Rural Human Services Board can't foretell. None of these can foretell how individuals will feel about their families. Agencies can offer research, assistance, and theory about how families can improve the ways they treat each other. Only the people who live in the families can decide if the families are good or bad or whole or broken.

Any of the people in any of the families can improve the quality of the living experiences they are offering to each other and to themselves at any time.

What Six People Are Doing About Their Families

Dale and Judi Hammel are improving their attitudes about teenagers. They don't especially like teenagers; they have heard a lot of bad things about young people recently. They have three girls who will soon be teenagers, so Judi and Dale are doing volunteer work with a group of teens in a community recreation project. Dale and Judi believe that if they learn about adolescents and improve their own attitudes towards teenagers, they will provide a more positive environment for their daughters.

1

Greg Brand and his son Bruce are constantly at odds about the family car. Greg would like Bruce to be more considerate and appreciative. Bruce takes the car without asking and leaves it without gas. The father's lectures on attitudes have not had the desired effect on Bruce. In fact, they don't seem to have had any effect at all. Greg has decided to make some fair and very firm rules about the use of the car which he will abide by and which he will demand that Bruce conform to. Greg is starting to improve the quality of experience that the family offers Bruce and himself by changing his own behavior. He will stop pleading and start firmly insisting.

Marcia and Dennis Olson are changing the way they talk to their son Paul. Paul is a bright, alert boy, but his nursery school teacher has noticed that he frequently refuses to try new things. When she offers activities that the children have not done before, Paul says, "I can't do that. I'm too dumb."

If the teacher gently chides Paul for negative behavior or for not doing something as well as he is able, he says, "That's because I'm a nuthead." The nursery school teacher reported Paul's remarks to Marcia and Dennis. They decided to find out why Paul might consider himself dumb.

As Marcia and Dennis listened to themselves talk to Paul, they noticed that both of them frequently reprimanded him by saying, "Paul, that was a dumb thing to do" or "Paul, that is a nutty way to act." They hadn't meant anything serious by these statements. But just in case Paul is saying he is dumb because of these remarks, they are changing the way they talk to him about what he does. Now when Paul makes a mistake, his parents say, "Not that way, Paul. Do it this way instead."

Sandy Hillstrom has just returned from a visit to her childhood home which she hasn't seen for several years. While she was home, Sandy bumped up against some of the values, rules, and expectations with which she was raised. She has been so busy raising her children and working that she had not examined her values and beliefs about children and parents for weeks. Or was it years? Now she is thinking through her beliefs so she can look at what she is offering her family and herself. She will see if it is consistent with what she really believes or whether it is leftover, unexamined behavior that gets her through each day but doesn't reflect her beliefs.

> *Dale, Judi, Greg, Marcia, Dennis, and Sandy are improving what they offer their families in different ways—Dale and Judi by examining attitudes, Greg by changing behavior, Marcia and Dennis by changing the words they use, Sandy by considering underlying values and beliefs. What they all share is a common belief that families and what they offer to each other are far too important to be left to chance.*

*When people talk about what they want to improve in their
families, several topics come up again and again:* **self-esteem,** [1]
*values, trust, love, discipline, responsibility, control and structure,
handling peer pressure, and understanding stages or developmental tasks. Self-esteem includes each of these topics in some way.*

Why Is Positive Self-Esteem Important?

*Positive self-esteem is important because when people experience
it, they feel good and look good, they are effective and productive,
and they respond to other people and themselves in healthy, positive, growing ways. People who have positive self-esteem know
that they are lovable and capable, and they care about themselves
and other people. They do not have to build themselves up by tear-
ing other people down or by patronizing less competent people.*

*Positive self-esteem is not to be confused with self-centeredness,
machismo, being a braggart, or acting superior, all of which are
attempts to hide negative feelings of self. "You are important as
long as you act tough, accomplished, or smart" is a negative, un-
healthy central message around which to organize one's life. "You
are a worthwhile person" is a positive, healthy message.*

Who Needs Positive Self-Esteem?

The Hammels think their three daughters need positive self-esteem. That's
one reason Judi and Dale are examining their own negative attitudes toward teenagers. Greg Brand has enough positive self-esteem to decide that
he doesn't need to spend hours arguing and feeling bad about his son or
the car. Marcia and Dennis Olson want Paul to have the confidence in his
own ability that comes from positive self-esteem. Sandy decided that self-
esteem is important, and she is considering how she fosters it in each of
her family members.

*Lots of people believe that self-esteem is important for children but
what about for adults? Can adults show children how to have
positive self-esteem if they don't have it themselves? Does self-
esteem play a role in physical health or in the severity of postpartum depression?*

Bill's parents are divorced, and he never knew his dad. Bill, who is scared
that he won't be a good parent, experienced worse baby blues than his wife
did after Stacy was born. He believes there is more to postpartum blues
than hormones and fatigue

Does the self-esteem of the adults play a role in child battering? One woman reported that she hit her child only when she was feeling bad about herself. What is the self-esteem level of a man while he is beating a woman? Or of the woman who allows herself to be beaten repeatedly?

Self-Esteem: A Family Affair

Self-esteem is a family affair. Because the family is the first place we decide who we are and observe and practice how to be that way. To the extent that we decide we are lovable and capable, we build positive self-esteem. Therefore, the parenting or nurturing that we give and receive in the family is important. During the formative years of a child's life, the parenting or nurturing and the offering of values are done by the original mother or father, by the new parent in a remarriage, by an adoptive or a foster parent, a day-care person, a grandparent, an older sibling and/or that ubiquitous new parent, the television set. Whatever the sources, parenting or nurturing is important. It is important for young children because it allows them to live, whether poorly or well. It is important for adults because it impacts not only the most obvious parts of their life styles, but also the very core of their beings—their own self-esteem.

Some aspects of society are not supportive to esteem building and give more prestige, power, and status to people for making money than for nurturing and sustaining families. And this is done without a lot of regard for how the making or spending or investing of that money impacts the quality of family life.

Currently, in many parts of the country, people are segregated by age. Some apartment houses don't allow children. Some nursery schools won't combine three and four year olds. Mixing kids of different ages in elementary classrooms is considered experimental and, therefore, suspect. Young couples from four different states find houses on a street lined with families the same ages as theirs. Grandma and Grandpa are moving to Retirement City and Great-Grandma is in a nursing home with sixty-four other geriatric cases. Mobility has a lot of advantages, excitements, and interests; but it is difficult to raise children in anonymous communities where people call the police instead of the parents when kids misbehave and where the constant interaction with people of all ages is limited or missing. This lack of cross-generational contact leaves gaps in our knowledge of how life is for people of different ages and of how to cope with the next set of problems in our own lives.

4

So we make do without the valuable cross-generational contact, or we fall back on the uneven teachings of television, that ever-present source of cultural information and living-color-video-values. For those of us who do not have an extended group of people living near us who care about our family in a committed, ongoing manner, the task of helping family members discover who they are and how to be that way is flung back onto the family unit with a force that can be perplexing or even overwhelming.

So this is where we are, and however we live, we can find better ways to build strong, functioning families. No matter who we are, while we do whatever we can to make our institutions more supportive and humane and to find new networks to replace extended family ties, we can each start, right now, to assess and improve the quality of living experiences we offer to ourselves and the other people in our immediate families.

What Contributes to Positive Self-Esteem?

We build our own brands of self-esteem from four ingredients: fate, the positive things life offers, the negative things life offers, and our own decisions about how to respond to fate, the positives, and the negatives.

Fate determines some very important items in our lives. That Marie was born female, Black, in Rochester, Minnesota, to her particular family on her particular birthday is not something she can change. Nor can she control the fact that she is firstborn in her family, that her mother is extremely beautiful, that her parents surround her with books, or that an airplane crashed into her house. What Marie can do with her fate is to make decisions about it and attempt to make sense out of it.

Neither fate nor decisions can be determined by other people in her life. No one can change fate, and although parents may tell their children what decisions to make, children have a way of thinking their own thoughts and making their own decisions. These decisions may be stated openly or may be revealed through repeated behavior. "I want my son to be a professional ball player. He was outstanding in Little League! But for the past three years he's been sick on the day for the high school baseball tryouts and didn't make the team." Many of us have experienced the difference between decisions we tell our children to make and decisions they actually make.

How Can We Offer Positive Self-Esteem to Children?

Since we can't control fate or force decisions, what about the other two ingredients of self-esteem: life's positive and life's negative offerings? These are the areas in which adults have great power and opportunity to impact self-esteem. All of the time that children are with us, we set a rich buffet of positive and negative messages or rewards from which children may choose building blocks for their own self-image.

Positive Offerings for Doing

Positive offerings for being capable and for doing well *are self-esteem building blocks that each of us needs every day of our lives. They come in great variety. The "You did that well!" message[2] is important, whether it is praise for a baby grasping a block, a comment on the height of the block tower built by an older child, or a remark on how fast the child can knock the tower down again. Telling an older child what a high jumper he is or telling the baby he can yell louder than anybody else can be a self-esteem building message if the message is delivered in an admiring tone.*

"You are capable!" is an important message to offer children at every age. Telling the baby he is clever for learning to call you by crying when he needs dry pants, complimenting a seven year old for figuring out what to take with her to play with in the car, commending the sixteen year old for passing his driver's test are "You are capable" messages. The offerings change as the child grows, but the message remains the same—"You can do well."

If you count, you will probably find that you give dozens of "You did well!" messages in a day. I avoid using the word good *in the compliments because it has a special moral and religious meaning for many people. When Mr. Williams told Heidi to "be a good girl," she didn't know what he meant until she had been bad; then he told her what she should have done. Give children guidelines by telling them what you want them to do instead of telling them to "be good." And tell them what you like about their behavior instead of calling them "good children."*

Positive Offerings for Being

The positive offering that is equally important to the "You are capable" message that children need to hear is "You are important and lovable just because you exist."[3] This self-esteem building block is a gift that the child does not have to earn. We give this gift when we say, "Hi! I'm glad to see you! . . . I love you! . . . How are you? . . . I'm glad you come to my house!" These and all of the other ways—through words, looks, or touch—that we let children know we are glad they were born are very important because these messages reinforce the belief that they are lovable.

Negative Messages Can Build Esteem

Sometimes adults have to send negative messages to children. Children deserve clear negative messages that tell them how to improve their behavior. If negative messages attack the child's being or define the child as incapable, they are destructive to self-esteem. "You dummy! You'll never make it!" invites the child to fail. Properly delivered, negative messages say to the child, "I care about you. You are a worthwhile person, and you can learn how to do things better." Saying "Stop that!" or "Don't do that!" or "Not that way!" does not invite a child to have positive self-esteem. However, a negative message given in a three-step manner can. Tell a child specifically what not to do and why and then give an alternative: 1. Don't do that . . . 2. because. . . . 3. Do this instead. . . .[4] This three-step process lets a child know that he is an important person capable of thinking and of taking care of himself. For example, say to a three year old, "Don't pull the kitty's tail because he may scratch you. I'll show you how to pet him gently. If you don't, I'll ask you to leave the kitty alone." This is more apt to produce a self-assured, gentle kitty-petter than is a screamed "Keep your hands off that cat!" Older children can be invited to think of their own alternatives. For example: "Don't throw that ball in the living room; it might break a window. You can find a safe toy to play with until we go outside." With both children and adults it is important not to tell them what you don't want unless you also tell them what you want them to do instead.

*There are two kinds of messages that do not help build positive self-esteem: **plastic** compliments and **"don't be" messages.** A plastic compliment is a compliment that starts out feeling good but ends up feeling bad. "You sound good for a kid who can't carry a tune," "That looks good considering you made it," or "I like you no matter what anybody says" are examples.[5] Some people call these plastic compliments "left-handed compliments." I think that is insulting to left-handed people, and I hope that we all give up using plastic compliments soon. A straight one feels better, and children deserve straight compliments.*

The most destructive message we can put on the buffet of life for children to choose from is a "don't be!" message. Who would deliberately say to a child, "Don't be!"? That is an invitation to suicide! But sometimes we carelessly say things that could be interpreted as "don't be!" messages by children, such as "Are you here again today?" or "If it weren't for you, I could be in Florida!" or "We planned on having three children, and now here is our little mistake!"[6] We might say these things without meaning them, but children often interpret our words literally.[7] It is not difficult to remember to say "I'm tired today" or "I need some time alone" instead of "I wish you kids were all somewhere else." We can be careful about the words we choose.[8]

Since children determine their self-worth from the decisions they make about their fate and the decisions they make about the positive and the negative messages they hear about who they are and what they do, adults can learn to offer a rich buffet of esteem building messages.

One way adults can improve the quality of positive and negative messages they offer is to practice the **Four Ways of Parenting** exercise. This is done by identifying one problem and responding to it in four different parenting styles: nurturing, structuring and protecting, marshmallowing, and criticizing.[9] The first two parenting styles build positive self-esteem. The latter two invite negative feelings about self.

Let us say that a child who was roller-skating broke a strap on his skate and skinned his knee. He comes crying to his parent. How will the four different parenting styles respond?

The soft, warm manner of parenting named **nurturing** in this exercise offers help and offers positive rewards for being. It affirms both the importance of the person, just for being, and the person's capacity to grow. For example: In the above situation, the nurturing parent might put a gentle hand on the child's shoulder and say words like "Oh, I'm sorry you hurt yourself."

The firm manner of parenting called **structuring and protecting** in this exercise offers support, protection, and ethical teaching. It also offers **positive rewards for doing well and for doing poorly**, and it expects the person to be capable and suggests ways to behave capably. Example: "We'll get new straps for your skates. Want me to help you clean your knee?"

The sweet but gooey manner of parenting called **marshmallowing** in this exercise may sound comfortable or seductive, but it is plastic or patronizing. It invites the person to be dependent, to stay stuck, or to assume that outside forces or other people are responsible for his life. Example: "Oh, dear, I was afraid that concrete was too rough for you to skate on."

The harsh manner of parenting called **criticizing** in this exercise offers negative rewards in a way that attacks the person, suggests ways to fail, and offers "don't be" messages. Example: "Clumsy! No more skates for you if you're going to break the straps! You're always falling and breaking things!"

There are a variety of other examples included at the end of each chapter in this book. Each situation is usually followed by four messages. If the problem situation is stated as if by a child, the four responses are given as an adult might give them. If the problem is stated by an adult, the responses are given as the adult might hear them in his or her own head.

To learn to recognize the responses of the four ways of parenting, one person can read all four messages or several people can role play the four different manners of parenting. Practicing all four types of responses allows people to hear and feel and decide which words and phrases to continue giving or to stop giving or to improve. Messages that are nurturing at one age may be marshmallowing at another age, so examples are given for different age groups. These role plays are not to be said to a child but are to be said, listened to, and thought through by adults for adult consideration.

The examples listed at the end of each chapter reflect the values of the author or other people who teach parenting classes based on this book. Every statement is only one example of the many different ways that a response can be given by the four different parenting types. You may not agree with the values reflected in the examples but you can learn to recognize and practice the four methods of parenting and substitute your own values and words. Since we adults respond in these ways not only to children but to other adults and to ourselves, each example has a description of the age or person with the problem so that the reader will know whether the messages were intended to be said to a six-year-old child, said to another adult, or said by the parent to himself in his own mind.

Many people who have used this Four Ways of Parenting practice method have reported that they are able to respond in all four ways but that the ways that are easiest to use are the ways in which they themselves were parented. This role play gives you an opportunity to recognize ways in which you have been parenting other people skillfully and to enjoy and to strengthen those ways. If you identify ways you have been parenting that you do not wish to continue, the role play offers you an opportunity to practice positive alternatives.[10]

What About Positive Self-Esteem for Adults?

While the adults earn the living, keep the households going, and provide all of the support that kids need—the driving, the school conferences, the skills, the clothing, the supervision, the worrying, the positive self-esteem building—who builds positive self-esteem in the adults? They themselves do, that's who! Some of them have already internalized a lot of positive self-esteem. But all adults need to add to that by getting self-esteem nourishment from other people.

It is the responsibility of adults to get positive self-esteem messages for themselves and to offer them to other adults. Sound like a big job? It doesn't take more time or energy than living with low self-esteem does. In fact, it takes far less of both, and it is much more exciting and fun than living in self-esteem poverty.

How do you build positive self-esteem in adults? In the same ways you do for children. Give yourself and others positive rewards for being, positive rewards for doing well, and appropriate negative rewards for doing poorly. Stop giving plastics or any kind of "don't be" messages to yourself or to others. If you realize you have said something that was plastic or sounded like a "don't be" message, take it back. Apologize, make a phone call, write a letter, do whatever you need to do to change the message. Messages people send are like kites—we can reel them back in and ask that the other person accepts our change of message. If plastics or "don't be" messages come your way, don't accept them, don't internalize them, don't believe them. Don't accept messages that damage your own self-esteem. It is much easier to improve or change your behavior when you believe you are lovable and capable.

In addition, be aware of the different messages that you hear in your own head and remember to turn up the volume on the messages that contribute to your positive self-esteem and to turn down

10

the volume on any message that encourages you to think negatively about your worth or ability. One way you can build your own self-esteem is to practice the four ways of parenting described earlier in this chapter and included in the worksheets at the end of each chapter.

You can improve the quality of messages you have in your head about being lovable and capable. For example, let us use the problem "I think I should be a better parent." Hear the warm supportive nurturing messages—"You are an important, caring, lovable person, and you can improve your ability to parent." Hear the strength and the how-to-do-it suggestions in the structuring and protecting messages—"I expect you to be a nurturing parent. Claim the ways you are doing an important job and identify the areas in which you need to improve. Get help if you need it. You can do it!" Hear and reject the siren song of the marshmallow inviting the parent to give up—"I think you're just fine the way you are. After all, you love your kids. And you did come from a broken family, so you couldn't be expected to know as much about parenting as a person from a normal home." Hear and reject the destructive gloom and doom and projections of the criticizing message—"You should be worried about being a better parent. What you did yesterday was really dumb! You keep that up, and your kids won't want to have anything to do with you."

Love yourself, appreciate your accomplishments, accept your mistakes, and change them without beating on yourself. Find some other people who will swap that kind of healthy relationship with you.

Can People Really Change?

Meanwhile, what's going on with those four families you met at the beginning of this chapter?

Dale and Judi were apprehensive when they first volunteered to work with the Teen Task Force. They didn't know quite what to expect from the kids. If Dale and Judi lived in a large extended family, they'd know a lot about teenagers because there would be cousins, nieces, and nephews moving in and out of teenage, showing and telling bits and pieces of the contemporary teenage experience. Dale and Judi don't live in an extended family. The Hammels gave that up generations ago and are glad to be out from under the bossiness of Grandpa Hammel, the complaints of old Aunt Myra, and the suspicious eyes of Uncle Harold and Aunt Agnes. But they also gave up their classroom for learning how people grow.[11] So Judi and Dale are finding another way to learn about teenagers. They are spending time with teenagers from other families, and it isn't as difficult as they thought it would be. What are they finding out?

So far they have observed that the kids often resist them but seem to lap up one-on-one approval, especially if other kids aren't watching. They hear the kids complain a lot about their parents—how unreasonable, out of touch, and arbitrary they are. They also hear kids delight when a parent has been mightily pleased about that kid's achievement. They notice that the kids like having adults other than their parents to check things out with, get approval from, or try to shock. They observe that peer pressure is important to the kids. And the kids seem to rely on peer pressure instead of self-esteem. The Hammels have changed their attitude toward teenagers from suspicion to interest.

And how is it with Greg and Bruce Brand and the family car? Greg worried about seeming unreasonable, but Bruce is following the rules and grousing less than before. Greg, however, is uneasy. He isn't spending as much time with Bruce as he did when they were feuding, and he misses that. Also, he has a sneaky feeling that he may have been using the car to keep some control over Bruce. He always prided himself on teaching Bruce to be responsible and independent, not to let others control him, so trying to control Bruce doesn't seem logical. Greg wonders if he has some of his own self-esteem tied up in controlling Bruce. If so, that won't help Bruce become independent. How do other dads handle this?

When Marcia and Dennis Olson first stopped calling what Paul did "dumb" and "nutty," they thought it was a superficial change. Now they realize how often they had been calling themselves and each other "dumb," even though the remarks had been in jest. The Olsons have decided that it's important to do less criticizing of each other and themselves. They give each other and Paul more compliments for doing things well, even though the old way of talking is more comfortable and the new way feels awkward.

Sandy Hillstrom has come up with a few problems. She discovered that she disagrees with her mother's teachings in some areas. But to her annoyance, she has been following some of those old rules because she feels guilty if she doesn't. Sandy is sorting through her own beliefs and values about behavior and responsibility.

Sandy made a list of all of the things that she learned when she was a little girl that "good mothers" do. She thought about each item on the list carefully and decided that at some time, to her mother or her grandmother or her father, the items on the list had made sense. But some of them no longer make sense in Sandy's environment. She went through the list and starred the items that she believes help her to be an effective mother to her children now. She crossed off the items that no longer seem to fit at all. She called those "buggy whip" items. The rest of the items she rewrote to keep the parts of them that were helpful and to update them so that they would help her and her children build self-esteem—be lovable, capable people who respect themselves and other people.[12]

Families come in different sizes and varieties, and any of the people in any of the families can improve the quality of living experiences that they offer to themselves and each other. You can use the exercises at the end of this chapter to explore the self-esteem building ideas in this chapter. The stories in the following chapters tell how the adults in several different families improved their own self images and offered "You are lovable and capable" self-esteem building messages to their children and to themselves at different ages and stages.

Notes

1. Words which have a special definition as presented in this book are set in boldface the first time they are used in this chapter. The definition of these words is given in the Glossary.

2. See the Rewards for Doing Well worksheet on page 18 for additional examples.

3. See the Rewards for Being worksheet on page 17 for additional examples.

4. See the Messages About Doing Poorly worksheet on page 19 for additional examples.

5. See the Plastics worksheet on page 20 for additional examples.

6. See the "Don't Be" Messages worksheet on page 21 for additional examples.

7. For additional reading see negative injunctions on pages 61–62 and 85–86 in *Scripts People Live* by Claude M. Steiner (New York: Grove Press, Inc., 1974). See also Robert Goulding, "New Directions in Transactional Analysis: Creating an Environment for Redecision and Change," *Progress in Group and Family Therapy*, ed. Clifford J. Sage and Helen Singer Kaplan (New York: Brunner/Mayer, 1972), p. 107.

8. To examine the kinds of messages you are sending, use Five Balloon worksheet on pages 22 and 23

9. See the Four Ways of Parenting description on page 14.

10. See the Four Ways of Parenting exercise on pages 15 and 16. See also *Four Ways of Parenting Description* and *Four Ways of Parenting Exercise* in Glossary.

11. Margaret Mead, *Culture and Commitment* (Garden City, N.Y.: Natural History Press, 1970).

12. See A Good Mother list and A Good Father list on pages 24-27.

Four Ways of Parenting Description

Nurturing

Invites a person to get needs met. Offers to help. Gives *permission to do things well*, to change, *to win*. AFFIRMS!

Recognizes and validates the personhood of the other as being important, having strength(s), having the capacity to grow, practicing self-control, being self-determining, having goals, being not intentionally hurtful or destructive, being loving and lovable.

Gives "I" messages about personal reactions to the other's behavior. Uses touch to say "I'm glad you're here. . . . I care about you. . . . I'm with you." Encourages others to get their needs met.

Descriptive words: *gentle, caring, supportive.*

Structuring

Shows or tells *how to do things well*, to change, *to win*. AFFIRMS!

Supports the other as a growing person who is capable and is building on strengths by offering choices, exploring alternatives and consequences, advocating traditions and ethics, demanding that preferred behavior be substituted for undesired behavior, setting conditions so others can be successful, removing obstacles. offering appropriate incentives, telling or showing ways to build skills and providing for practice and feedback, negotiating contracts and goals. Asks people to state what they want or need in a problem situation.

Descriptive words: *assertive, sets limits, demands performance, offers tools.*

Marshmallowing

Sounds supportive but invites dependence. Gives *permission to fail*. NEGATES!

Judges the other as weak and inadequate—lacking strengths, the ability to grow and learn, self-control, self-determination.

Blames other people, situations, or fate. Uses "You" messages: "You poor thing. . . . I'll do it for you. . . . You must have had a lucky/bad break. . . . There's nothing you can do."

Enables self-destructive behavior and leads the other person to wish for magic. Carries the other person's burden or invites a person to be responsible for other people's feelings.

Descriptive words: *smothers, subtly destroys, sticky, patronizing, seductive.*

Criticizing

Ridicules, tears down, shows or tells *how to fail*. NEGATES!

Judges the other as unacceptable by blaming and fault finding, comparing the person with others, using global words: "You always. . . . You never. . . ." labeling or name-calling, using "why" questions to accuse or trap the other, offering no solutions.

Encourages a person to do poorly or to do self-destructive acts. Assumes a person is responsible for other people's feelings. Uses touch in hurtful or punishing ways. Uses caustic, sarcastic, or cruel humor.

Descriptive words: *harsh, hurtful, blaming, shaming, discouraging.*

Four Ways of Parenting*

For any situation that requires parenting—advising and supporting—there are four possible ways of responding. Nurturing and structuring and protecting ways encourage positive self-esteem. Marshmallowing and criticizing ways tear down self-esteem. Below are situations. Each situation has a response given by a nurturing, a structuring and protecting, a marshmallowing, and a criticizing parent.

Read each of the four responses to each situation. Allow yourself to hear the positive and the negative implications of each. Rewrite each answer to fit your own value system where needed.

Parent Messages

Nurturing

This message is gentle, supportive, caring. It invites the person to get his or her needs met. It offers to help. It gives permission to succeed and affirms.

Marshmallowing

This message sounds supportive, but it invites dependence, suggests person will fail, and negates.

Structuring and Protecting

This message sets limits, protects, asserts, demands, advocates ethics and traditions. It tells ways to succeed and affirms.

Criticizing

This message ridicules, tears down, tells ways to fail, and negates.

Situation: Adult says, "I'm going to read a book called *Self-Esteem: A Family Affair*, and I don't really know if I'll find it helpful."

Nurturing

I hope it will be helpful, interesting, and fun.

Marshmallowing

Do you have to? I'm sure you know all that stuff already. Books can't teach you anything.

Structuring and Protecting

I trust you to think things through and to decide what will be helpful for you.

Criticizing

You shouldn't have to read a book. You should just automatically know how to run a family.

*See Glossary, pages 269-270, for further information.

Situation: Adult says, "I often get lost when I'm driving."

Nurturing

Getting lost doesn't sound very good.

Structuring and Protecting

Learn to read a road map and use one. Pay attention to street signs. Stop getting lost.

Marshmallowing

Well, lots of people get lost.

Criticizing

You never pay attention. You shouldn't be allowed to drive.

Situation: Eleven-year-old girl says, "I want to stay overnight with my girl friend. Her parents are out of town, but her sixteen-year-old brother will be there."

Nurturing

I know you want to have fun with your friend. She can come here for the night.

Structuring and Protecting

No, you can't stay overnight with your friend unless her parents are home.

Marshmallowing

Well, I don't think you should, but I suppose that just this one time would be okay.

Criticizing

Of course you can't go! What kind of parents would people think we are? Do you know what sixteen-year-old boys want?

Rewards for Being

On this and the following pages are examples of the five ways of rewarding or stroking or communicating with other people. You may look at the examples and use the Five-Balloon Strokes worksheet to record ways in which you are offering self-esteem building messages in your family. You can celebrate the ways in which you are doing well and make any changes that you want to make.

Statements

I'm lucky to know you!
You're a pleasure!
You are important.
You are unique.
I like to (see, hug, hold, rock, kiss) you.
I love you.
It's good to see you.
Good morning!
I'm glad I'm getting to know you.
I'm glad to share this (day, time, lunch) with you.
I'm glad you're here.
I'm glad you live in our house.
Glad you came today.
I enjoy you.
I enjoy being with you.
I like to sit by you.
I'm glad we're (riding, walking, playing, working) together.
I thought about you during the week.
I like you.
I'm glad you're in my (house, class, group, life).
I think you're a neat kid.
I'm glad you're my friend.
Will you play with me?
Thanks for being you.

Actions

smile
hugs, pats, kisses (if acceptable to the person)
handshake
listening to a person
sharing something important
spending time with the person
initiating contact
using a person's name

Rewards for being start at birth and help people of all ages live!

Rewards for Doing Well

Statements

Neat work.
Nice job.
I like the way you did that.
Much better, keep it up.
I like the way you wear your hair.
You have a good eye for color.
Thank you for picking up the papers
You're a good cook.
You're one great carpenter.
Wow, do you read fast!
Your work is impressive.
Fantastic painting!
I'm amazed at your improvement.
You're the fastest runner I know.
You make beautiful music.
Nice job of planning.
Great carry through.

I LIKE WHAT YOU DO.

FOR DOING WELL

You're a super (mom, dad, son, daughter, teacher, worker, entertainer, problem solver . . .).
I love the way you use your voice.
You think well.
You certainly are clever.
Thanks for the gift.
I like the way you listen.
I hear you did a great job. Congratulations!
What you said is very interesting.
I appreciate your support.
You're a good team member.
You encourage me to think.
You take great pictures.
You do know how to survive.
You put things together in an amazing way.
Thank you for being so patient.
I'm proud of the way you did that.
Excellent results!

Rewards for doing start at six months and encourage people of all ages to do things well.

Messages About Doing Poorly
Or, you are an important person
—here are ways you can improve!

Messages about doing poorly often sound like accusations or blaming. Examples: You forgot to shut the door. . . . You're late again. . . . You look sloppy. . . . You tracked mud on the floor. . . . You forgot my birthday. . . . Another F! . . . You don't make enough money. . . . You spend too much money. . . . Stop butting your nose into my affairs. . . . Clumsy! . . . NO SELF-ESTEEM BUILDING HERE!

Messages about doing poorly can build self-esteem when they honor the other person, show that you care enough to set limits, and invite the person to be a winner. Messages about behavior that you want changed can be given in a loving way. (Example: Don't do this . . . because you are important.) Or they can be given in a respectful way. (Example: Don't do this . . . because it may hurt you or someone else; you can figure out a better way to do it.) Or these messages can be given in a way that owns feelings. (Example: Don't do this . . . because I don't like it; do this instead.) The tone of voice must be respectful or loving, not sarcastic.

Statements

I resent your being late. You're an important member of this group. Do you want us to delay our meeting time?

Don't wear those pants to school; they're dirty. Put on clean ones.

Don't track mud on the floor. I just cleaned the floor, and I get mad when you track. Clean it up.

When you forget my birthday, I feel sad. Will you give me a present on my birthday?

Stop failing math—you can't go to summer school because we are all going on a long trip. Study an hour every night and turn this grade around!

When you interfere I get mixed up. Let me do this my way.

That's the third dish you've broken this week—you must be in another growth spurt. Will you carry the dishes extra carefully while you get used to your new size?

Messages about doing things incorrectly should start at eighteen months and should encourage people of all ages to do better. These messages should continue all the rest of our lives.

I DON'T LIKE WHAT YOU DID!

FOR DOING POORLY

Plastics

Statements

No matter what anybody says, I like you.

You're pretty good-looking for a bunch of librarians.

You are really good at math for a girl.

You run really fast for an old man.

You certainly look good considering your age.

You look nice. That has always been my favorite dress.

You cook well for a man.

How come you're so smart?

How come you *always* know the answer?

Oh you, you *never* make a mistake.

You always do *everything* so *perfectly*!

Everything you touch turns out to be beautiful!

I know you must be happy about being pregnant even though you walk like an awkward goose.

Positive rewards for being or rewards for doing can be turned into plastics by being said or done in a sarcastic way, by being insincere, by being patronizing, by being grandiose. (Example: Our little Millie is *the most marvelous* little cook.) Or, they can be changed by adding negative riders. (Examples: considering it's you . . . for a change

. . . finally . . . but when will you . . . but you should have . . . if only.)

Plastics should not be given at any age.

YOU THINK WELL FOR A GIRL!

PLASTIC

"Don't Be" Messages Or "Don't be who you are."

Statements

I never had migraines before I had you.

If I didn't have children, I would have time to read.

I wish you hadn't been born.

You could be replaced.

Your parents should have used birth control.

Get lost.

Drop dead.

If you hadn't been born, I could have had a career.

You were a mistake.

We planned to have three children, and then you came along.

Go play with knives.

Go play on the street.

If I hadn't married you, my life would be happy.

If you see a stork, hold it; I want to send this baby back.

I bet your folks were disappointed when they saw you.

Go away!

Are you here again?

Actions

constant ignoring

battering

acting and speaking as if the child were not there when the child *is* there

"Don't be" messages should not be given at any age.

Five Balloon Worksheet

Name __Kristen Baker__

Day __Tuesday__   Time __9:00 – 9:20 A.M.__

I LIKE YOU.

Hi!
How are you?
Would you like
to go with me
to the store?
BE.

I LIKE WHAT YOU DO.
You did a
great job of
pulling up weeds.
The garden looks better.
Thanks for the letter
you sent.
DO.

I DON'T LIKE WHAT
YOU DID.
You didn't finish
that gardening job!
After you stop, please
clean up and put
away your tools.

DON'T DO.

YOU THINK WELL
FOR A GIRL.
You must be the
best ball player in
the world! (Global!
Changed to:
You're fun to play
b ball with.)
PLASTIC

I DON'T WANT YOU
AROUND.
You again? What do you want?
(Took back and changed to:
Go and play for a while.)
DON'T BE.

Name _____

Day _____ **Time** _____

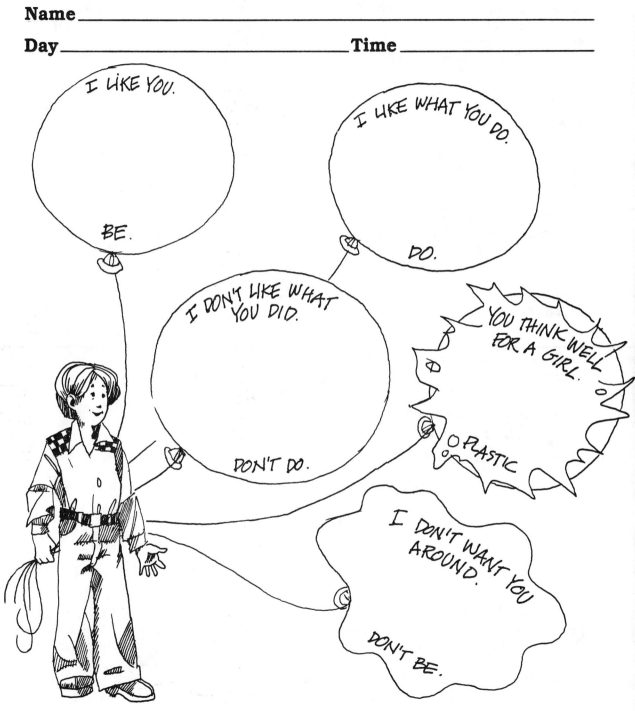

A Good Father . . .

(How John revised the list)

helps kids learn how to ride a bike
doesn't do homework
~~schedules~~ *helps out*
says "Don't put your elbows on the table."
reads stories *to the kids*
works a lot* *(but not all the time)*
drinks with his friends
keeps room clean
says "Don't eat mud."
says "If I say no I mean no."
doesn't do housework*
makes money to feed family
loves★ *when asked to explain*
explains ~~and explains~~
goes to church and Sunday school
goes to the basement ~~a lot~~ *to work on tools*
teaches children ~~not to pick their nose~~ *social rules*
helps with school work
makes sacrifices for clarinets and college
is ~~gone~~ *home* a lot*
is tired from working*
fixes anything
thinks to himself *and talks about it*
listens well★

is an active member of the family
is open about problems and solutions
helps around the house

reads the newspaper every morning
tells me I'm good at things like drawing,
    singing, dancing
~~makes me feel safe*~~ *protects me*
lets my friends come in to play
takes family on trips
doesn't touch kids, ~~leaves that to Mom~~
loves me all the time
takes me fishing
~~spanks~~ *provides discipline*
is quiet, doesn't talk much
is conservative *in some ways*
works hard
helps me★
believes in other people's concerns
spends time with children★
~~crabs a lot~~ *is crabby sometimes*
works with machines
earns the living*
is strong and silent
holds me★
disciplines the kids when he ~~gets home from work~~ *sees them do something that calls for discipline*
doesn't go away from me
gives me some rules
says I did well when I did★

The lists of things that "good mothers" and "good fathers" do were collected from groups of people. The items that are starred appeared on more than one list. Add your own items to the list and then update the entire list by starring the items that help you build positive self-esteem in yourself and your children, by crossing out any items that no longer fit, and by rewriting or adding any items you want to.

A Good Father . . .

helps kids learn how to ride a bike
doesn't do homework
schedules
says "Don't put your elbows on the table."
reads stories
works a lot*
drinks with his friends
keeps room clean
says "Don't eat mud."
says "If I say no I mean no."
doesn't do housework*
makes money to feed family
loves
explains and explains
goes to church and Sunday school
goes to the basement a lot
teaches children not to pick their nose
helps with school work
makes sacrifices for clarinets and college
is gone a lot*
is tired from working*
fixes anything
thinks to himself
listens well

reads the newspaper every morning
tells me I'm good at things like drawing,
      singing, dancing
makes me feel safe*
lets my friends come in to play
takes family on trips
doesn't touch kids, leaves that to Mom
loves me all the time
takes me fishing
spanks
is quiet, doesn't talk much
is conservative
works hard
helps me
believes in other people's concerns
spends time with children
crabs a lot
works with machines
earns the living*
is strong and silent
holds me
disciplines the kids when he gets home from
      work
doesn't go away from me
gives me some rules
says I did well when I did

A Good Mother . . .
(How Sandy revised the List)

~~doesn't have children who are obnoxious in stores~~

takes care of her children* *and herself*

keeps the house clean ~~at all~~ *most* times*

cooks for the family *often*

doesn't smoke*

thinks of her children ~~first~~ *whenever she can*

is an affectionate, warm, caring person ★

is right* *sometimes*

eats leftovers*

~~bakes = loves*~~

doesn't yell at kids

~~caters to Daddy~~ *respects Dad*

loves father ~~before~~ *and* kids

sings a lot

doesn't drink liquor* *too much*

~~is passive and always obeys her husband~~

is virtuous, religious*

chauffeurs kids

gives children lessons

~~is long suffering~~

works hard*

is self-sacrificing* *only when necessary*

keeps peace in the family

is fair ★

teaches her kids to do things by themselves

takes time to be alone, when she really needs it

~~spanks naughty children~~ *disciplines*

takes part in community activities*

loves her family ★

is ~~strict~~ *firm when she needs to be*

is overworked and underpaid

~~is always short on money~~

keeps things together

is there when kids are hurting

~~gives up her career for her family~~

is strong

~~saves~~ *sheds* her tears ~~for at night in bed~~

gets up with her family and makes breakfast for them

is home with her children enough to listen to them and to be an influence in their lives

~~is from~~ *builds* a happy marriage ★

fills in as a parent for other children who need parenting *if she wants to*

supports and is a team with her husband—

~~doesn't~~ disagrees *when she must*

~~takes care of children so they don't bother Daddy~~ *lets kids + Dad work it out*

entertains ~~whenever Dad wants to~~ *sometimes*

~~is always tired~~

talks over problems before they get too big to handle

is flexible

looks for a good babysitter for her kids

A Good Mother . . .

doesn't have children who are obnoxious in stores

takes care of her children*

keeps the house clean at all times*

cooks for the family

doesn't smoke*

thinks of her children first

is an affectionate, warm, caring person

is right*

eats leftovers*

bakes = loves*

doesn't yell at kids

caters to Daddy

loves father before kids

sings a lot

doesn't drink liquor*

is passive and always obeys her husband

is virtuous, religious*

chauffeurs kids

gives children lessons

is long suffering

works hard*

is self-sacrificing*

keeps peace in the family

is fair

spanks naughty children

takes part in community activities*

loves her family

is strict

is overworked and underpaid

is always short on money

keeps things together

is there when kids are hurting

gives up her career for her family

is strong

saves her tears for at night in bed

gets up with her family and makes breakfast for them

is home with her children enough to listen to them and to be an influence in their lives

is from a happy marriage

fills in as a parent for other children who need parenting

supports and is a team with her husband—doesn't disagree

takes care of children so they don't bother Daddy

entertains whenever Dad wants to

is always tired

2

Happiness
Is Having a Baby
and Other Cherished Notions

There has never been a baby like Jason! He is beautiful, special, unique, and surprising, and he has turned the Banner home upside down. He eats in the middle of the night when his mother, Julia, should be sleeping, and he sleeps in the middle of the day when Julia should be awake. He insists upon being walked at 6:00 P.M. when his father, Bernie, would like to read the evening paper and rest from all of the people he has been with during the day and Julia would like to interrupt his reading with household news, because she hasn't had any adults to talk with all day.

Jason is special and surprising because he's new and because he's here! The Banners have been wanting him and feeling scared about him since long before he started to grow. They are enormously proud of and excited about him. When Uncle Adolph, who thinks new babies look like wrinkled monkeys, came by and said, "Now that is a baby!" both Julia and Bernie were pleased. The grandparents are proud; Great-Aunt Elda sent a silver cereal spoon; the Hammels loaned a cradle; and the minister called.

The only problem is the colic. Jason cries so hard!

Of course everyone is very happy about Jason. Well, Julia and Bernie do get tired sometimes, but they had expected that. Their coming and going is restricted; they can't suddenly decide to take off for the weekend. But they had expected that also. What they had not expected was the colic!

Jason stiffens and screams until his face is crimson, and both Julia and Bernie feel scared! Only walking—fast, bumpy walking—soothes Jason. The moment they stop walking, Jason starts screaming again for the duration of the daily colic hour—or, more accurately, an hour and twenty minutes.

The screaming annoys and frightens Bernie. He is alternately irritated and perplexed by it. Julia seems to be such a good mother. "What goes on during the day while I'm gone?" Bernie wonders. "The fault can't be with Julia. Jason cries on the nights when I've been home all day, too." Sometimes Bernie toys with the idea of working late to miss the noise. "That's a tempting thought, but not fair," he concludes.

Julia is scared. "Why my baby?" she wonders. Julia was so sure she would be a good mother. Doctor Wellsley is frustratingly unconcerned, almost bored, with Julia's repeated pleas for help. "Jason is healthy," Wellsley says. "Walk him and wait. He'll grow out of it." Wait! Who can wait with that piercing wail and that scary stiffening?

Somehow, this wasn't what Julia and Bernie had expected. They talked with Francie and Ned Bauer who have just adopted two-month-old Jana. Jana doesn't have colic, but Ned and Francie talk about how tired they are and how they worry when Jana's breathing is jerky.

> *The Banners and Bauers have concerns that are shared by many families—"It doesn't turn out the way we expected. . . . How can we help our baby? . . . How can we help ourselves?"*

Somehow I Wasn't Prepared for This, or How Does a New Member Affect a Family?

> *The arrival of a new child in a family may be greeted with joy, but it also causes stress. Physical space must be shared; there are alterations in sounds and smells, and the financial impact can be frightening. Other people respond in new ways to the family, and family members have new feelings about themselves. The addition of a child by birth, adoption, or foster care is a major event in the life of any family. So is the loss of a child—by death, run away, termination of foster care, or growing up and leaving. Each of these events has impact on the self-esteem of each family member.*

> *Parents who give birth to their first child walk through a door in their own lives. They have to deal not only with their infant but also with their own internal expectations of what it means to be a mother or a father. Becoming a parent is an irreversible step. Even if the child does not live or is placed for adoption, the parents cannot go back to the personal space they lived in before the mother gave birth. The woman who adopts or marries a man with young children takes that step as surely as the woman who gives birth.*

> *The man who has made the adjustment to being a father rather than just a husband takes another irreversible step in his journey when he takes a foster child. Even if the child stays only a short time, the man has moved into that experience and can never again return totally to his previous position. Each of us has deep-seated expectations of what it means to be single, married, childless, parent, or grandparent, and when people have tasted any of those experiences, they can never go back.*

It's like travel. Once people have traveled abroad, they cannot return to the position of never having left their homeland. It is impossible, and the experiences and impressions of the travel will be with them for the rest of their lives, even if these experiences are not in their immediate awareness.

Where Do Families Get Support?

Who supports people on their various family journeys? Support comes from other families, from institutions, from individuals, and sometimes, if people are lucky, from their own families of origin. But often these families are not around. Grandma is in Northfield and the brothers and sisters are in Virginia or Colorado or abroad. A loving telephone conversation is not the same as having Grandma bathe the baby! And the one aunt who lives nearby is on a different wavelength. Often families with young children are coping with child rearing as best they can with the help of the coffee break and the car pool, the barber and the bartender. Caring for young children can be a lonely journey—for the parents at home, if they are alone with the children, missing the stimulation of the jobs they had before the babies came, and for the parents away from home, especially if they are constantly with people who do not care about families.

Bernie's boss may say, "I know your wife recently had a new baby, Bernie, and congratulations of course, fine things, children; but I hope the crying during the night does not interfere with your work. We are under a great deal of pressure right now and we expect. . . ." And Bernie may add his own expectations—"I'll work harder than ever, I'll show them that having a baby won't make any difference. And I'll be a good father, too; probably the best there ever has been."

Whatever the messages in Bernie's head about being a "good father" are, they are probably messages he has had for a long time, and they are likely to be charged with emotion. If he is scared about the responsibility for this new person—the money needs for his new family; the job of guiding another human being, emotionally, physically, and spiritually into a complicated world; any fear that he can't do it or do it well enough, or that his wife won't have as much time for him now—he can face those fears and come to terms with his new role or he can bury his fears under work or alcohol or both.

What of the father who isn't living with his children? When he wonders about how someone else is raising his child, when he has fears, what does he do with them? Where does he go for support?

Julia and Bernie had planned for Jason so long that they had everything ready before the baby's arrival. But they weren't prepared themselves—for the fatigue or the fear or the frustration or for the fact that sometimes they longed for someone to reassure and take care of them. Parents of young children need support from other adults—people who care, people who are willing to share information and experiences, and people who will give reassurance and encouragement. They need people who will help them cope with the baby, with themselves, and with their fears, hopes, and wishes.

Bernie and Julia Banner get some support from their friends, the Hammels. The Hammels supply, among other things, baby furniture and talk. The Hammel girls are six, nine, and eleven years old, and they are excited about holding Jason and giving him their stroller and crib. Judi Hammel calls Julia with advice and encouragement and assures her that Jason will grow up before she knows it.[1] But Julia and Bernie get most of their support from Francie and Ned Bauer. Before Jana came to the Bauers', Francie and Ned took a class about parenting taught by Francie's Aunt Sheila in which they used the concepts in *Self-Esteem: A Family Affair*. They learned about different kinds of **strokes**[2] and how to give them to children and to each other. The Bauers practice giving **affirmations** (confirming that a person is lovable and capable) and **visualizing** (imagining how we want people to be) to build positive **self-esteem** in Jana and in themselves. They often discuss with the Banners the importance of understanding the **four ways of parenting**[3] and the importance of strokes.

How Can We Build Positive Self-Esteem in Infants?

Three ways that adults can build positive self-esteem in infants are by giving them lots of positive strokes, by affirming their beings so they develop trust in themselves and in the world, and by visualizing them as having confidence in themselves.

Positive Strokes

Babies need food, water, air, protection, and strokes. Yes, strokes—being caressed, being sung to, being cuddled, being touched, being talked to, being rocked, being touched, being carried, being handled, being touched. In his helpful book Touching—the Human Significance of the Skin, *Ashley Montagu says, "Among the most important of the newborn infant's needs are the signals it receives through the skin, its first medium of communication with the outside world."[4] Babies who are not touched can experience depression, lack of appetite, weight loss, and death. This condition*

*is called **marasmus** or wasting away. Touching a baby's
skin stimulates growth, both physical and mental. So, if you want
your baby to grow up healthy and smart—cuddle her. Often.*

*The talking and touching that the baby gets are called uncondi-
tional strokes. They are **positive rewards for being**. The baby
does not have to earn them. She does not get them on the condition
that she behave in a certain way. She gets them just because she
is there. They are strokes for being and are very important since
the job of the infant is to decide to be. "To be, or not to be: that is
the question." If she gets enough care, if her needs are met, she
will decide to be, to trust her caretakers, to trust herself, and later,
to trust her world.*

*The frequency and quality of the strokes we give to infants are im-
portant because children define themselves in terms of the strokes
that they get.[5] Warm, tender, loving responses to a baby's cry will
invite her to decide that she can get her needs met, that she is OK.
There's lots of positive self-esteem in that. A grumpy, rough response invites her to decide that she is not OK and maybe that
other people are not very OK either. She may still decide to live, to
be, but it will be a less confident, less joyful decision. Not much
positive self-esteem in that.*

*Unlucky is the child who is told not to be. "I wish you had never
been born" is an invitation to a child to decide not to be. They are
"don't be" messages. She may end her life quickly with an au-
tomobile or slowly with alcohol or other drugs or she may live her
life without really being, by living only a small part of the life she
is capable of living. There's little positive self-esteem there.*

Julia and Francie were discussing positive strokes one day when the
postman delivered a package from Jana's Great-Aunt Sheila. She had embroidered engaging designs and messages on the quilt. The messages are
the **affirmations for being** that Aunt Sheila taught Francie and wants
Jana to be surrounded by. Each affirmation had its own block on the quilt:
"You have every right to be here, Jana. . . . Your needs are OK with
me. . . . I'm glad you're a girl. . . . You don't have to hurry. . . . I like to
hold you." Around the border, she had embroidered over and over in green
so it looked like a leafy design—"I'm glad you are here. . . . I'm glad you
are here. . . . I'm glad you are here."

Affirmations for Being

Affirmations are things we say to people or ways we treat them or things that we say about them that indicate how we expect them to act and to view themselves. Any time we credit another person verbally or nonverbally in a positive way, we affirm that person. For example: "Jim is a good problem solver" or "This boy is delightful." Any time we attribute a negative quality to a person we negate him. For example: "Jim is a dummy" or "Jim is our one who is not good at math" or "This kid is going to be a real heller." Negations also tell Jim who he is and how to expect to be treated.

The affirmations for being are from Pam Levin's book Becoming the Way We Are *and are the messages that people need to hear from birth on—*
1. *You have every right to be here.*
2. *Your needs are OK with me.*
3. *I'm glad you're a boy or a girl.*
4. *You don't have to hurry.*
5. *I like to hold you.*[6]

These are the bare bones of the messages. Parents flesh them out according to their own individual parenting styles and the age of the child.

Do infants "hear" the messages? Yes. They may not understand the exact words, but they get the meanings. These affirmations are core messages. They are given in many ways—directly and indirectly—by word, touch, attention, and care.

All of the preparations that Julia and Bernie made for Jason and that important fuss the family made over his arrival tell Jason that *he has every right to be here*, that they are glad he is here. Their delight with having a boy, the fact that they named him Jason (an unmistakable male name), and the proud way they call him son send him the message *We are glad you're a boy.*

Affirming a child's sex has nothing to do with sexism, with giving one sex preferential treatment over the other. That would happen if they later taught him that boys are smarter than girls or that boys should not cry. Jason needs to accept that it is great for him to be a boy if later on he is to accept that it's great for his sister to be a girl.

Julia and Bernie like to hold Jason very much. So he gets the message *I like to hold you.* Except maybe when they are in a hurry or when he has colic? *You don't have to hurry* means you don't have to hurry and grow up, be cute, learn to patty cake, sit up, crawl, grow hair. Some afternoons

34

Julia wishes very much that Jason would hurry and grow out of the colic though.

Your needs are OK with me means all of the needs. Julia is good at that. She feeds him when he is hungry and burps him when he is full. She easily changes diapers. Somehow she understands that all of his needs are OK. Except maybe the need to be walked when he has colic? Julia knows that she has to believe the affirmations or they won't work. Saying one thing and meaning another invites confusion rather than positive self-esteem.

Francie looks at the quilt squares and thinks that Jana's needs are OK with her. She is happy to have a girl. She definitely is not in a hurry for her to grow up and perform. After all, she waited so long for her baby. And she does love to hold her. But how can she be sure that she will know that *she has every right to be here*? Jana was adopted at two months. She may find it difficult to decide that she belongs in the Bauer family. Or she may wait a long time to be sure.

Francie and Ned have two things in their favor. One is that they are both completely sure that Jana has every right to be with them. The other is that human beings recycle developmental tasks.

> *The process of recycling is described by Pam Levin in* Becoming the Way We Are. **Recycling** *early developmental tasks means that people reexperience earlier developmental tasks in a more sophisticated form at a later age. For example, infants have high oral needs—they suck, taste, experience their worlds through their mouths. Thirteen year olds often recycle early oral needs as they eat continuously or seem to devour books or activities. They are replaying early oral needs. And if the needs were not adequately satisfied for the infant, the thirteen year old has the opportunity to get those needs satisfied, perhaps to decide more firmly to be.*

So if Jana doesn't believe that she has every right to be in the Bauer home immediately, Francie and Ned can continue to demonstrate that she does have that right and to expect that Jana will join them in that belief.[7] The issue is trust. When Francie and Ned let Jana make her needs known, let her tell them with a good loud cry that she needs them, and then respond immediately, when they figure out what she needs and give her what she needs so that she feels satisfied or comforted, they invite Jana to trust, to decide that it's OK to be. Deciding it's OK to be is the first step of positive self-esteem. And if a child decides to be and trust, if she feels a strong bond or attachment between herself and one or both of her parents, she will have the necessary groundwork for separation later on. That is another step in positive self-esteem.

The loving messages that Jason and Jana need to hear during their first six months are assurances we all need to hear in some way during later stages of our lives.[8]

Jason's teenage cousin Susan needs to know that *she has every right to be in this world* that seems unsure about how to treat its teenagers. She needs to be sure that *her needs are OK* even though sometimes she's not sure what her needs are.

Susan can be encouraged to separate her wants and her needs. She wants to listen to loud rock music; she needs to figure out who she is. She needs reassurance that her age and stage is all right and that *she doesn't have to hurry and grow up.* The culture is sending her mixed messages about how to be a girl.

While she is considering whether she wants to be a "Total Woman," a "Liberated Woman," or her own version of female, she needs extra assurance that *it is great that she's a girl.* She still needs to be held or touched, and since she has been fortunate, like Jason, to have been held lovingly in a non-seductive way ever since she was a baby, she has help separating her need to be touched from her new sexual urges.

It is unfortunate when a teenage girl does not know how to get affectional needs met, uses her sexuality to get some longed for love and affection, and then becomes pregnant, not because she is ready to be a mother but because she didn't know how to get affection without sex. She is then faced with an overwhelming nurturing job to do for her baby when she, herself, is in great need of affection and nurturing and is not ready to provide the twenty-four hour environment of love, care, safety, comfort, and encouragement necessary for a baby to be free to grow and develop.

Infants and teenagers are not the only ones who need to hear those five loving messages which affirm being. Jason's great-grandmother is eighty-four, senile, and living in a nursing home. She asks, "Are you sure it's all right for me to stay here? Are you willing to help me again today? I need so much help now." She needs to hear, "Yes, I am sure it's *OK for you to stay here.* We want you to stay. Yes, *we will be glad to help you* today. Are you ready to get dressed now? Let's find some beads for you to wear with that dress. There, *you look so feminine! There is plenty of time* to get your hair combed before breakfast."

And the nurse combs Grandma's hair and pats her arm. And Grandma needs every one of those loving messages, just as much as Jason and Susan do. We all do. *You have every right to be here. . . . Your needs are OK with me. . . . I'm glad you're a girl (or a boy). . . . You don't have to hurry. . . . I like to hold you.*

Visualization

To visualize is to close your eyes and imagine the child as if she has already accepted the affirmations. Look at her in your mind's eye and see her as she will appear when she knows that she belongs here and that her needs are OK, when she likes being a girl, when she knows that she can grow at her own pace and that people love to hold her. See her. Visualize her. Daily.

Why visualize? Because it helps the adults. It helps them give up old fears and admonitions. Adults who visualize their hopes for a child become more consistent in their own behavior. They stop saying things that negate the child.

When Bernie is walking Jason and Jason screams and stiffens, Bernie visualizes Jason healthy and comfortable. Bernie can see, in his mind's eye, Jason, smiling, alert, his eyes bright and interested, his body relaxed and moving naturally. As Bernie focuses on the visualization, his arms and chest relax a bit, and sometimes Jason's crying ceases.

These three gifts—strokes, affirmations, and visualizations—help adults lay the foundation for infants' positive self-esteem for competent, healthy, happy adult lives. Give lots of high quality positive strokes, give and live the affirmations for being, and practice visualization. Meanwhile. . . .

Who Takes Care of the Caretakers, and What About the Self-Esteem of Parents?

Julia says she understands about strokes and how important they are for Jason and she is willing to give them and to care for him in a consistent, loving way. The only trouble is that she is tired, she needs a haircut, she is lonesome for some stimulating adult talk, and when she thinks about how hard Jason cries, she cries.

Bernie says that he understands about strokes and how important they are for Jason, and he wishes Julia would give him, Bernie, some. He says if strokes are good for boys they must be good for Dads and he would like more. Julia and Bernie agree that babies drain strokes. And time. And energy. And even though they love Jason a lot and want the very best for him, sometimes they are cross or depressed. Sometimes they quarrel and then disagree about what they quarrelled about. What can they do?

An old country doctor once said that what a new mother needs is her mother. But mothers are often unavailable, so new mothers need to find some other sources of nurturing. And although the old doctor didn't mention new dads, they, too, need special nurturing. In a **nuclear family** —one like the Banners where only the mother, father, and their children live in a home—arrangements should be made before the baby is born to have some outside help to give the parents time to rest and play after the baby arrives. Some families have a regular sitter come in every afternoon for an hour or two so the mother can have some time for herself. Some families swap sitting, and some have child care or willing relatives available to help.

These arrangements should not be left to chance, because the care of the parents of infants is extremely important. It may be tempting for parents to say, "We won't need that. We want to take care of our baby ourselves" or "We can't afford that" or "We will help each other." That isn't enough. That attitude sets the family up for the day when both parents have scraped the bottom of their energy-and-patience barrels with the result that that baby doesn't get proper care and both parents feel resentful and possibly guilty in addition and the stage is set for violence. Parents who do not have strong rules in their heads against physical or verbal abuse or leaving the baby alone are most apt to engage in that destructive behavior when they are tired and frustrated.

The demands of an infant are so great that they act as a **stroke drain** on many parents. Special care should be taken to keep the parents' stroke needs met.

What are parents' stroke needs? Do moms and dads need to be cuddled and held and cooed to and rocked? Yes. Sometimes. Even if they don't admit it. But adults have long since substituted a wide variety of human contacts for much of the touching that babies get. Any interaction between two people is a stroke. Any act that lets a person know she has been recognized—a greeting, a smile, a punch in the nose, a letter, a gift, a phone call—all of these are strokes. And adults need strokes every day just as infants do.

One of the contributing factors in postpartum depression for the woman who has been leading a busy, interesting life is that when she finds herself alone in her apartment, day after day, with her infant whom she loves dearly, she suffers from a lack of the strokes she was accustomed to. Or, if the parents are working outside the home and caring for their infant, they may be suffering from a lack of privacy—the world of personal internal strokes to which they were accustomed. Each may experience a loss of strokes from the other because they are busy or preoccupied with the baby. I know mothers who have adopted babies and who report having baby blues and fathers who insist that they experienced postpartum depression. To avoid feeling blue, adults who are caring for an infant must make careful plans to get their own needs met.

One way they can do this is to schedule time for their own rest and play. Another way is for couples to schedule quality time with each other. For one couple it will be a favorite kind of play. For another it will be nurturing time. **Separating sex and nurturing** is especially important at this time.

Many men have been taught how to nurture conditionally and are comfortable with the **structuring and protecting** part of caring for themselves and other people. They work hard, provide money, buy insurance, fix the leaky roof, and check the brakes on the car. They may be less comfortable with the soft part of **nurturing**—the encouraging, listening, empathizing, touching part of the nurturing environment—that is needed by all children and adults and especially by adults who are vulnerable or ill or tired or who have new babies.

A woman who has been holding a fretting baby most of the day may be feeling vulnerable and in need of nurturing herself by the time her husband gets home. He realizes she needs nurturing, but already tired from a long day at work and feeling awkward because he doesn't know how to do soft nurturing well, he offers her sex instead. In this situation, a woman who usually enjoys sex very much may feel "Shucks, I've taken care of the baby all day and now this! I wish he'd just talk to me for a little while and then take care of the baby while I rest for an hour." A clear agreement to nurture—to hold, rub the back, talk to, wait on—for twenty minutes, with no sexual invitation is very satisfying to many people. They may find that the quality of their sexual relationship improves also. Whatever strokes the parents need, it is important that they help each other get them.

Recycling

Recycling is doing early developmental tasks again at an older age in a more grown-up way. The idea of recycling is exciting! The assurance that I have more than one chance in life to get what I need, the idea that I have many chances to resolve my problems is *reassuring. Since adults often recycle their own early experiences as they watch their children go through each age and stage, it is not surprising that the parents of infants often find comfort and strength in the same affirmations for being that are so crucial for their baby.*

When Bernie's older brother, Calvin, brought his daughter Polly to meet Jason, Calvin recalled the recycling that he had done when Polly was an infant. Cal was determined to be a super good father to Polly. Cal planned, of course, to do well all the things his father had done well. In addition, Cal resolved to do well all the things his own father had not done well. Cal helped with infant care—he held, fed, and diapered the baby; he got up for one of the night feedings; he gave his wife some time for herself each evening. In addition, he embarked on some ambitious new plans at work, determined to prove to his boss that he would be more rather than less efficient at work now that he had an infant at home. He felt exhilarated; his energy was high. He was determined to prove that he would be a good father and a highly productive worker at the same time. For the first few weeks, he felt high and his energy seemed boundless. Then he started making careless mistakes at work; he felt like snapping at his co-workers; and one night he was irritated with his wife for spending her "time off" writing a letter to her mother instead of cleaning the living room. He admitted that something was wrong.

Cal had been trying to prove that he could be a good father by doing everything perfectly. He had forgotten that part of being a good dad is just taking time to be, to look at the baby with wonder, to savor the experience of having a newborn baby in his care. And Cal had neglected to take care of his own needs for sleep, for play, and for time alone. Cal started saying the affirmations for being to himself: *I have every right to be a father. . . . I'm glad I'm a father. . . . It's still OK for me to have needs. . . . I don't have to hurry and do all of the fathering perfectly this month. . . . and I'm lovable as well as loving.*

After a few days, Cal decided to slow down. He planned to continue to devote the high amount of time and energy that an infant under six months needs, to do the same adequate job at work he had been doing before Polly was born, but not to become super worker of the year right now. He also decided to make whatever arrangements were necessary to catch needed naps and have some fun. Cal, like so many new parents, was reexperiencing the developmental task of deciding that he is important for being. That does not mean that achievement is not important. It does mean that an infant deserves a father who feels important just for being and who is also willing and capable of doing the demanding care that an infant needs. Cal recommended that Bernie use the affirmations for himself as well as for Jason.

Julia and Bernie already had the list of affirmations for being from Jana's quilt-making Aunt Sheila. They've been experimenting with different ways of giving the affirmations to each other as well as to Jason. At first they felt awkward, and after a few days, they stopped. Then they decided that they had less energy and were more quarrelsome than when they were using the affirmations, so they started saying them again.

Julia likes them best when Jason is asleep and Bernie holds her on his lap and whispers them. But she also likes it when he calls her during the day and asks her what she needs and tells her that she is important. Bernie likes best to hear the affirmations while Julia is rubbing his back, but he also liked it last week when he had to go out of town and found a note Julia stuck in his shirt pocket that used their own private love words to tell how glad she is that he is a man and she is a woman!

Julia has written the affirmations on some cards and put one set by the phone and another where she can see them while she is nursing Jason. This reminds her to say them to him and to herself and helps her avoid baby blues.[9]

Visualization for Grown-Ups

Adults who are experiencing the joy or the stress of caring for an infant can help themselves by visualizing themselves as excellent parents and as persons who have already accepted the affirmations.

When Francie gets tired and is tempted to worry because adopted baby Jana seems unresponsive, she closes her eyes and allows herself to see the Francie who is a warm, loving, capable mother, who knows, bone deep, that she has every right to be the mother to this infant, and who realizes that she has a right to feel tired and that she will arrange to get some rest. She sees a strong Francie who does not have to prove her love to Jana in a hurry, a soft Francie whom Jana will learn to enjoy cuddling with. Francie says visualizing helps.

Three ways to care for the caretakers—three ways to give strength and positive self-esteem to parents or anyone who is caring for infants—are to get lots of positive strokes, to take comfort and strength from the affirmations, and to visualize success.

How Did It Turn Out?

And what about the Banners? Has anything changed during the colic hour? Apparently not with Jason; he still has colic more nights than not. And things haven't changed with Dr. Wellsley. He is still unconcerned; he knows babies outgrow colic attacks.

But Julia and Bernie have both made changes. They gave up an old worry about spoiling by picking Jason up every time he cried, and they installed a new rule that said "The way to spoil a baby is to feed him before he asks or to delay response to his requests." They decided to stop worrying about being perfect parents and raising a perfect son and to take one day at a time. They can learn to take good care of Jason without being martyrs. During the day, Jason's needs will be met and so will some of Julia's and some of Bernie's. There aren't going to be any more poverty days when adults give care the whole day and don't get any strokes for themselves. Bernie says twenty minutes of undivided quality time and attention from Julia is great, but ten minutes will do it, and that the really important thing is not to skip a day.

Julia and Bernie suffered a jolt the day that Bernie's mother came and told them that they were spoiling the baby, that he should not have colic, that her babies had never had colic, that the pacifier would ruin his jaw, and that, if they continued to pick him up every time he cried, he would grow up with a weak character. Julia and Bernie were alternately furious with her negativism and lack of support and scared that there might be some truth in what she said.

What they did to help themselves was to visualize themselves as successful, caring parents. Moreover, the next time Bernie's mother called on the phone to ask if they had gotten rid of that horrid pacifier yet, he silently read the affirmation cards propped by the phone and calmly told his mother that he and Julia had decided that pacifiers are beautiful and that he hoped his mom and dad were both well and enjoying themselves.

What Julia and Bernie did about the colic was to trust Dr. Wellsley's medical advice that Jason really is a healthy boy. They decided to let *his needs be OK with them.* That means that they can give all of the affirmations. Now when he cries and demands to be walked in that fast, bumpy rhythm that is the only thing that seems to soothe him, instead of being scared that they are not good parents or instead of feeling angry that Jason has interrupted the dinner hour, Julia and Bernie take turns walking him. They tell him that he is beautiful and special and unique and surprising and that they are glad he is demanding the walking that he so obviously needs. And they enjoy dinner together, after Jason is asleep.

42

Notes

1. See the Parenting Tips for Raising the Birth- to Six-Month-Old Infant on pages 44-45.

2. Words which have a special definition as presented in this book are set in boldface the first time they are used in this chapter. The definition of these words is given in the Glossary.

3. See the Four Ways of Parenting exercises on pages 46-47.

4. Ashley Montagu, *Touching: The Human Significance of the Skin* (New York: Harper & Row, 1971), pp. 58, 92–184.

5. See *What You Stroke Is What You Get* in Glossary. See also the worksheet on page 52 for examples of ways the Banners stroke Jason to help him develop his ability to feel and to think. On the worksheet on page 53 , list ways you can encourage a specific person to grow by stroking different personality parts.

6. Pam Levin, *Becoming the Way We Are: A Transactional Guide to Personal Development* (Berkeley, Calif.: Transactional Publications, 1974), p. 27.

7. For more about how children hear and incorporate parental messages, read Ken Ernst, *Pre-Scription: A TA Look at Child Development* (Millbrae, Calif.: Celestial Arts, 1976).

8. See the Affirmations for Being sampler on page 50.

9. See the Affirmations for Being worksheets on pages 48 and 49.

Parenting Tips for Raising
the Birth- to Six-Month-Old Infant

I. The job of the infant is being. Jason needs to establish a relationship with his caring adults so that he can begin to learn three things.
    A. He needs to learn to trust them.
    B. After which, he can learn to trust himself—"I can cope and get my needs taken care of; it is OK for me to be."
    C. After which, Jason can learn to trust his world—"My environment will respond to my needs and take care of me. This is an OK world for me to be in."

II. The job of the caring adults is to care for the baby in such a way that the baby will decide to be—to live, to enjoy being the sex he is, to get his needs met. The enormous time and energy that the adults give are an investment in vitality for the infant's entire life. Jason feels and expresses needs but doesn't yet think about how to get those needs met or how to make judgments. This means the adults must think for the baby.

A. The adults think for Jason, respond to him, figure out what he needs after he has indicated his needs. Jason may need food, sleep, more stimulation, less stimulation, dry clothes, to be warmer or cooler. He may need movement, to be rocked or walked, or protection from overwhelming stimuli. When Jason cries or roots and the adult figures out what he needs and cares for him, he experiences that he can get his needs taken care of, that it is OK for him to be.

B. The adults nurture and protect Jason. They care for the baby in a gentle, loving way that encourages him to be joyful. It will be easier for him to learn to take good care of himself and others, to become independent and responsible, at a later age if he is allowed to be dependent while he is an infant. He needs time to experience having his needs met in a loving, protected environment before he is expected to learn to please other people. Parents start laying the groundwork for independence and self-responsibility by allowing the baby to come to a full cry or to root vigorously and then by giving immediate response to his needs. Babies who receive marshmallow parenting at this age are cared for before they make their needs known. Babies whose needs are anticipated may expect to be taken care of when they grow up. This is often done to girl babies who are treated as if they are more delicate than boy babies. Another way of encouraging children to be passive is

44

to ignore them. Criticism or even demands are not appropriate for this age child. When Jason cries and is told to be quiet or when no one responds, the message he hears is "My needs are not important. I can't get them met." He may even have difficulty learning to know what his needs are.

C. The adults affirm the baby's being by doing the thinking for him, by nurturing and protecting him, and by verbally saying the affirmations for being. They visualize Jason as if he has already accepted the affirmations.

III. The job of the caring adults is to take care of themselves. Meeting the full-time needs of a completely dependent human being is a huge task. Mothers often feel depressed and fathers often feel rejected, so it is important for both of them to get lots of strokes from other people, from themselves, and from each other. They sometimes need reassurance that they are capable—that they can learn to care for an infant. Since adults recycle their own early experiences as their children go through each stage of development, adults also need to hear the being affirmations. If the adults have unresolved problems about being, they should help themselves or each other or get outside help. They should not use the infant to help them work through those problems. The father who buys a catcher's mitt or the mother who gets pink ballet slippers for an infant should resolve their sexual identity or achievement needs another way and leave the infant free to become who he or she wants to be. Separating sex and nurturing is especially important during this period. Satisfying sexual activity may not be restored for some time after the birth of a baby, and couples who depend on sex alone for intimacy will deprive themselves of needed support. Often both parents need extra nurturing while they adjust to an infant, and they should arrange outside sources of support to supplement what they offer each other.

Remember that your parents did the best they could. You have done the best that you could. If you want to use these new tools, it is never too late to start.

Four Ways of Parenting*

For any situation that requires parenting—advising and supporting—there are four possible ways of responding. Nurturing and structuring and protecting ways encourage positive self-esteem. Marshmallowing and criticizing ways tear down self-esteem. Below are situations. Each situation has a response given by a nurturing, a structuring and protecting, a marshmallowing, and a criticizing parent.

Read each of the four responses to each situation. Allow yourself to hear the positive and the negative implications of each. Rewrite each answer to fit your own value system where needed.

Parent Messages

Nurturing

This message is gentle, supportive, caring. It invites the person to get his or her needs met. It offers to help. It gives permission to succeed and affirms.

Marshmallowing

This message sounds supportive, but it invites dependence, suggests person will fail, and negates.

Structuring and Protecting

This message sets limits, protects, asserts, demands, advocates ethics and traditions. It tells ways to succeed and affirms.

Criticizing

This message ridicules, tears down, tells ways to fail, and negates.

Situation: Parent says, "My baby likes a pacifier, and my mother says it will ruin his mouth."

Nurturing

You're smart. You care about your baby. You can decide.

Marshmallowing

It's important to please your mother.

Structuring and Protecting

Put the baby's sucking needs first. Talk to a professional person about pacifiers and then decide for yourself what is best for your baby.

Criticizing

You must be doing something wrong, or he wouldn't want it. Pacifiers look terrible—throw it away!

*See Glossary, pages 269-270, for further information.

Situation: Parent says, "We thought having Laura would strengthen our marriage, but now we fight about her, too."

Nurturing

I hear that you're concerned about your marriage. You deserve happiness, and Laura deserves the chance to do her growing up without being responsible for your happiness.

Marshmallowing

I'm sorry she isn't working out the way you had hoped.

Structuring and Protecting

You and your spouse resolve your marriage problems. Leave Laura out of it. Get help if you need it.

Criticizing

Wait till Laura is in bed to argue. You damage her when you fight in front of her.

Situation: Parent says, "My spouse is gone for six weeks. The baby is driving me up the wall, but I hate to ask for help."

Nurturing

Ask! You deserve it. And the baby needs a parent who is not up the wall. Nobody should be expected to raise children all alone.

Marshmallowing

Well, I hope you make it. Poor thing! There just isn't any good help available these days.

Structuring and Protecting

Get help! Find a way. Call a friend. Find a church group that has baby-sitting service. Call an agency. Take care of yourself and the baby. Do it!

Criticizing

Be strong! You can last for six weeks!

Situation: Six year old says, "The kids at school tease me because I'm adopted."

Nurturing

I'm glad we adopted you! You are important to me, and I love you.

Marshmallowing

Poor baby. I wish you had been born to us!

Structuring and Protecting

I've watched you solve lots of problems. You're bright, and you can think how to outsmart those kids when they tease.

Criticizing

You understand about adoption. You must not be explaining it well enough.

Affirmations for Being—Deciding to Live:
Birth to Six Months

We tell people how we expect them to behave and feel about themselves by what we say to them and about them. Pam Levin, in her book *Becoming the Way We Are*, lists the messages that people need to hear and identifies the approximate ages at which each starts.

These affirmations for being are particularly important from birth to six months, for early teenagers, for people who are ill or tired or hurt or vulnerable, and for everyone else.

TO SEAN – 3 months

I'm glad you came to live with us.
Good morning, Sean!

You have every right to be here.

TO RUTHIE – 12 year old

Hi, with a big hug.

TO JEAN – adult

I'm glad to see you!
Hello!

Oh, so you're hungry again? OK!
You're wet — I'll change your diapers now.

Your needs are OK with me.

I'm willing to help you out.

It's OK for you to mourn for your dad;
I'll help you and sympathize.

I hoped that you would be a boy.

I'm glad you're a (boy, girl).

Your looks are changing.
I like the way you look!

That dress looks nice on you —
so feminine.
You're pretty.

Ignore them, Sean.
You'll sit up when you are ready.

You don't have to hurry (and grow up).

Sure, I'll help you pick out your clothes.

You can do that for enjoyment —
you don't have to rush through it.

You are so huggable!
I like to hold you on my lap, Sean.

I like to hold you.

I'll be glad to give you a back rub.
Let's cuddle!

(I'm glad you're here.)

Want me to hold you?
How about a big hug?

Affirmations for Being

Follow the **Directions for Others** or the **Directions for Self** below and fill in this worksheet.

Directions for Others

1. Think of a person you want to send affirmations to. The person can be any age.
2. Write each affirmation the way you want to convey it to that person (words, touch, attention, listening).
3. Visualize the person as if he or she has already accepted your message.

Directions for Self

1. Write each affirmation the way you want to hear it.
2. Write the name of someone you want to hear it from. Name at least three different people.
3. Get the messages in a way that is constructive for you and for other people.
4. Give the messages to yourself, even if you don't believe them at first.
5. Visualize yourself as if you already believe them.

You have every right to be here.

Your needs are OK with me.

I'm glad you're a (boy, girl).

You don't have to hurry (and grow up).

I like to hold you.

People who hear a message and consistently observe opposite behavior can feel confused or crazy. Send only the messages that you believe.

Sampler: Affirmations for Being—Deciding to Live

Here are ways to offer the affirmations for being to people of different ages.

———————

To two-month-old baby Tommy his dad can say, "Hello, sweet baby! I'm so glad you're here! Oh, I see you're wet. Well, I can fix that. Here is a dry diaper. Have I told you today how happy I am that you're a boy? I have? Oh, well, I'll tell you again, you wonderful boy. Tommy, you are stronger than you were last week, and you look bigger. You go ahead and grow at your own speed; you don't have to hurry to please me. You're so cuddly; I love to hold you."

Dad can say all of the affirmations to Tommy at one time or can say them at different times during the day.

———————

When thirteen-year-old Wayne is recycling birth- to six-month developmental tasks and feeling dependent, as he is here, Mom gives all of the affirmations for being in a cluster. On other days Mom gives each one at an appropriate time.

Wayne: Hi, Mom.

Mom: Hi, Wayne.

Wayne: Mom, what should I pack for the camping trip?

Mom: Wayne, you've packed for many camps and cookouts. You know what to take.

Wayne: No, I don't, Mom. I've never gone to this camp before!

Mom: Wayne, would you like to have me help you make a list of things you need to take?

Wayne: Ya, that would be great.

Mom: I can help you about 8 o'clock.

Wayne: Gee, thanks.

By 8 o'clock Wayne may have heard his mother's willingness to help and, satisfied, gone off to pack by himself. Or, he may make a list with her.

———————

A group leader offered the affirmation for being during the first meeting of a parenting class:

Adult: "Hello. I believe that you have every right to be here, and you don't have to explain or defend your needs. Since I like to work with women and I like to work with men, I'm happy to see all of you. I'm looking forward to the time we will spend together. You don't have to hurry and solve all of life's problems immediately. You look lovable, and each of you is an important person."

On the way to the class the leader thought, "I can give myself the same affirmations that Tommy's dad and Wayne's mom can say to themselves—I have every right to be alive and competent. It's OK for me to have needs, and I can see to it that my needs are met. I'm glad I am a (woman, man). I don't have to hurry and become a perfect parent or leader! I *am* lovable."

What You Stroke Is What You Get

name ————————————————— age ————————— time —————————

To encourage people to become whole and well balanced, compliment all aspects of their personalities.

Encourage nurturing, structuring and protecting, having and using morals and ethics, and doing things for self and others by complimenting others when they . . .

judge, protect, moralize, criticize,
direct, control, organize,
offer opinions, display ethics and
morals, nurture, take care of,
teach, comfort, support

Encourage dealing with current reality, gathering facts, estimating probability, and solving problems by complimenting others when they . . .

gather and consider data,
estimate probability,
solve problems,
give information

Encourage feeling and acting naturally and adaptively by complimenting others when they are

cute, adaptive, clever, rebellious,
compliant, wishful, fun, intuitive,
creative, imaginative, angry, curious, tricky

What You Stroke Is What You Get

name ___Jason Banner___ age __4 months__ time __Tues. morning__

To encourage people to become whole and well balanced, compliment all aspects of their personalities.

Encourage nurturing, structuring and protecting, having and using morals and ethics, and doing things for self and others.

(A child under 6 months should not be expected to comfort other people.)

Encourage dealing with current reality, gathering facts, estimating probability, and solving problems.

(Adults think for the child: Thanks for hollering when you need me!)

Encourage feeling and acting naturally and adaptively. *

(Adults comfort the child when he cries:
I like holding you, Jason.
You are a darling.)

*See page 51 for more examples of what to stroke and how to stroke

What You Stroke Is What You Get

name _____ **age** _____ **time** _____

To encourage people to become whole and well balanced, compliment all aspects of their personalities.

Encourage nurturing, structuring and protecting, having and using morals and ethics, and doing things for self and others.

Encourage dealing with current reality, gathering facts, estimating probability, and solving problems.

Encourage feeling and acting naturally and adaptively. *

*See page 51 for more examples of what to stroke and how to stroke.

3

I Love You No Matter What You Do, but Do You Have to Do So Much of It?

Eleanor Holmes is a woman in a hurry. She does her job well; she hopes to go back to school sometime in the near future; she and her daughters are almost settled in the new apartment; and tonight she is giving a birthday party. Janny Holmes is one year old today, and Eleanor has invited the Sanchez family for cake and balloons. Linda Sanchez is Janny's favorite babysitter, and the Sanchez family has been very helpful to Eleanor since she and the girls moved into the Garden Court Apartments.

Eleanor leans briefly against the bakery counter and looks at the rows and rows of cookies as she waits for the special birthday cake she ordered. "I can let the bakery help me with this party," Eleanor thinks, although she knows she should have made the cake herself. Even without the extra time for baking, she has been up since 5:30 A.M. decorating the apartment, wrapping Jan's presents, and getting Jan and four-year-old Addie to the day-care center by 7:30 and then working all day. As she waits for the cake, Eleanor remembers how excited the girls were this morning about the party.

The cake is beautiful, and Eleanor scoops up the box and rushes off to pick up her daughters. This party is an important event, the first birthday without Holden, Jan and Addie's father. The Sanchez family will be laughing and warm, but afterwards the apartment will be a mess. Jan can make a mess without tissue paper and cake, and Eleanor is already tired.

Expectations

When Eleanor and Holden got married, Eleanor never dreamed that her life would turn out like this. They had talked about having children. Eleanor had assumed that she would stay home, at least until the youngest child was in school, and she had definitely planned that she and Holden would live happily ever after. Now he is gone and she is alone, the working mother of two preschoolers.

Holden's death left a huge hole in Eleanor's life. The loss of intimacy had instant impact. Now the loss of adult-to-adult sharing, support, and talk throbs through each day. What a big adjustment!

Eleanor tried briefly to stay in their old house, but every corner held painful memories. She couldn't handle the financial drain or the energy expenditure. Even in the small apartment with no yard to care for and no memories, energy is one of Eleanor's biggest daily problems—that and her loneliness and Jan's fantastic ability to go in all directions and get into all things at once.

Eleanor understands baby Jan's constant activity. Eleanor had learned about the six- to eighteen-month-old child's needs three years ago with Addie. When Addie started to creep, Eleanor and Holden baby-proofed the family room and kept the living room for adults, by putting a gate across the doorway. This gave the parents a place away from the clutter of the young explorer's world. Eleanor understood the importance of exploration, and when Holden was concerned about Addie's need to climb everywhere and taste everything, Eleanor reminded him that this stage of seige on order and tranquillity would only last about a year. The two of them put into effect temporary exploratory house rules based on "Messy is Beautiful."

> The time and energy spent protecting a six- to eighteen-month-old child during his explorations is like an insurance policy that protects his spontaneity, creativity, motivation, grace, ability to solve problems, and his ability to see, hear, feel, smell, and talk. His job at this age is to explore, not to learn to restrain himself, so it is important for him to have a safe place to explore without rules and restrictions. Expecting him to remember not to touch a vase at this age hinders his growth and sets him up to lack motivation later on.[1]

Eleanor arranged to have some hours away from Addie's rambling. That was one of the parent survival rules Eleanor learned from Grace Greely. The Holmes' friends, Dan and Grace Greely, had three older children plus an explorer. Eleanor and Holden watched the way the Greelys let ten-month-old Brett explore and the way they protected him while he was exploring. They watched Dan and Grace divert Brett without disciplinary action. "Here, Brett, pull the train or the duck, not the lamp cord," they would say. On the other hand, they had started to discipline the two-year-old Jane. "Don't color on the book," Grace would say. "I have to take it back to the library the same way I got it, with no coloring. Find an old magazine or your coloring book. Otherwise, I will put the crayons away for the rest of the morning."[2]

They also watched the Greelys allow Brett to have the bottle until he threw it away, firmly and finally. They saw Brett defined as assertive and independent rather than messy. "You are very good at opening cupboard doors and finding out what is inside the cupboard!" Dan would say proudly. Eleanor learned from Grace how to make Christmas ornaments of safe materials that the children could put on and off the lower branches of the tree as often as they wished. Grace said, "Christmas is a time for touching and smelling and tasting."

Eleanor and Grace discussed how easy it is to give **negative strokes**[3] to little explorers. Eleanor said that when she was in a hurry it was easy for her to speak sharply and then feel guilty about scolding Addie. Grace taught Eleanor the difference between the **criticizing** and the positive **structuring and protecting parenting** that explorers need. Grace and Eleanor discussed the **four ways of parenting** and Eleanor practiced them. Separating **nurturing** and gooey **marshmallowing** was not a problem for Eleanor. (For Holden, maybe; for Eleanor, no.) But turning criticizing into protecting took more effort.[4]

When the Greelys have to say no to Brett, they say two yesses at the same time. Their yesses come in the form of two things Brett can do. For example: "Don't chew that cigarette butt, chew on this plastic toy or this rubber ring." Grace explained that she believes that children probably decide early how many good strokes and how many bad strokes they will get from life, so the Greelys are limiting the negatives they give to Brett. They hope that they are inviting Brett to be a winner who will expect good things from life and who will respect other people at the same time.[5]

Stroke Quotient Decision Theory

The **stroke quotient decision theory** states that young children decide that the proportion of positive and negative strokes they receive must be what life has to offer them, so they go through life making that happen. For example, in order for him to survive, baby Tommy has certain needs that must be met: food, protection, warmth, and a certain level of strokes. Let us assume that baby Tommy needs one hundred strokes per day to live—to stay alive (knowing that he could actually need more or less than one hundred). If his environment offers him seventy positive strokes per day rather consistently, he will have to get thirty more to stay alive. To do this he cries. A baby could get thirty positive strokes for this in some families, but baby Tommy gets thirty negatives. The thirty negatives don't feel as good as positives, but they do keep him alive! Later he notices that some children get one hundred positives and he wonders why he doesn't. In order to make sense *out of his stroke economy, he makes a decision. He decides that the world has seventy positives and thirty negatives to offer him— that's just how it is. Once he has made that type of decision he will look for his quota each day. If he goes to nursery school and a loving teacher offers him one hundred positives, he may take seventy, **discount** the rest, and go home to get his thirty negatives. And so on.*[6]

This is a theory. It could explain why some wives stay with husbands who batter and why some people criticize themselves. It could also explain why people hear some channels louder than others in the Four Ways of Parenting exercise.

Stroke quotient decision theory[7] *explains why when we invite a child to change stroke patterns, the child sometimes seems to resist, and why encouraging a person to change a little bit at a time rather than to make a sudden, dramatic change often works more smoothly.*

Holden and Eleanor learned how to say two yesses with every no and how to offer options to Addie. "Play with this old purse or this toy, not with Grandma's handbag," they would say. This was harder for Eleanor than for Holden. Even when Holden was alive, Eleanor was a hurrying person, and she often viewed life in an either/or fashion—either Addie could do something or she couldn't. It wasn't easy and natural for Eleanor to offer Addie alternatives. Holden, however, liked to offer Addie options and often headed her off at the pass before safety became an issue. "Here, Addie, catch this teddy bear and let me have that fork," he'd say. Or, "Carry this ball or this doll while you run, but give me the pencil." Eleanor listened to Holden and practiced adding alternatives to her "don'ts" and "no's."

Affirmations

Holden and Eleanor had been giving Addie lots of verbal and nonverbal **affirmations for being** which are **positive strokes for being** she did nothing to earn: "*I love you, sweet Addie. . . . I'm glad to see you. . . . You're a wonderful girl! . . . Take your time.*" At about six months, when Addie started to wriggle across the floor, they began giving her **positive strokes for doing**. This was the start of support for achievement, of **affirmations for doing**—"Addie, you move so quickly! . . . You certainly can creep well! . . . Wow, can you ever see tiny things and pick them up well! . . . Look what you found!"

The *You don't have to do tricks to get approval* **affirmation**, puzzled Eleanor and Holden until they watched Grandma Lois play with Addie.

Grandma urged her to play patty cake, wave bye-bye, and smile. Then they heard Grandma say, "What a smart, dear baby she is and so responsive to me. Little Jason is her age and he isn't nearly as nice a baby as she is." It sounded like Grandma's love for Addie depended on Addie's brightness, cuteness, and tricks. So Eleanor found many ways to say, "Hey, Addie, baby, you are OK with me whether you feel like pattying-a-cake or waving bye-bye or not. However you are today, I love you."

The meaning of the *It's OK to do things and get support at the same time* affirmation wasn't obvious to Holden and Eleanor at first. They figured it out with the help of the playpen. Eleanor had a playpen[8] which she sometimes put Addie in briefly. Addie objected strenuously, but occasionally Eleanor could not watch Addie and had to have a safe place to deposit her for a few minutes. The day that Addie piled her toys in the corner and climbed up on them and got out of the playpen, Eleanor remembered the affirmation. She picked Addie up, hugged her, and said, "What a smart baby you are to figure out how to get out of the playpen!" *It's OK to do things.* And Eleanor did not put that particular combination of toys in the playpen again. Providing for safety is giving support.

> *By providing safe environments in which a child can actually do things, parents give the child the affirmation* It's OK to do things and get support at the same time. *Six- to eighteen-month-old children are too young to be given responsibility for their actions. Their need to explore enlarges the responsibility of the parents when they act on* Your needs are OK with me. *Russell Osnes talks about fences[9] and the idea that the parents' job is to know what kind of fence to provide at which age. Surely nothing changes the appearance of a household more than switching from the soft, protective fence of the crib, the lap, and the blanket to the room-sized fence that the reaching, tasting, squeezing, dropping explorer needs. The child's need to explore everything is affirmed with the earlier* You don't have to hurry and grow up *affirmation[10] and protected with the* You don't have to do tricks to get approval *affirmation.*

> *If children have to be cute or sick or smart or tough or delicate or any special way to get attention, it takes energy from their needed exploring, just as it does if they have "don't touch the pretty breakables" rules, which should not begin this early. Of course, children can learn not to touch earlier, but it is easy to store breakables for a few months. It may be much more difficult to restore restricted initiative or creativity at a later age than to "baby-proof" part of the house and let the six- to eighteen-month-old child thoroughly explore his environment.*

Visualization

Eleanor and Holden both practiced **visualizing** Addie with high **self-esteem.** They would close their eyes and see Addie as a child who was sure of her physical abilities, who was confident she could master her world, and who knew for sure that her very important adults loved her. When Jan was born and Addie was alternately excited about the "pretty baby" and resentful of the "yucky baby," Eleanor and Holden visualized Addie as sure of her place of importance and uniqueness in the family. But Eleanor isn't visualizing either Addie or Jan now. There is so much to do that Eleanor forgets about it.

Holden is gone. Addie is four and rather quiet now, and a new explorer is in the family, Jan.

Parents of Explorers Need Strokes Too!!

Eleanor's **stroke economy** changed suddenly and dramatically after Holden's death. For the first few weeks, there was the disbelief, hurt, and shock. There were the overwhelming business tasks to be done. Eleanor's parents came from Arizona and stayed with her for three weeks. With other adults to talk to, Eleanor resisted the urge to depend on her daughters to fill the emotional void left by Holden's death. After her folks left, it was harder for Eleanor not to turn to the tiny girls for constant support, but she realized that that was not fair to them so she looked for adults to talk to. Her brother Allen dropped by occasionally and that helped.

Eleanor talked with several other single parents. One thing she noticed that many of them had in common was that for a while after a death, divorce, or desertion, they didn't seem to feel anything. It was as if the stress was too great to bear and the feeling machine shut off for a while so the person didn't feel pain. But in the process of shutting out the pain, it shut out other feelings also.

Something like this happened to Eleanor the night of Jan's birthday when she leaned against the counter in the bakery and suddenly felt how tired she was. She couldn't have gotten that tired suddenly, but she had not felt it until that moment.

Eleanor remembered one woman who said that she didn't feel anything for weeks, and when she did, she was so angry she wanted to beat her children. The urge to batter! When she heard that, Eleanor wondered if it was directly related to **stroke level,** how many good strokes a person is getting and keeping, and to self-esteem. When a person's self-esteem is low, does it take more energy not to hit kids?

60

Eleanor looks as if she is "adjusting very well," as her friends say, but she has been so busy getting life organized that she is only now beginning to feel the huge impact of the everyday losses. She misses Holden's support and understanding; she misses the way he helped her see options; she misses his friendship; she misses loving. She even misses their fights! The pleasant memories are painful, and there is a hollowness inside that rattles when she walks.

Eleanor believes that self-esteem is a family affair. "But how can you have it unless you have a whole family?" she wonders now. "How can I have positive self-esteem without Holden to love me, to tell me how important I am?" she thinks. Eleanor doesn't feel like telling herself she is important

Although she has decided to look ahead rather than backwards, each family celebration or holiday brings a new awareness of her loss. Eleanor is busy, and she is confident that she and the girls will survive and be all right, but her stroke level is low.

> *Grief increases stroke needs and drains stroke reserves and the lower one's stroke level is, the easier it is for old patterns to surface—to push up through new decisions that are not yet firmly entrenched and thoroughly practiced.*

Eleanor had some old **stroke rules** that say, "If you have to ask, you don't deserve them and anyway, they aren't any good if you had to ask. Furthermore, strokes are only good from other people. Don't brag about yourself." She understands the negative impact of those rules on her life.

These rules had caused some of the fights between Holden and her. Eleanor remembered one night clearly. Addie had been fussy and uncomfortable from her three months' immunization shots, and by the time Holden got home, Eleanor was tired and blue. She wanted Holden to understand, to hold her, to help her with the baby, and above all, to let her go to bed early. When Holden walked in, Eleanor said, "Hi, honey, how was your day?" Holden rubbed the back of his neck and said, "Exhausting! I sure hope Addie lets me get some sleep tonight." Instead of saying, "The baby has fussed all day and I need some time out and some rest, too," Eleanor had remained silent about her own needs and had cared for Holden as well as the baby. Days later, when the tension had built to the blow up point, Eleanor accused Holden of being insensitive and caring only about himself. At the end of a stormy scene, he yelled, "How can I come home tired from a day's work and guess what you want? I don't have a magic ball to look in and see what you need. Damn it, woman, you have to tell me!"

That was when Eleanor had started to think through those old rules about not asking for what she needed—rules that had worked so well for her in her childhood home where each person tried to guess what the other people needed before they asked. Even there the "don't tell what you need" rules had not worked perfectly. Sometimes people had guessed wrong about what Eleanor wanted, and she was expected to appreciate what she got, just because the person giving it had meant well. Eleanor had decided that Holden's rule "Say what you need and want" was less apt to lead to hurt feelings and fights.

Eleanor had started asking Holden for what she wanted. She had been saying affirmations to herself and a few times she had even complimented herself for doing something well.

Now, with the vulnerability of her grief, she has slipped back into the old familiar rules. When she has given and given all day and no adult has sent her any love or appreciation, she doesn't ask anyone to tell her she did a good job. And she certainly doesn't ask anyone to tell her she is nice or important just because she's Eleanor. She thinks, "Maybe I'm not really a lovable person. Holden said I was, and I believed him. But he was the only person who loved me just for me. And now he is dead! It was hard enough to ask Holden for what I wanted; I can't ask anyone else." And then that old rule about strokes being worthwhile only if they come from other people seems stronger than ever. She thinks, "I want other people to tell me I'm important. I don't want to hear it from myself."[11]

Eleanor is doing the best she can, working hard, taking good care of the girls, but that doesn't seem to make her feel better. Maybe it is because Holden died.

Would it be different if something else had happened to her marriage? Eleanor thinks about the other single parents she talks to. One woman went from one therapy group to another looking for ways to improve her husband until he left her. One man who changed himself from a quiet "Yes, dear" husband to "Mr. Assertive" split because his wife didn't keep up with his changes. He couldn't wait for her and had to get on with his own life and find some other woman worthy of the new him. One couple had nothing to say to each other after the alcoholic wife stopped drinking. One woman couldn't stand her husband, so she gave him custody of the three children in order to get out of a dull marriage. A young couple has been divorced for almost a year, and they still don't know what went wrong. Eleanor works with an unmarried woman who has a son. She knows another man who divorced his wife and married a woman the age of his daughter.

62

"How is it for all these people?" she wonders. "How do they feel about themselves? Where do they get the good strokes everyone needs? Do any of them have little explorers like Jan who have to be watched constantly? Where do they get the energy to meet their children's needs?" Eleanor often wonders about the woman who felt so angry she wanted to batter her children. "How did she recapture enough self-esteem to protect her children? Does she feel good about herself now? Do any of these people feel the same kind of grief I do?"

Anytime or any way a marriage breaks there will be grief. Sadness for the loss of a dream of happiness or of a relationship with a living person can be as intense as the grief over a death. The depression, sadness, and loss from divorce or desertion deserve the same careful attention and working through that they do following a death. Grief includes not only depression, sadness, and loss, but it also includes anger. The anger at the loss of a marriage can be intense.

Sometimes anger as a part of grief is denied or considered socially unacceptable. People who have lost a spouse, in whatever way, may not get help with their rage. All grievers must at some time come to terms with the anger. It may be reasonable anger or unreasonable—no matter. The anger of the divorced parent may be "Here I am, left with this mess. I have to be responsible all of the time while the other parent is off having a good time." Whether that is true, or whether that is only how it seems, the anger must be accepted and dealt with.

The widow or widower often has a similar anger, whether the death was suicide, from disease, or accidental. They think, "Why didn't he drive safely? Why didn't she take care of her health? Why did he desert me by going away, by dying?"

Besides blaming the other person, any single parent can have some self-blame, some guilt. Society says to the divorced person, "You didn't try hard enough, you didn't care enough. If only. . . ." The more grief-locked people feel, the more important it is to get help with the situation. If the anger has not been dealt with and the urge to batter rushes up, they should get help immediately.

Eleanor thought about ways of expressing anger at the Single Parents' meeting she attended where people had shared ideas about what to do instead of hitting children. "When I get that feeling I call a friend on the phone. . . . I put on a record I like. . . . I remember how I hated it when my mother beat me and I sing loud instead. . . . I remember that my parents didn't batter me and I appreciate that. . . . I call a Hot Line number and talk with somebody about my urge. . . . I slam doors. . . . I call my neighbor to come over for coffee. . . . I ask my mother-in-law to take the baby for a couple of hours. . . . I don't ever hit. There are always alternatives." Everyone had ideas. Eleanor didn't exactly feel like battering Jan or Addie, but there were times when she was mighty frustrated!

> *Anyone who feels like battering can get help. Help can come from family, friends, church, social agencies, support groups, oneself, from anywhere, but get it! Help and support are important for anyone who has experienced a great loss, but help is especially important for a parent raising children because the children feel their own feelings and look to the parent for ways to handle the feelings. They need to see how to act and for how long, even how much, to feel the feelings.*

Art had left Sharon, an acquaintance of Eleanor's, and the marriage had been terminated, but young Charlie remained sad, quiet, and pale. Sharon consulted a child psychiatrist who said, "Sure he is sad, any boy is sad to lose his dad, but things have not been so good at your house. I wonder why he is keeping so much sadness for so long. I think it is for you. You need to do your depression-and-anger work. Try this for the boy. The next time he says, 'I wish my dad would call,' you say, 'Yes, I'm sure you do and I hope he calls you soon. But sometimes doesn't it feel good to have him out of here, to have the fighting stopped?' This is a way of telling Charlie to own all of his feelings." Sharon only asked the question once and after that Charlie's sad times were short and his spontaneity returned.

> *The parents show the children the way through grief and separation. Openly owning and working through grief, depression, sadness, anger, and guilt gives the children permission to do the same; it is modeling for owning and working through their own feelings. Some parts of society offer more support to widows and widowers than to divorced people, as if death is more acceptable than divorce. Actually, people who are experiencing a family separation need support, no matter what the cause of the separation.*

> *It is a questionable practice to withhold support from children in order to punish their parents for divorcing. Some parents separate because the family system they have developed together is destructive to their children. The divorced person often suffers double grief—grief for the loss of a person once loved, the intimacy that might have been, and grief for the loss of a dream, the dream of building one happy marriage. Many people don't want a second chance; they wanted to make it the first time; they have an enormous sense of failure. Their grief work is double, and it is doubly important to do it.*

64

Affirmations for the Parent

Sometimes people who are carefully watching the ways in which they affirm and visualize their children forget to affirm the most important model for their children, themselves.

Eleanor had dealt with her grief by turning off her feelings. She has decided to turn her feelings back on, and now she is not only exhausted from her new job, the move, and the caring for Jan and Addie, but she is mourning for her lost marriage. Fortunately, she has also decided that her girls deserve a mother who takes care of herself as well as them. Eleanor has started taking care of herself by saying affirmations to herself night and morning. This is a way to start stroking herself positively, something that is very important for any single parent to do. Eleanor had an old rule that she had to deserve positive strokes, so the unearned being affirmations have been especially supportive for her. *I have every right to be here* is the easiest to say. *I'm glad I'm a girl* is OK too. *I'm holdable.* "Yes," Eleanor thinks, "the girls both like to cuddle with me!" Not so easy to say is *I don't have to hurry!* "Oh," Eleanor thinks, "but I do hurry every day! I remember that that affirmation means that I don't have to hurry to solve every problem today. I can slow down. I can pause and think of three options instead of staying stuck in my old either/or way of thinking."

When Eleanor gets to *My needs are OK*, she has a block. "How can they be OK?" she thinks. "They are overwhelming." Then she remembers that her needs are OK, even if they are not being met. And it is up to her to find ways to get them met.

Eleanor also says the doing affirmations. *"I don't have to do tricks to get approval,"* she says to herself. And she wonders, "How much of the hurrying which I've been doing is to get approval? To show people that single parent, Eleanor Holmes, even without Holden, can raise healthy, happy children? To prove my competence? Have I been adding competence tricks to my already busy life?"

When Eleanor told herself, *"It's OK to do things and get support at the same time,"* she said, "Garbage. People sympathize and say they care and say that they want to help. Then they say, 'Let me know if there is anything I can do.' What kind of offer is that?" Eleanor wondered. "It's no offer at all!" she concluded. "But wait, maybe it is. Maybe my friends don't really know what I need. Maybe I'll ask."

So the *It's OK to be powerful and get help at the same time* affirmation Eleanor translated into *It's OK to become a functioning, competent, single parent and get help at the same time.* Eleanor thought, "This means I don't have to choose between being competent and asking for help. Maybe learning to ask for and get the right kind of help is competence. And I don't have to decide between getting the girls' needs met or mine. I can figure out a way to take care of the girls and me."

Eleanor finds after saying the affirmations that it is easier for her to stroke herself in other ways, to say, "Yes, I'm doing a good job!"[12]

Visualization of a Family with High Self-Esteem

Eleanor has started visualizing the girls and herself again, morning and night, along with saying and feeling the power of the affirmations. What a positive way to start and end each day! When she visualizes herself, she sees an Eleanor who is rested, has proper diet, and a high level of strokes. She has some stimulation and time just for herself, not related to her job or to her children. She does not minimize other people or the situation or herself. She remembers that she must keep high energy to care for Jan, Addie, and herself. She sets priorities and uses them to keep herself from getting into a daily hassle with urgencies. She is nurtured by other people. How this future Eleanor looks and acts is starting to come into focus for the now Eleanor.

The now Eleanor is starting to make some changes to have the visualized Eleanor come true. Eleanor's self-esteem is rising.

How Is That Young Woman with the Two Little Girls Getting Along?

Eleanor Holmes? Quite well. She has decided to give up her longing for the perfect family of her dreams, to stop viewing her current home as broken, and to start defining herself, Addie, and Jan as "our family"—a family that deserves positive self-esteem, a family of loving people who are competent. She has also decided that she doesn't need to do it all alone; she is asking for and getting some help for herself and the girls.

What were the risks that she took? Eleanor changed her attitude about herself. That was scary at first. She thought a single parent was someone to be pitied, a loser. She decided to define herself as a winner, to set her priorities and take charge of her life rather than to run her days as a long, hurried set of responses to circumstances. She also decided to ask for help, which was the biggest risk, because she might be turned down.

How successful has she been? First Eleanor assessed her wins. She has sustained her children and talked to them about their grief. She has sold her house and moved into an apartment. She has found a satisfying job. She has found a supportive day-care situation for the girls. Next, Eleanor ordered her priorities and thought of several ways to protect each priority from the emergencies that regularly crop up in her life. Although her system does not work perfectly, it does work. Eleanor is hurrying less and enjoying life more. Eleanor reassessed her first assumption that she must spend all of her non-working time with the girls and decided that she needs some regular time for herself. She and Linda Sanchez have an agreement that Linda will babysit for one hour on two nights during the week and longer at least once each weekend. This gives Eleanor two spots to do errands, rest, or take a bubble bath during the week. Weekends are the loneliest time, and this way Eleanor can plan fun away from the girls on the weekend.

Linda sometimes takes the girls to the Sanchez apartment where they get a larger family experience, with people of many ages—a contrast to their own home and to their day-care experience with other young children.

And while Jan explores the Sanchez apartment under Linda's constant eye, Addie explores the people, moving her quiet eyes from person to person. When the cost of sitting goes above the amount Eleanor can budget for it, Linda has agreed that Eleanor can give her sewing lessons as payment.

Eleanor bought two season tickets to the Community Theater. She can invite a different person to go with her each time.

Allen, Eleanor's younger brother, has agreed to come to dinner one night a week so the girls will get some regular exposure to a man and so that Eleanor will get a hug from a grown-up. This will also give the little girls the opportunity to observe adults interacting, an important learning experience that could be neglected in a **single-parent family**.

And What of the Future?

Eleanor is still reluctant to ask friends to help her, but she is going to continue doing it. She has thought about all those people who said, "Let me know," and she is going to ask them if they will invite her family to join their family for some holiday celebration. Any type will do—an all day Memorial Day picnic or a half hour for Valentine's Day. She expects that some people will say no, some will hedge, and some will say yes and never call, but she is going to ask anyway. And she is going to accept Grace's invitation to bring the girls to the Greely cottage for a weekend.

Eleanor has talked to enough other single parents to know that her circle of friends may change completely. Married friends may forget to call or assume that Eleanor is no longer interested in couple activities. Eleanor will use those theater tickets to help make some new friends. There are a series of workshops on grieving at her church, and Eleanor plans to go to those to get help for herself and for her girls. Jan seems to be doing well, but Eleanor is thinking about Addie's quietness and how to help her regain her spontaneity.

When Eleanor did her priority listing, she decided that going back to school could wait at least until after Jan is three. Or maybe Eleanor will go back to school when both girls are in school, but right now she is going to use time away from the girls to relax and learn a new skill just for fun. She may do some **recycling** of her own exploratory needs. She thinks the slender time she has away from her girls will be better spent exploring a new skill for herself than studying child development.

Eleanor has decided to accept herself, to stop suffering about the unfairness of death, and to look at how other people are managing families with one parent.

She is looking for more ways to get nurturing, and she will join a support group. She accepts that her loss is great and that even after she has made all of these efforts, some loneliness for the loss of intimacy will still be there. She is making new friends. She could find an interesting man friend. Well, after she has finished grieving is time enough to decide about a new involvement. She doesn't have to hurry.

Meanwhile, next Tuesday, when Linda comes for an hour with the busy little girls, Eleanor is going to find an orderly, spacious, beautiful place to sit and do nothing for one half hour!

Notes

1. See the Parenting Tips for Raising the Six- to Eighteen-Month-Old Creeper and Toddler on page 70.

2. See page 7 for further explanation of how to offer negative messages about doing in ways that build positive self-esteem.

3. Words which have a special definition as presented in this book are set in boldface the first time they are used in this chapter. The definition of these words is given in the Glossary.

4. See the Four Ways of Parenting exercises on pages 72-73.

5. See the What You Stroke Is What You Get worksheet on page 74 for examples of the ways Eleanor strokes one-year-old Janny to encourage her thinking and feeling. See page 75, choose a specific person, and write ways you can invite that person to grow by stroking different personality areas.

6. See the Stroke Quotient Theory worksheet on page 81.

7. Hedges Capers and Glen Holland, "Stroke Survivor Quotient or Stroke Grading," *Transactional Analysis Journal* 1, no. 3 (July 1971): 40.

8. So-called playpens prevent freedom for exploration and should be called "temporary safe-holding pens."

9. Russell Osnes, "Fences " an unpublished paper.

10. See Chapter 2, pages 34-36, for more on this affirmation for being.

11. See the Stroke Rules worksheets on pages 76-79.

12. See the Affirmations for Doing worksheets on pages 82-83 and the Affirmations for Doing sampler on page 84.

Parenting Tips for Raising the Six-
to Eighteen-Month-Old Creeper and Toddler

I. The job of the toddler is doing. Jan needs to explore (see, touch, smell, taste, chew, hear, push, pull, grasp, and later drop) her environment. She needs to expand her sensory experiences. Being asked not to explore is like being asked not to eat at this stage. The toddler needs an environment in which she is free to explore and experiment so she can do three things.

   A. She can begin to trust that she can experience her environment for herself. (Example: She may find out how wood tastes.)

   B. She can continue to trust herself to get her needs taken care of (example: learning to feed herself) to lay the groundwork for the independence that will allow her to break away from her parents later.

   C. She can start to learn that there are options, that life is not all win or lose, and that not all problems are easily solved. (Example: Calling Mom or biting won't stop the pain of a new tooth pushing through the gum.)

II. The job of the caring adults is to care for the toddler in such a way that she will decide to do as well as to be. The exhausting care that adults give during this period is an investment in Jan's ability to achieve, to become independent, to use her senses, and to think. Since six- to eighteen-month-old children think with their whole bodies, the adults will do seven things.

   A. They will provide protection.

      1. They will provide the baby with a safe environment. They will baby-proof part of the living area and put the knickknacks up— store the delicate, fragile, precious, dangerous items and let "herself" explore! She is too young to learn self-discipline, so teaching her not to touch is taking precious energy away from her job of exploring and thinking. Inhibiting her exploration invites passivity and lack of motivation later in life.

      2. They will protect the child from other people who want her to sit up, be neat, be cute, be toilet trained. (Let her sit on the pot if she insists, but wait until her sphincter muscles are ready before you expect her to perform.)

   B. They will provide experience.

      1. They will provide the baby with a variety of things to experience—different textures, colors, shapes, sizes, temperatures, odors, flavors.

      2. They will provide her with doing tasks she can experiment with. (When she wants to feed herself, offer soft, finger foods instead of baby food. For the six to eighteen month old, "Messy is beautiful!")

   C. They will offer options.

      1. They will limit no's to important issues.

      2. They will use two yesses with each no. (Examples: "Don't bite your brother, chew on a biscuit or this rubber duck. . . . You can squeeze the ball or the doll, not the cat. . . . You can play in the water in the kitchen sink or the bathtub, not the toilet. . . . Color on the paper or the box, not the wall.")

D. They will say simple words, such as *milk, nose, block, hot, sticky*, to identify or describe whatever the toddler is interested in at the moment.

E. They will play with the baby when she initiates play.

F. They will not expect her to share since she is too young.

G. They will affirm the toddler's being and her doing.

   1. They will visualize the baby as if she has already accepted the affirmations.

   2. They will give positive strokes for doing. (Example: "Look, Jim, Diane is starting to feed herself!") They will also give positive strokes for being. (Example: "I love you!")

III. The job of the caring adults is to take care of themselves.

A. They will protect their own health. Meeting the needs of a creeper or toddler can be a more exhausting job than caring for an infant. Adults arrange for a good diet and for time off, so they can rest and play while someone else cares for the busy toddler.

B. They will protect themselves from their own guilt. Adults put aside demanding household standards and go on temporary "Messy is beautiful" standards. They keep Jan out of certain parts of the house, or they go out to some orderly place to satisfy their own neatness needs. Adults also keep a framed picture of a baby food magazine ad to look at when they want to see a neat, clean baby. They allow themselves to feel comfortable seeing their own baby that way for only short periods of time.

C. They will find ways to protect the toddler and themselves at the same time—a playpen is convenient. An adult can sit in a playpen to get away from the explorer and still be able to watch her.

D. They will remember that they will be recycling their own exploratory needs. If adults feel restricted, they can take a class in photography. If they feel locked in a power struggle with the busy little miss, they can create situations where both people's needs get met.

E. They will get lots of strokes—from others, from self, from spouse. They will continue separating sex and nurturing. Adults who do the demanding job of nurturing toddlers need nurturing themselves.

Remember that your parents did the best they could. You have done the best that you could. If you want to use these new tools, it is never too late to start.

Four Ways of Parenting*

For any situation that requires parenting—advising and supporting—there are four possible ways of responding. Nurturing and structuring and protecting ways encourage positive self-esteem. Marshmallowing and criticizing ways tear down self-esteem. Below are situations. Each situation has a response given by a nurturing, a structuring and protecting, a marshmallowing, and a criticizing parent.

Read each of the four responses to each situation. Allow yourself to hear the positive and the negative implications of each. Rewrite each answer to fit your own value system where needed.

Parent Messages

Nurturing

This message is gentle, supportive, caring. It invites the person to get his or her needs met. It offers to help. It gives permission to succeed and affirms.

Marshmallowing

This message sounds supportive, but it invites dependence, suggests person will fail, and negates.

Structuring and Protecting

This message sets limits, protects, asserts, demands, advocates ethics and traditions. It tells ways to succeed and affirms.

Criticizing

This message ridicules, tears down, tells ways to fail, and negates.

Situation: Seven year old says, "I don't want to spend the weekend at Daddy's house. He and his new wife drink a lot, and then they sleep a long time, and I get hungry."

Nurturing

How do you feel about that? What would you rather do instead? How can I help you?

Marshmallowing

I'll pack you a bag lunch, honey

Structuring and Protecting

Would you like me or some other adult to stand beside you while you tell your dad how you feel and what you want?

Criticizing

Don't tell me about it. I'm only responsible for you when you're here.

*See Glossary, pages 269-270, for further information.

Situation: Seventeen month old starts to tear the evening paper.

Nurturing

(Take paper gently but firmly. Say, "You can't have that one because we haven't read it. Here is a magazine you can tear, or you can play with this toy.")

Marshmallowing

Go ahead, honey. I'll go out and buy another copy.

Structuring and Protecting

(Same as for nurturing message. Until eighteen months, structure and protection is the job of the parents, not the child. Say two yesses with every no.)

Criticizing

(Slap child's hands and say, "You have to learn not to touch the evening paper!")

Situation: Parent says, "When I ask my fourteen year old to do a five-minute job he hassles me for ten minutes, and then sometimes he does the job and sometimes he doesn't."

Nurturing

Hassling is an important skill. You can find a way to hassle that is enjoyable for you.

Marshmallowing

Boys will be boys. If the job only takes five minutes, you can do it for him. After all, he is your son.

Structuring and Protecting

Tell him when you want to stop hassling and then stop. Establish family responsibilities together and identify a consequence for jobs not done. Carry through on that.

Criticizing

Good kids don't hassle.

Situation: Adult says, "I have to arrange for a speaker for my group by August, and the person I want is out of town all summer. What shall I do?"

Nurturing

If this is the speaker you really want, I know that you can figure out a way to arrange it.

Marshmallowing

Oh, dear, what a pity. Well, I'll find another speaker for you.

Structuring and Protecting

Make the contact by phone or mail. Make the plans by mail, phone, or cassette tape. Do you want a notice in the newsletter asking if any member will be visiting the area and can talk with the trainer for you?

Criticizing

You should have made your contact earlier. I certainly hope you don't run late on your programming all year.

What You Stroke Is What You Get

name _Jan Holmes_   age _1 year_   time _Sat. afternoon_

To encourage people to become whole and well balanced, compliment all aspects of their personalities.

Encourage nurturing, structuring and protecting, having and using morals and ethics, and doing things for self and others .

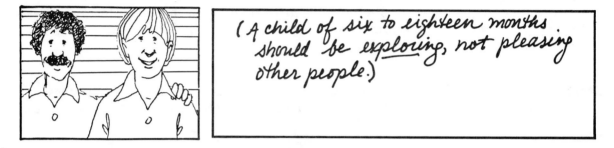

(A child of six to eighteen months should be ex*plor*ing, not pleasing other people.)

Encourage dealing with current reality, gathering facts, estimating probability, and solving problems.

You do a good job of finding things and tasting them!

I'm glad you come to me and try on my leg when you need me.

Encourage feeling and acting naturally and adaptively . *

I like to cuddle you!
You are a wonderfully curious baby, Jannie.

*See page 51 for more examples of what to stroke and how to stroke.

What You Stroke Is What You Get

name _____ age _____ time _____

To encourage people to become whole and well balanced, compliment all aspects of their personalities.

Encourage nurturing, structuring and protecting, having and using morals and ethics, and doing things for self and others.

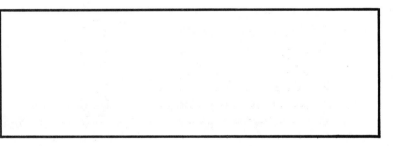

Encourage dealing with current reality, gathering facts, estimating probability, and solving problems.

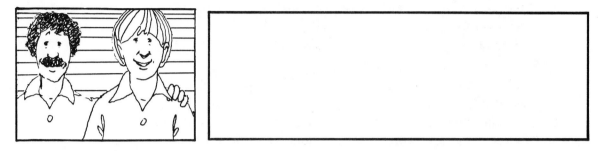

Encourage feeling and acting naturally and adaptively · *

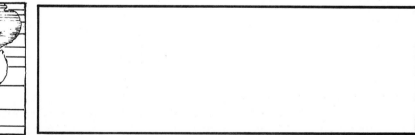

*See page 51 for more examples of what to stroke and how to stroke.

Stroke Rules, Old and New, False and True/Women

(collected from a group of women)

1. When feeling bad, don't accept strokes.
2. Strokes from one's self are best.
3. Strokes must be earned.
4. If you get a stroke, reduce its importance.
5. You have to take a stroke if it's offered.
6. You should know what kind of strokes I need and want.
7. Strokes have to be verbally acknowledged.
8. Too many strokes will spoil the baby.
9. Don't brag too loudly.
10. Stroke others before yourself. Your needs are less important.
11. Strokes from those who know you best are better.
12. Don't ask for strokes for things you should do.
13. Strokes from males are better than from females.
14. Strokes from Mother are best.
15. Be selective about whom you give strokes.
16. Strokes are not unlimited in effect. The more you give, the less effective they are.
17. Physical strokes are the best.
18. Strokes asked for are not as good as those not asked for.
19. If someone asks for a stroke, you have to give it to him or her.
20. Negative strokes are more true than positive strokes are.
21. Husband strokes are golden.
22. Loving strokes are essential to a person's well-being.

When it was originally adopted, each stroke rule on these two pages had some functional purpose. However, rules that once helped us get along or stay alive will no longer help us if in our present life they discount ourselves, others, or the situation. On pages 78 and 79 are examples of how two people revised these lists to reflect their present needs. Look over these two revised lists. Then select one of the four lists, star the statements that help you get a good stroke now, cross out or rewrite the rest, and add any new ones that you want.

Stroke Rules, Old and New, False and True/Men

(collected from a group of men)

1. Specific strokes from another businessman are more meaningful than general ones.
2. Strokes are more meaningful from a person who understands a similar situation or problem.
3. A stroke from my daughter who does not know my environment is not as good as one from another businessman.
4. A stroke has to be justified before I'll give it or accept it.
5. My wife thinks strokes for bowling are better than for cooking for the family.
6. You're only successful if you have money.
7. It's important to ask for strokes.
8. People are supposed to know when you need strokes.
9. If offered a stroke, pass it on. (I'm strong and don't need it.)
10. If you get a gift, you'll have to prove you were a good boy and deserved it.
11. You don't need compliments.
12. Too many compliments give a child a big head.
13. You don't need to be complimented for everything you do.
14. If you're *good*, you don't need compliments. Compliments are ways to get you to work harder.
15. This gift costs so much blood, sweat, and tears that you'd better be worth it.
16. Strokes from people who love you well are best.
17. Strokes from strangers are better.
18. If you get a stroke, give it back.
19. If you get a stroke, you have to take it.

Stroke Rules, Old and New, False and True/Women

(collected from a group of women)

(How one woman revised the list)

1. When feeling bad, ~~don't~~ accept strokes.
2. Strokes from one's self are ~~best.~~ *good and so are strokes from others.*
3. Strokes ~~must~~ *can* be earned. *keep it if you want it.*
4. If you get a stroke, ~~reduce its importance.~~
5. You ^*don't* have to take a stroke if it's offered.
6. You ~~should~~ *don't* know what kind of strokes I need and want, *so I'll tell you.*
7. Strokes ~~have to~~ *can* be verbally acknowledged.
8. ~~Too~~ many strokes will ~~spoil the~~ *make a good* baby.
9. ~~Don't brag too loudly.~~ *Learn to compliment yourself.*
10. Stroke others ~~before~~ *and* yourself. Your needs are ~~less~~ *equally* important.
11. Strokes from those who know you best are ~~better~~ *good*.
12. ~~Don't~~ ask for strokes for things you should do.
13. Strokes from males are ~~better than~~ *good and so are strokes* from females.
14. Strokes from Mother are ~~best.~~ *good*.
15. ~~Be selective about whom you~~ give strokes; *they're good for people.*
16. ~~Strokes are not unlimited in effect. The more you give, the less effective they are.~~ *Figure out how many strokes to give and don't skimp.*
17. Physical strokes are the best, *and verbal strokes are the best.*
18. Strokes asked for are ~~not~~ as good as those not asked for.
19. If someone asks for a stroke, you ^*don't* have to give it to him or her.
20. Negative strokes ~~are more~~ *may be* true ~~than positive strokes are.~~
21. Husband strokes are golden, *too.*
22. Loving strokes are essential to a person's well-being. ⭐

Stroke Rules, Old and New, False and True/Men

(collected from a group of men)

(How one man revised the list)

1. Specific strokes from another businessman
   are ~~more~~ meaningful ~~than general ones.~~

2. Strokes are more meaningful from a person
   who understands a similar situation or problem. *when they're about that problem.*

3. A stroke from my daughter ~~who does not know~~ *is great!!*
   ~~my environment is not as good as one from~~
   ~~another businessman.~~

4. ~~A stroke has to be justified before I'll~~
   ~~give it or accept it.~~ *I will get good strokes.*

5. ~~My wife thinks strokes for bowling are~~
   ~~better than for cooking for the family.~~

6. ~~You're only successful if you have money.~~

7. It's important to ask for strokes. *★*

8. People ~~are supposed to~~ know when you need strokes, *often don't* *so ask.*

9. If offered a stroke, ~~pass it on. (I'm strong~~ *good*
   ~~and don't need it.)~~ *take it!*

10. If you get a gift, ~~you'll have to prove you~~
    ~~were a good boy and deserved it.~~ *enjoy it!*

11. ~~You don't~~ need compliments. *I*

12. ~~Too~~ many compliments ~~give~~ a child ~~a big head.~~ *help* *grow physically and mentally.*

13. ~~You don't need to be complimented for~~
    ~~everything you do.~~ *We all*

14. ~~If you're good, you don't~~ need compliments. *we all*
    ~~Compliments are ways to get you to work harder.~~

15. ~~This gift costs so much blood, sweat, and~~
    ~~tears that you'd better be worth it.~~

16. Strokes from people who love you well are ~~best.~~ *great!*

17. Strokes from strangers are ~~better.~~ *great, too.*

18. If you get a ~~stroke,~~ *good* ~~give it back.~~ *Keep it!*

19. If you get a stroke, you *don't* have to take it.

Thoughts About Changing Stroke Rules

Don't prejudge the response that you will get from family members or close associates. They may be delighted to support you, or they may try to pull you back into old, familiar patterns. Families and other ongoing groups of people operate as systems. Systems have rules. Think of a family as a mobile.*

Bill's family rule about change is "Don't rock the boat—don't make changes!" The family mobile will bounce when Bill starts to change, and family members will try to pull Bill back into old, familiar patterns, perhaps without realizing that they're doing it. He may want to move slowly and give "I" messages and reassurances. For example: "I know that I'm changing the way I act. I believe this is a better way for me, and you may like it better too. I love you just as much as I did before."

Fred's family rule is that it's OK to try new things, so Fred announces his changes, talks about them, asks for compliments for how well he is doing, and invites people to tell him their feelings about his changes. His mobile will flutter.

Get some support from people outside your immediate systems while you are making changes. Find a friend who is willing to listen to you and who will periodically cheer you on.

*Virginia Satir, *Peoplemaking* (Palo Alto, Calif.: Science and Behavior Books, 1975), p. 119.

80

Stroke Quotient Theory

The idea that each person has a stroke quotient is a theory. Here is a way that you can explore it for yourself.

1. List ten adjectives, positive or negative, that describe you.

Put a plus or a minus beside each adjective—plus if this is a positive thing in your life and minus if it is negative.

Add the number of pluses and the number of minuses.
Total +_____ –_____

2. If you have a stroke quotient as described on page 57, think what number it is.
Write those numbers. +_____ –_____

3. If the stroke quotient numbers you indicated are similar to the proportion of pluses and minuses you listed by your adjectives, could this indicate how you have set up your personality to make your stroke quotient decision come true?

4. If the theory makes sense to you, pause for a moment and say some words of appreciation to yourself for finding a quota that would help you survive. Try out, "I'm glad I found a way to make sense of my world" or "I was a smart kid to figure that out."

5. If this theory fits, if you decided on a daily quota of positive and negative strokes, you can decide to change those numbers. (The person with a +70 and −30 quotient can move to +75 and −25 and practice that for a while. Her family may try to pull her back to old ways, just because familiar ways are comfortable, even if they are partly negative.)

Affirmations for Doing—Starting to Do Things on Our Own: Six Months to Eighteen Months

These affirmations for doing are particularly important for six- to eighteen-month-old children, for thirteen- and fourteen-year-old children, for people starting a new job or a new relationship, for people starting to learn any new skill, and for everybody else.

You don't have to do tricks (be smart, cute, stupid, sick, happy, tough, fragile, busy) to get strokes.

To BRENT — 14 months

Hi, Brent. How are you?
(pat, pat, pat)
What are you doing there, Brent?
Oh, I see.
Very interesting!

To GLORIA — 16 years

Go on in there, Gloria, and cream that driving test — but remember, honey, I love you whether you pass on the first try or not.

To LAURIE — adult

You don't have to act tired to get nurtured; I can help you.

You can celebrate your Mom's birthday simply! No big party — just a few friends.

It's OK to do things (try things, initiate, be curious, be intuitive) and get support and protection at the same time.

Hey, Brent, where are you going with that big bucket of water?
Let me take you and the water outdoors.
You're washing rocks?
Makes them wet, doesn't it?

Gloria, I know it's scary to volunteer in the emergency room of a hospital, but I think it's a great thing to do. I'll help you any way I can.

You can go ahead and enroll in some night classes; I'll help you with the housework.

(I am glad you're here, and I see you're doing things.)

82

Affirmations for Doing

Follow the **Directions for Others** or the **Directions for Self** below and fill in this worksheet.

Directions for Others

1. Think of a person you want to send affirmations to. The person can be any age.
2. Write each affirmation the way you want to convey it to that person (words, touch, attention, listening).
3. Visualize the person as if he or she has already accepted your message.

Directions for Self

1. Write each affirmation the way you want to hear it.
2. Write the name of someone you want to hear it from. Name at least three different people.
3. Get the messages in a way that is constructive for you and for other people.
4. Give the messages to yourself, even if you don't believe them at first.
5. Visualize yourself as if you already believe them.

You don't have to do tricks (be smart, cute, stupid, sick, happy, tough, fragile, busy) to get strokes.

It's OK to do things (try things, initiate, be curious, be intuitive) and get support and protection at the same time.

People who hear a message and consistently observe opposite behavior can feel confused or crazy. Send only the messages that you believe.

Sampler: Affirmations for Doing—
Starting to Do Things on Our Own

To sixteen-month-old Annie

"I'm glad you're getting into everything: opening cupboards, sorting through closets, climbing on tables, moving chairs to reach what you want. I'll give you full attention without your having to get into mischief to attract my attention. I'll pick you up and hug you when you are playing quietly, not just when you are clinging to my knee." (Baby-proof a room and give the child time and space to explore and positive strokes for exploring. Store the pretty breakables or other objects that the adults do not want fingered, mouthed, smelled, and dropped, and replace them with baby-safe objects of different textures, colors, and shapes.)

To thirteen-year-old Joshua

"I like you. You are important to me. I see that you are doing many new things. Explore, think, feel, decide what things you want to do well. You don't have to do special things to please me. You don't have to be a hunter because your father was, or a super achiever, or always busy. You can have my attention without getting sick. Your macho act is not necessary to get me to notice that you're growing up. I love you just because you're you. I see that you're trying many new things. You can try different activities and ways of thinking and feelings without cutting yourself off or having to do them all alone. You can get protection from me or other people whenever you need it, and I'll support you in your explorations. When you make mistakes, I'll listen to you and support you and help you learn from them."

To an adult starting a new job or a new relationship

"It may be exciting or it may be scary, but remember, if you do well or even if you decide not to pursue this, I will love you. It is all right for you to go ahead, try things, and make a place for yourself. I know that you are curious. That is wonderful. You can initiate things and figure out things and be intuitive. I am here and I love you."

To myself

"I'm OK. I find safe places and ways to try out new things. I'm curious, and I learn new things no matter how old I am or how competent I am. I don't have to get sick to get time for myself. I take time everyday for me. I don't have to be tricky or outstanding to be noticed. I'm glad I'm me."

4

I'm Glad You're Growing Up, but Do You Have to Say No So Often?

"Raise happy, healthy children in beautiful, friendly Oak Park," the real estate brochure said. When the grain company bought the house for Curtis James and moved his family to suburban Oak Park, both Curt and Ann hoped it would be a good place to raise their long-awaited baby. Carrie was born shortly after the move. Curt and Ann expected to be involved in the community; they planned to do a lot of work on their house. They anticipated that life in Oak Park would be friendly and busy.

For the James family life in Oak Park is lonely and busy!

Ann had hoped her mother could visit when Carrie was born. But her mother wasn't able to come, and Ann's folks have seen Carrie only once.

When the couple came to Oak Park, Curt was excited about his promotion to the position of comptroller, and Ann was sure she would find friends in this beautiful area. She has found some, but everyone seems so busy. Ann has been busy, too, taking care of Carrie, and Ann hasn't kept in close touch with her old friends. Oak Park is lovely, but it isn't like home. Curt at least has one friend, Philip North, who shares his office.

Shortly after Carrie's second birthday, Ann decided to return to work as a data processor. She waited until then because she believes that the learning and growth which take place during a child's first two years are too important to be left to strangers, and Ann has no family close enough to help her.

Now Carrie goes to Mrs. Ames' newly-licensed day-care home while Ann works. Mrs. Ames seems pleasant, and she says she runs a very casual operation. She has lots of toys and a big, new color TV set which is on all day, so the children have plenty to do. Mrs. Ames seems competent. If only she wouldn't look so worried each time she mentions Carrie's temper, Ann would feel better about leaving Carrie there. And Mrs. Ames does mention Carrie's temper every day, just when Ann is ready to leave for home with Carrie.

Since she's started working again, life is less lonely for Ann. The hours at work fly, and in the evenings, she and Curt scramble to make supper, do the housework, and spend some playtime with Carrie. Curt is usually cooperative with this busy, new schedule. Carrie is usually not. Still, Ann has trouble thinking of Carrie as a child with an unpleasant disposition. "She was such a sweet infant," Ann thinks, "but now Carrie says no almost as regularly as she breathes and she seldom cooperates." After Ann does succeed in getting a dirty, reluctant Carrie into the bathtub, the splashing, water-loving Carrie refuses to get out.

Carrie is an appealing toddler with the healthy good looks of a child who was a cuddled infant and an eager explorer. She was allowed and encouraged to explore as soon as she was able to hitch herself around. But she is not acting like a happy child. She resists every rule, every suggestion of everyone, including Mrs. Ames. Ann and Curt think it is time to find ways to discipline Carrie. So Ann has joined a group of people at the Neighborhood Center in a class about taking care of children and raising them with positive **self-esteem**[1]. Curt considered attending too, but he decided to stay home with Carrie. He agrees that they need some better ways to handle Miss Two.

How Can We Build Positive Self-Esteem in Somebody Who Even Says No to Ice Cream?

In her group, Ann learned, to her immense relief, that it is normal and desirable for a two year old to say no often—that saying no is one way children start to become separate and independent. Ann realized that her worry about Carrie's need for discipline came from her own wish to have Carrie be cooperative, a wish that Ann promptly shifted to a later age when it will be more appropriate for Carrie's developmental tasks. Ann decided to focus on positive self-esteem and see how discipline fits with that. She learned that there are three kinds of **strokes** that offer positive self-esteem to children eighteen months or older. She understands that **positive strokes for being** are all the ways she lets Carrie know that she is loved. Ann also understands **positive strokes for doing**. They are easy to give to Carrie; she does such cute things.

Ann has trouble with **negative strokes for doing**—those are the ones she had heard were bad for children. But when Ann's anger overflows she gives them anyway. Sometimes she yells a big bunch of negatives at Carrie all at once, and later Ann feels guilty. Ann is glad for a chance to practice constructive ways of saying, "No, don't, not that way."[2]

Ann thinks, "Carrie has reached the age when I should be giving her some 'don'ts.' After all, I can't be responsible for her all her life!" Ann is replacing her old rules—if you can't say something nice don't say anything at all—with a new rule, "Say what I want, set limits, provide discipline in ways that tell Carrie how I expect her to act and what I am going to do about her actions."

> *Until a child reaches eighteen months, parents are totally respon-sible for her safety and comfort. At about eighteen months, parents start the gradual shift of responsibility to the child, a process which will take the next sixteen or seventeen years to complete. Three of the ways that adults start to transfer responsibility are by starting to expect the child to use cause-and-effect thinking, start-ing to set limits or to discipline the child (without using punish-ment), and starting to expect the child to become aware of other people's feelings.*

Encouraging Cause-and-Effect Thinking

Ann wanted specific examples of ways to strengthen cause-and-effect thinking by Carrie and by herself. Each person in her class offered Ann one possible way to encourage a person to connect cause with effect in-stead of confusing that person implying that some outside power controls her life. Examples: "You spilled the juice, wipe it up." Not, "Why did you spill the juice?" Or, "You got mud on your shoes. Would you like me to help you clean the mud off?" Not, "Your shoes got muddy." Or, "How did you do on the test?" Not, "How was the test?" Or, "I am not spelling correctly today." Not, "This typewriter can't spell worth a darn today." Or, "How did your first day of school go?" Not, "How did school go?"

One woman told the class, "When my son mutters, 'Stupid piano won't play right!' I say, 'You're not playing as well as you usually do. Go ride your bike for a while and then come back and play well.'"

> *Another way to help children learn cause-and-effect thinking is to be specific about requests. For example, consider the father who said to his two year old, "I have worked hard to finish painting the garage. Don't play in it until the paint is dry." So the child took the paint and "worked" as she had seen her father do. The father said, "I told you not to play in the garage, and now you have paint all over!" Father could have said, "Do not touch the paint!" "Work," "play," "good," and "bad" are not specific distinctions for a young child. Instead of telling children to be good, tell them what be-havior you want.*

Mel, a father in Ann's class, told how he made the switch from good be-havior to specific behavior. Each morning Mel had been saying to his four year old, "Bye, Michael, be a good boy for your mother today." Now he says, "Bye, Michael. I've noticed that you have sharp eyes. Look for unusual things to see with your eyes today." Or he says, "You are a careful listener, Michael. Count how many different sounds you can hear in the back yard today. Tell me tonight. Bye now." Michael checks out big words with Mom and goes off on his search. At five o'clock when Dad gets home, he and Michael have something concrete to share. The counting may not have been accurate, but there is a whole new interaction, full of positive strokes for both father and son. This surely beats being a "good" boy.

Discipline or Setting Limits— Don't Do This, Because, Do This Instead

Eighteen months to three years is the age at which it is appropriate for parents to start some clear, gentle discipline.

Ann practiced being clear and specific with Carrie (especially with negatives) about the behavior she wanted and about the consequences. Previously, when Carrie stood on a chair, Ann moved her off and said, "Chairs are for sitting." But chairs are also for standing on; Ann stands on a chair when she waters her hanging fern. In class, she practiced setting limits and giving options by saying, "I don't want you to stand on the blue chair; you might get it dirty. Stand on your toy chest instead." She went home and tried it on Carrie, who said no, which is what a two year old needs to say. Ann lifted Carrie off the chair, adding, "I expect you to remember not to stand on that chair." Ann was firm but not rough. She remembered that gentle consistent discipline or limits at two years will make other separating processes—especially the fourteen-year-old experience—smoother for both Carrie and her parents.[3]

Ann also learned from the **Four Ways of Parenting** exercise[4] that people role played in class. When Ann first watched the Four Ways of Parenting role playing, she thought it was arbitrary and phony. Then as the weeks went by, she realized that messages from the four kinds of parents could be done in numerous ways, depending on the individual's value system and personal styles, and she paid more attention to the exercise. Ann understands the need to give Carrie permission to grow, be, win. That way of parenting is called **nurturing parent** and Ann does it easily and well. She says, "I love you, Carrie girl, and you can do it."

Ann also understands the need to give Carrie clear **structuring-parent** messages about how to do things, but Ann had some reluctance about actually giving the structuring messages because they include so many shoulds. Ann had an idea that shoulds were bad. Repeated practice and some long discussions with Curtis clarified the difference between structuring, security-giving shoulds with reasons and consequences and arbitrary, don't-think-for-yourself shoulds. Now Ann is practicing giving clear structuring messages in a loving way—"I insist that you hold my hand while we walk through the parking lot, but you can walk by yourself on the sidewalk."

The **marshmallowing-parent** messages Ann hated! She had heard too many of them in her life and she thought it was dumb to practice them. It felt like affirming them. However, after Ann role played the marshmallow way of parenting a few times, she announced that she was through giving marshmallows. She affirmed herself as a positive, nurturing parent, and she sharpened her ability to catch her own marshmallow messages to Carrie. Role playing these messages had brought them into her awareness and had made it easier for her to hear them and to change them. Now when she catches herself saying, "Here, I'll do it for you, Carrie," she stops to think, "Is this something Carrie can do for herself?"

Giving **criticizing-parent** messages is not a problem for Ann. As a youngster, she experienced the sting of name-calling and decided early that degrading names and destructive criticism would not be allowed in her home when she became a mother.

Are Ann's new ways of discipline and setting limits helping Carrie? Mrs. Ames hasn't noticed any difference. And Carrie has so many nos to say that the other night she even said no to ice cream. Ann can't tell yet if Carrie's self-esteem is more positive. What she does know is that she, Ann, feels more positive about herself and about Carrie! Ann hopes her own increased self-esteem is contagious.

Thinking Affirmations, Starting at Eighteen Months

In her class, Ann learned **affirmations** to enhance Carrie's self-esteem and give her confidence in her new job of becoming independent. These affirmations help Carrie begin to think for herself. These thinking affirmations are

> I'm glad you're growing up.
> I'm not afraid of your anger.
> You can think about what you feel.
> You don't have to take care of me by thinking for me.
> You can think to take care of yourself.
> You can be sure about what you need and want and think.[5]

Ann likes the affirmations. In her group she listened to Lillian tell how she tested the thinking affirmations. Lillian said, "Shortly after I learned these thinking affirmations, I was visiting my grand-niece and grand-nephew, Miss Six and Mr. Thirty-three Months. The family was bragging about the girl's thinking and negating the boy's. My nephew, the father, said, 'Oh, yes, our girl loves school. She brings home smiling faces on all of her papers. She always has been a bright child. Now our boy is another story. He is just full of it! He is so active; we don't know how he will ever sit still in school long enough to learn anything. Daughter, get your paper to show Aunt Lillian.' Mr. Thirty-three Months diverted attention from the paper display by demanding candy in a loud voice. His mother said, 'No candy until after dinner.' Quietly Mr. Thirty-three Months got a wrapped candy, unwrapped it, showed Mother the wrapper. She said, 'Oh, well, as long as it is unwrapped, you can eat just that one.'"

Lillian continued her story, "He came over and stood by me. I thought, 'How easy it would be to tell him how smart he was to get what he wanted.' Instead, I asked him to sit on my lap. I thought, 'This is the time to find out if a child this young understands the affirmations.' I said to him, 'I think I know a lot about kids your age. Will you listen to what I know and tell me if it is really true?' He nodded yes. So I cuddled him and whispered, 'I know that *kids your age are growing up.*' He nodded yes. Again I continued, 'I see that you get mad at your sister or your mom sometimes. You know, *I'm not scared of you when you're mad.* I just watch you to see how well you are thinking while you are mad. I watched you do it today. I could be wrong, but I guessed that you were mad at your sister for being so smart and you thought what to do about it.'

"He looked up at me and then snuggled closer with his head tucked against my shoulder."

"So I went on. I said, 'I see that *you can feel mad and think what to do. You can feel mad and not hurt yourself or anyone else.*'

"He nodded yes. 'I also know that *kids your age know what they need and what they want.* Inside of themselves they really know. Is that true?' He nodded yes. 'Sometimes little people take care of big people by making them happy or cheering them up when they are sad. Is that true?' He nodded yes again. '*You don't have to do that for me* anytime when I am with you.' He stole another glance at my face. 'Tell me, am I right about kids your age?' 'Uh huh.' 'Am I right about you, that you are a very good thinker?'

"'Uh huh.'

"Fantastic! My grand-nephew is not yet three and is already a master manipulator," Lillian said. "I decided to try an affirmation from the three- to six-year-old set of messages.[6] So I said, 'One more thing. I see that you are skillful at tricking your mother to get what you want. I also know that kids your age really know what they want. Instead of tricking they can just say what they want. Is that true?' He nodded yes again. 'Will you tell me what you want whenever you are with me?' 'Yes,' he whispered.

"The other people in the room continued talking," Lillian confided. "They didn't even notice that we two good thinkers had been whispering. When I left, Mr. Thirty-three Months looked into my eyes for a long time and gave me a mooshed chocolate chip cookie to put in my pocket."

Lillian had explored the thinking affirmations with her thirty-three-month-old grand-nephew. She had held him, listened to him, and talked to him without using big words. There is no way of knowing exactly what or how much the small boy understood or what decisions he made about the experience. Adults can offer affirmations in a variety of ways—it is up to the children to internalize and make decisions about them. The important issue is that adults mean what they say. If adults say one thing and believe or mean another, they invite the child to feel confused or crazy.

Curt got interested in affirmations when he listened to Ann chant them to Carrie during her bath. Ann started with the **affirmations for being** and the **doing affirmations**. Now she has added the **thinking affirmations**. Ann and Curt are examining each affirmation to be certain that they believe it and to decide ways to give Carrie each message. They want Carrie to be able to think well.

I'm glad you're growing up. Yes, that affirmation is easy. Carrie doesn't have to stay an infant. It is all right for her to start separating, to be independent, to dig in her heels, and to say no even to ice cream.

You can think and feel at the same time. Of course. Many times when Curt has been most frightened, he has had to do some of his quickest thinking. When Curt heard someone at work say he was so mad he couldn't think, Curt thought, "Man, when you are mad or scared is when you better think fast and well!"

The *I'm not afraid of your anger* affirmation is a problem for Ann. Mrs. Ames says the other children are afraid of Carrie's temper tantrums and that Ann should do something about them. And furthermore, Mrs. Ames adds, a good mother would have her child toilet trained by Carrie's age! Then Ann feels angry herself, although she thinks she shouldn't. Ann decides to skip that affirmation till later.

The *You don't have to take care of me by thinking for me* affirmation was meaningless to Curt until Ann and he listed some of the statements they had heard as children that encouraged them to accept responsibility for the feelings of other people or that invited them to think that other people were responsible for their feelings. Curt and Ann's list said—

You drive me up the wall!

If she heard what you did, your mother would perish!

You make me so mad!

Don't feel that way.

You hurt my feelings.

That teacher bores me to death.

Now you've done it; you've made her cry!

Make me proud of you, Son.

You made me feel like a failure as a father.

You should feel glad about that.

Ann and Curt thought of ways to rephrase each statement, ways to talk to Carrie to teach her to be aware of other people's feelings without thinking she has to be responsible for them. They changed the list to read—

I'm upset.

Your mother doesn't approve of that behavior.

I'm mad.

It's OK to feel the way you feel; control how you act.

I feel hurt.

I'm bored.

She's crying.

I'm proud of you.

I feel sad about that.

Do you feel glad about that?

Ann and Curt decided to change the way they say their first list of things to each other as well as to Carrie.

The last thinking affirmation is *You can be sure about what you need.* Ann doesn't have the confidence to say that yet. How can she tell Carrie to know what she needs when Ann doesn't know what she herself needs sometimes. What does she need? Her family? Old friends? Ways to deal with the loneliness? Ann will not say that affirmation until she figures it out for herself.

Ann returned to *I'm not afraid of your anger* and decided to start dealing with that affirmation by stroking Carrie for positive behavior, not for being angry,[7] and by visualizing.

Visualizing a Smiling, Problem-Solving, Independent Two Year Old

Sometimes Ann listens to Mrs. Ames' fear of Carrie's anger and wonders if Mrs. Ames is right, if Carrie really is a problem child. Ann doesn't think so, but sometimes when Carrie shouts "I won't," ripples of tension stream through Ann's tired body. Ann has started the practice of **visualization**, so when she feels impatient with Carrie's resistance, Ann visualizes Carrie as the smiling, glowing, problem-solving, considerate person she can become. If that isn't enough, if Ann still feels irritated with Carrie's "I don't want tos," Ann visualizes an older Carrie who was not allowed to express her "I won'ts" when she was two and has given up her ability to say no.

Ann pretends to see Carrie at fourteen, with her peer group pushing her to take drugs. There is Carrie without the protection of being able to say "No," "I won't," or "I don't want to." Ann doesn't want a fourteen-year-old Carrie who can't say no, and Ann feels her impatience melt. Then Ann flips back to the real two-year-old Carrie, gives her a hug, and says, "You say no really well!" Being able to say no at the right time is essential for positive self-esteem!

Ann has come to realize that what she called Carrie's need for discipline is also her own need to have some time away from the nos of a normal, independent, separating two year old. Once Ann accepted the importance of Carrie's resistance, Ann was able to sort out when to ignore or compliment Carrie's resistance and when to limit Carrie's behavior.

There Ought to Be Federal Insurance for Stroke Banks, or Are You Sure This Is All My Responsibility?

The stroke bank theory [8] *proposes that one's stroke level affects one's feelings of well-being and that a person can say what her stroke level is, just like she can determine how much money is in her bank account.*

Ann is considering the stroke bank theory. It helps her make sense of her moods. She can feel her spirits rise when people tell her she looks nice or when her boss compliments her on work. She is putting positive strokes in the bank. She knows that sinking feeling when she stops to pick up Carrie and Mrs. Ames gives her a friendly smile but has a worried look in her eyes as she murmurs, "Carrie had two of her temper spells today. And she's wet, Mrs. James." An encounter with Mrs. Ames lowers the level of strokes in Ann's bank.

Ann agrees with the idea that any stress, like moving to a new home, can pull one's stroke level down. When she counted the stresses in her life in the past two years, she got a long list. Besides the new house, there was Carrie's birth and with it the stress for both Curt and Ann of changing from being a married couple to being parents. First, she missed her job, and then she missed being home. The death of Curt's father added more stress; they both keenly felt this loss. During that first year, the sadness lingered as each holiday or special event dragged by without his telephone call. Ann mourned for what had been. It is easy for Ann to understand that with all of the stroke-draining stresses, she needs extra strokes now.

So do the Blakes. They are in Ann's class. They have had a death in their family. The Blakes lost an infant in a crib death. At first they tried to pretend that the loss was not great because they had not had their baby long. She was hardly a person to them. But that didn't work. **Discounting** grief seldom works; so they came to the class to get some support for themselves, some tips on handling their two boys. They think the class may help them face their loss and anger at losing what might have been. They want to get their sadness and anger out in the open, feel it, and express it, so they will be free to focus their energy back on their two boys. The class leader told them about a grief group they can attend.

> *People's stroke bank levels are lowered by many different experiences. For some people, fatigue, illness, and grief drain strokes like a series of bank robberies. For other people, the daily monotony of a job or the constant irritation of an unpleasant co-worker or family members drain strokes. What can people do about a stroke bank drain?*

At first Ann resented even the thought that she was responsible for her own stroke level. She wanted Curt to make her happy. But the more she thought about it the more she realized that while Curt can offer her love, he cannot be responsible for her every up and down. That's too much for any one person. He has his job, his Village Task Force, Carrie, and himself to think of. To be totally responsible for Ann's feelings in addition is an unreasonable expectation. Besides, sometimes Curt is out of town for a few days, and Ann is left to her own stroke devices. Ann took a long look at her old stroke rule that said "Husband strokes are golden and strokes from anybody else don't count, or at least they don't count as much." Ann revised the rule to read "Husband strokes are golden; there are special strokes I want from him. I need positive strokes from lots of people; those are golden too. Curt deserves *not* to be responsible for my positive self-esteem."

Ann likes the part of the stroke bank theory that proposes the idea of a savings account that she can fill with strokes. Before Curt goes out of town, Ann always plans to have an especially good time with him. This helps her feel good while he is gone. While he is away, she goes to the movie with a friend, and she calls her folks and talks long distance with them.

Now Ann doesn't just store strokes for times when Curt can't give them to her. On days when she knows there will be extra stress at work, she wears the ring that she and Curt bought for her on a happy vacation. When she feels the stress in her stomach or her shoulder muscles, she looks at the ring and recaptures some good memories and feelings to help her through the current situation. Or she tucks the birthday card her mother sent to her into her purse. She glances at it when she needs a stroke boost.

One of the secretaries with whom Ann lunches has another way of managing her stroke savings account. She has a very mercurial boss. One day he is sunny, and the next he is Mr. Storm. Ann's friend went to her boss on a sunny day and asked him to write a letter of recommendation. She told him that she had no intention of quitting, that she just wanted to know what the boss liked about her work. She keeps the letter in her desk drawer, and on stormy days she reads it.

One thing Ann noticed about her stroke level is that the higher the level is, the more strokes she gets and keeps. Also, the higher her stroke bank is, the easier it is for her to give other people high-quality strokes. This doesn't seem fair or logical, but that's how it works. When Ann is below a certain stroke level, she feels so terrible that she doesn't ask for help and she doesn't even know what she needs. She just feels terrible! Her self-esteem is at low ebb. At that time she does not need admonitions to pull herself together to realize how lucky she is! She needs nurturing and affirmations for being.

Affirmations for Adults, or You Can Be Sure About What You Need!

Carrie was playing happily with her blocks; Curt was watching a football game on the tube, and Ann was feeling terrible. She had felt droopy all evening. At half time, she stood some distance from Curt and said, "I feel terrible; help me."

"What's the matter?" Curt asked.

"I don't know," Ann admitted.

"Well, cheer up, Annie," Curt advised.

Ann responded by bursting into tears.

Curt had been practicing the thinking affirmations on Carrie so they were on the top of his mind. *"You can figure out what you need*, Ann," Curt reminded her.

"No, I can't," Ann said and more tears spilled over.

When someone is in pain and admonitions and compliments don't work, try affirmations. If You can be sure about what you need doesn't help, experiment with one from the affirmation for being set.[9]

Curt says, "Annie, *I love you!* You know how *important you are*[10] to me and *I love you* so much!" and gives her a comforting hug.

Ann says, "You wouldn't love me if you knew how mad I am." True, Ann and Curt are sometimes frightened of each other's anger, and sometimes quarrel over it—each insisting that the other should not be angry!

Curt takes a chance and says, "Try me, Annie. Tonight I will listen to you and not get scared at how mad you are. Tell me."

"Well," Ann hesitated, "I've been thinking about Carrie. I'm mad at Mrs. Ames!" Ann started speaking faster. "And I'm scared that we are doing the wrong thing by leaving Carrie with her. Curt, I thought about how it would feel to be two years old. If I had been dependent and totally cared for all of my life and suddenly a growing push within me kept urging me to get free, be independent, go it alone, I'd be scared. I'd be very angry. Angry at having to leave the nest, angry at the people who had cared for me and in the future could never again care for me in the same enveloping way. I'd continue to be mad until I was separate enough to know that I could make it, and that my adults would still be there, even when I was mad. I think Mrs. Ames should understand that and not be so all-fired upset about the anger of one tiny two-year-old girl![11] Also, I worry about Carrie watching so much TV. Mrs. Ames has it on all day. Do you suppose the violence will hurt Carrie?"

Curt hugged her again and said, "Hey, Annie, I can see why you're mad. Stop blaming yourself, pretty Annie. You're a good mother; you've been doing the best you could. We'll figure out how to do it better. Let's both think what to do. I'll ask at work tomorrow if anybody knows any good places for Carrie. You ask, too. Then let's go out to dinner Friday night and talk about it. Can you get some suggestions from your class tomorrow night?"

When people go about solving problems and making changes, it works better if they collect data and evaluate possible courses of action rather than blaming or telling other people how to feel or how to change. Curt did not criticize Ann; he comforted her, listened, and made suggestions. He did not tell her how to feel. He didn't say, "Don't be angry!"

Ann had decided before she started her class that she would not come home and make Curt take the class secondhand. She had told him that people in her class shared ideas. He asked about affirmations when he heard her saying them to Carrie. Ann had been busy looking at her own beliefs and changing her own behavior. Now Curt had asked her to get help from the class for both of them.

Curt was interested in the ideas Ann was gathering. This could be just because he was interested, or it could be partly because Ann had been working on herself and not trying to make him over.

People often resent being "improved" or "fixed" by someone else— even if it is by someone they love. Geneva and Bart Knapp's experience is one example of how fixing someone doesn't work.

Geneva Knapp, a member of Ann's class, made a different decision from Ann's. Geneva and Bart have three boys; they are considering adopting a girl. When Geneva heard about the class starting at the Center, she pushed Bart to join. She didn't come right out and insist that Bart go with her, because that's not the way Geneva does things. She hinted and dropped comments. She thought it would be good for Bart and give him a chance to think more clearly about the adoption. She had a squiggly feeling about taking a baby, someone else's baby, and raising it like her own. Bart didn't have any questions about adopting. He went along to the group with Geneva because he knew Geneva had decided it would be good for him. He resented that. "But," he thought, "if it helps get my girl, it will be worth it! Anyway, it might be good for Geneva. Sometimes the boys are a handful and there are days when she doesn't manage too well."

Geneva and Bart only came to two classes. Ann never did find out if they decided to try to adopt a girl. Ann thought a lot about the difference between trying to make over and affirming family members to become whole people. Sometimes the idea of "making over" seemed appealing, but Ann didn't like it if Curt tried to change her, so she decided to stay with affirmations.

Affirmations

*Parents of eighteen-month- to three-year-old children need all of the affirmations, but they especially need the thinking messages in case they are **recycling** some of their own old problems, dependence, anger, or separation. "I'm glad you're solving your problems; tell me about your anger; own it as yours; don't direct it at me; I will not be afraid of it but will listen to it. . . . We can both have strong feelings and think clearly at the same time. . . . We can* figure out what we need and plan how to get it." *All these are messages that adults can give each other and themselves to believe and act upon.*[12]

Visualize Adults Whose Needs Are Met

One way for adults to stop discounting their own needs is for them to visualize themselves as they will be when their needs are met.

Ann visualizes. She sees a mental, technicolor, three-dimensional image of herself as she will look and act when she has tons of positive self-esteem, when she has played for ten hours a week, when she is well-loved and nurtured, and when she has accepted that it is OK for her to be angry. After she has visualized herself that way, she is more able to enjoy Carrie's pushing thrust for independence, which she sees as growth rather than negativism.

Becoming

Will Oak Park be a good place for Ann and Curtis to raise Carrie? It's still too early for them to be certain. But life will be better than it was! Two people in Ann's class offered suggestions on ways to help three year olds have opportunities to say no. The one that Curt liked best was "Shall I eat all the ice cream?"

Ann and Curt decided that Mrs. Ames' fear of Carrie's anger was too distressing and found another day-care person, Eva Larson. Eva is young and slight-looking; she loves two year olds, and she doesn't have a TV set in the day-care room. When Carrie stamps her foot and yells, Eva looks at Carrie with admiration, waits until the outburst is over, and says she is glad Carrie is learning how to say no so well. Then Eva gives Carrie a hug and whispers, "*I'm glad you're here.*" Eva says she expects Carrie will soon be getting to the age when she will keep herself dry all day.

Ann and Curtis are making some changes for themselves, too. Ann has stopped taking care of Carrie and Curtis full time and is spending more time on herself. She asks Curt for what she wants instead of feeling hurt when he doesn't guess what she wants and doesn't deliver it.

Ann and Curt are talking about their anger openly, and although they still fight, sometimes, they are moving on from their fights to problem solving. The two of them are deliberately spending more fun time together and are comforting each other when they are lonely rather than pretending they

100

have to be strong and ignore the loneliness. Each of them is making a deliberate effort to find some new friends who are positive, outgoing, nurturing people. Ann's class is going to continue to meet as a support group. Curt and his friend, Philip North, are planning to attend a similar class, a tribute to Ann's decision not to try to change Curt but to make changes in herself.

Notes

1. Words which have a special definition as presented in this book are set in boldface the first time they are used in this chapter. The definition of these words is given in the Glossary.

2. See page 7.

3. See *Recycling* in Glossary and in Chapter 7 on pages 184-191.

4. See the Four Ways of Parenting exercises on pages 104-105.

5. Pam Levin, *Becoming the Way We Are: A Transactional Guide to Personal Development* (Berkeley, Calif.: Transactional Publications, 1974), p. 36.

6. These age designations are guidelines, not set times.

7. See the What You Stroke Is What You Get worksheet on page 106 for examples of ways the James encourage Carrie to grow by stroking her for nurturing, for thinking, and for expressing her feelings. Use page 107 to think of ways you can stroke a specific person to encourage him or her to develop in a well-balanced way.

8. See the Stroke Bank worksheets on pages 108-109.

9. This assumes that one believes and feels the affirmations. Do not say an affirmation if you do not mean it!

10. *You are important* is a way of saying *You have every right to be here.*

11. See Affirmations for Thinking sampler on page 112 and the Affirmations for Thinking worksheets on pages 110-111.

12. See the Parenting Tips for Raising the Eighteen-Month- to Three-Year-Old Child on pages 102-103.

Parenting Tips for Raising the Eighteen-Montn-to Three-Year-Old Child

I. The job of the eighteen-month- to three-year-old child is thinking. Carrie needs an environment in which she is free to assert herself and to express anger. Being asked not to be angry at eighteen months to three years is like being asked not to explore at six to eighteen months. She needs caring adults who are starting to demand cause-and-effect thinking so that she can do many things.
   A. She can learn to think for herself.
   B. She can learn about using feelings, especially anger, and start to separate feeling and thinking.
   C. She can start to separate from her parents, become independent, and learn to say no.
   D. She can continue to be dependent when she needs to be.

II. The job of the caring adults is to take care of themselves by setting limits and to continue to care for the child while demanding that she start to think for herself. The energy and self-control that the adults expend during this period of assertion is an investment in Carrie's independence and preparation for smooth separation during her teenage years. The eighteen-month- to three-year-old child needs to learn to think, to say no, and to learn about feelings.
   A. Adults will encourage thinking.
      1. They will provide reasons, how to's, and information. (Example: "The puppy runs away and hides when you hurt her. I'll show you how to hold her gently.") They will use "do's" instead of "don'ts."
      2. They will provide limits. (Example: "I want you to stop hurting the puppy. If you don't stop, I'll insist that you sit by yourself until you're willing to control yourself.")
      3. They will provide time and space for Carrie to start to organize her own thinking.
         a. They will allow Carrie to play *near* other children without expecting her to play *with* them. They will not expect her to share. She needs time to experience ownership before she can be expected to share.
         b. They will tell her about activities ahead of time. (Example: "We are going on a picnic.")
         c. They will limit television time.
         d. They will demand that Carrie start caring for herself. (Example: "You carry your teddy bear.")
         e. They will let Carrie think for Carrie and will not invite her to take care of the adults. (Example: Don't say "I'm so unhappy with your daddy I could cry, but you'll make me smile, won't you, Ryan?" Say instead, "I'm sad because I had a scrap with your dad, but he and I will solve that tonight. What are you building?" Don't say, "I'm going on a business trip. Be a big boy and take care of Mommy while I'm gone." Say instead, "I'm going on a business trip. Mommy will take care of you while I'm gone, and I'll be back soon." Don't say, "Shame on you!" Say instead,

"Don't do that; because . . .;
do this instead.")

B. Adults will encourage learning
about feelings and separating
thinking and feeling.
1. They will accept Carrie's anger
and label it. (Example: "You look
angry.")
2. They will show her how to
handle anger by being open
about their own anger.
3. They will start negative strokes
for doing poorly and insist on
thinking. (Example: "I feel angry
when you kick me. Either figure
out how to climb up beside me
without hurting my leg with
your foot or don't climb up, or
ask me to move. Now, try it
again.")
4. They will keep their emotions
separated from the child's.
(Example: "I am sad because
Carrie is so negative; I must not
be a good mother," shows that
Mom needs to get her OKness
separated from Carrie! It's better
to say, "I am a lovable, capable
person. Carrie's no's bug me if
I'm tired, so I make it a point to
get enough sleep.")

C. Adults will encourage separation
which will lead to independence.
1. They will expect Carrie to say,
"No. . . . I won't. . . . I
can't. . . . I don't care. . . . I
don't want to."
2. They will set reasonable limits.
(Example: "You may not eat on
my bed; you may eat your lunch
at the counter or on the table.")
Carrie will repeatedly test; adults
will repeatedly remain firm.
3. They will show Carrie where
people put body wastes and expect her to put hers there also.

Toilet training sounds like a
program to train toilets. In fact,
it is usually a program to train
mothers. A two-and-a-half- to
three-year-old child is able to
think enough to use a pot if she
is allowed to see adults use one
and is told in a matter-of-fact
way that adults expect her to do ·
the same.
4. They will assure Carrie that she
will be cared for when she needs
care, and they will continue positive support with a loving attitude.

D. They will affirm the child's thinking. They will visualize her as if she
has already accepted the being, doing, and thinking affirmations.

III. The job of the caring adults is to take
care of themselves.
A. They will remember not to attempt
to get their own positive self-esteem
from producing a positive two year
old. Forget it! It's not supposed to
be!
B. They will play (some of the time
away from Miss Two), dance, eat,
sing, make love, but will do no ex-
tensive travel—Carrie's separation
is just starting. Instead they will
wait until after she is three.
C. They will get nurturing! Adults who
take care of eighteen-month- to
three-year-olds deserve it!
D. They will remember that they will be
reworking feelings about separation, dependence, independence,
and anger. It is better to get any
problems sorted out now than to
wait until Carrie is a teenager.

Remember that your parents did the best
they could. You have done the best that you
could. If you want to use these new tools,
do so now. It is never too late to start.

Four Ways of Parenting*

For any situation that requires parenting—advising and supporting—there are four possible ways of responding. Nurturing and structuring and protecting ways encourage positive self-esteem. Marshmallowing and criticizing ways tear down self-esteem. Below are situations. Each situation has a response given by a nurturing, a structuring and protecting, a marshmallowing, and a criticizing parent.

Read each of the four responses to each situation. Allow yourself to hear the positive and the negative implications of each. Rewrite each answer to fit your own value system where needed.

Parent Messages

Nurturing

This message is gentle, supportive, caring. It invites the person to get his or her needs met. It offers to help. It gives permission to succeed and affirms.

Marshmallowing

This message sounds supportive, but it invites dependence, suggests person will fail, and negates.

Structuring and Protecting

This message sets limits, protects, asserts, demands, advocates ethics and traditions. It tells ways to succeed and affirms

Criticizing

This message ridicules, tears down, tells ways to fail, and negates.

Situation: Eighteen-month-old child pulls the kitty's tail.

Nurturing

(Firmly separate cat and child. Give hug another time during the day.)

Marshmallowing

(Gently separate child and cat.)

Structuring and Protecting

Don't pull the kitty's tail because that hurts him and he may scratch you. Here is how to hold him gently. If you pull the kitty's tail, I will insist that you sit in the corner until you are willing to control yourself.

Criticizing

I've told you a hundred times not to pull the cat's tail. If he scratches you, it serves you right. You'll never learn.

*See Glossary, pages 269-270, for further information.

Situation: Parent says, "My two year old isn't toilet trained, and my relatives are giving me fits."

Nurturing

Get some space away from them. You can decide how to be a good parent. It's OK for you to decide how to treat your child.

Marshmallowing

There is nothing you can do but train her.

Structuring and Protecting

Protect yourself and your child from them. Many children do battle at two but train themselves around three. Make your own decision.

Criticizing

What!? Not trained yet? She will have to carry a diaper bag to kindergarten. Shameful!

Situation: Fourteen year old says, "I said I would babysit on Saturday night, and now I don't want to. I want to go to my friend's house for a slumber party instead."

Nurturing

You are a good babysitter and care about the kids. You also care about yourself. Trust your feelings to help you know what to do.

Marshmallowing

That's too tough a problem to solve satisfactorily. There is no happy ending.

Structuring and Protecting

You have a right to have fun with your friend and you have an obligation to fulfill. I bet you can come up with at least three alternative solutions to your problem. You're a good thinker.

Criticizing

It's too bad your friend is having a party on the same night. Stop feeling sorry for yourself and do your duty. Babysit.

Situation: Adult says, "I am thinking about changing careers."

Nurturing

I am willing to take extra good care of you while you make that decision. Think what you need from me, and I'll do it.

Marshmallowing

Oh, my, that sounds like a lot of work. Wouldn't that be scary? Are you sure you can do it?

Structuring and Protecting

That's an interesting and exciting idea. You can get the information you need to make a good decision. Don't forget to check your feelings, and opinions as well as the facts involved.

Criticizing

At your age? And with all the responsibilities you have! I don't know where you get such crazy ideas!

What You Stroke Is What You Get

name __Carrie James__   age __2 years__   time __Wed. evening__

To encourage people to become whole and well balanced, compliment all aspects of their personalities.

Encourage nurturing, structuring and protecting, having and using morals and ethics, and doing things for self and others

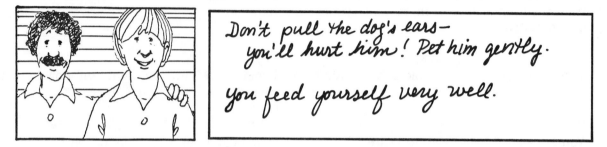

> Don't pull the dog's ears— you'll hurt him! Pet him gently.
>
> You feed yourself very well.

Encourage dealing with current reality, gathering facts, estimating probability, and solving problems.

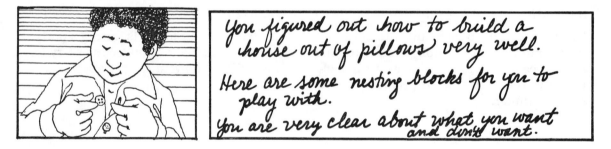

> You figured out how to build a house out of pillows very well.
>
> Here are some nesting blocks for you to play with.
>
> You are very clear about what you want and don't want.

Encourage feeling and acting naturally and adaptively . *

> Wow, Carrie — you say "I don't" better than anyone I ever heard!
>
> You are a cute, cuddly girl. (kisses, pats, and hugs)

*See page 51 for more examples of what to stroke and how to stroke.

What You Stroke Is What You Get

name _____ **age** _____ **time** _____

To encourage people to become whole and well balanced, compliment all aspects of their personalities.

Encourage nurturing, structuring and protecting, having and using morals and ethics, and doing things for self and others.

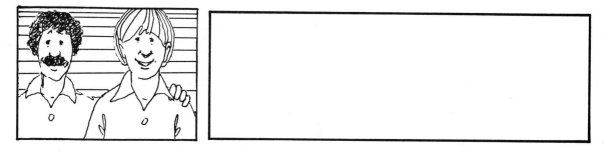

Encourage dealing with current reality, gathering facts, estimating probability, and solving problems.

Encourage feeling and acting naturally and adaptively . *

*See page 51 for more examples of what to stroke and how to stroke.

Stroke Bank

(How Sue filled in)

This page is an example of how one person might fill in a stroke bank worksheet. On the next page, you can fill in your own stroke bank worksheet.

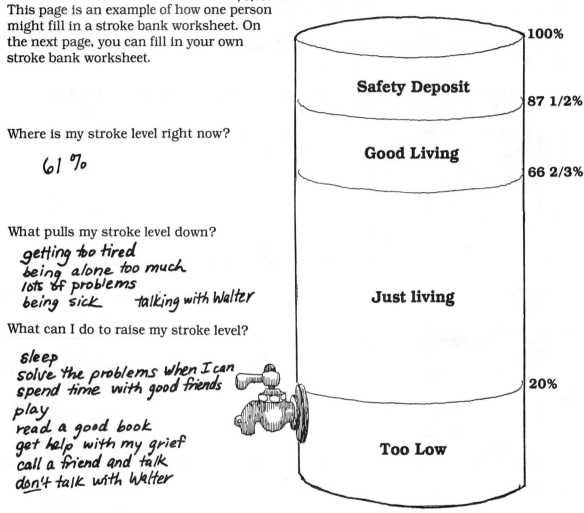

Safety Deposit

100%

87 1/2%

Good Living

66 2/3%

Where is my stroke level right now?

61 %

Just living

What pulls my stroke level down?

getting too tired
being alone too much
lots of problems
being sick   talking with Walter

What can I do to raise my stroke level?

sleep
solve the problems when I can
spend time with good friends
play
read a good book
get help with my grief
call a friend and talk
don't talk with Walter

20%

Too Low

When I let situations pull my stroke level down, there are many ways that I can help myself. What stroke rules do I believe which make it difficult for me to help myself?

Don't ask for strokes; if you have to ask, they aren't any good.
Keep a stiff upper lip and ignore your feelings.

What new rules do I need to help me be responsible for myself?

Ask and get what you need.
Feel your feelings and take responsibility to do
something about them.

108

Stroke Bank

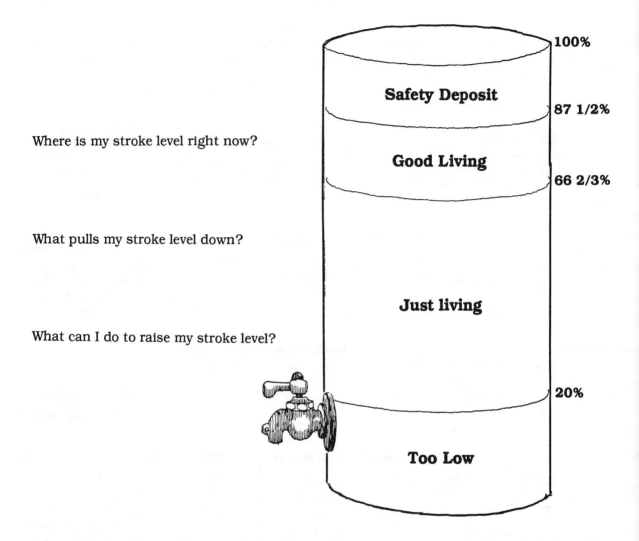

Where is my stroke level right now?

What pulls my stroke level down?

What can I do to raise my stroke level?

When I let situations pull my stroke level down, there are many ways that I can help myself. What stroke rules do I believe which make it difficult for me to help myself?

What new rules do I need to help me be responsible for myself?

Affirmations for Thinking—Deciding It's OK to Think: Eighteen Months to Three Years

These affirmations for thinking are of special importance to children who are eighteen months to three years old, to young people in the middle teens, and to everyone else.

To DAVID - 24 months
You need new shoes;
you're getting bigger!
(said lovingly)

I'm glad you're growing up.
To CARLA - 16 year old
You look very grown up
in your new outfit!

To ME - adult
You can start
a new career
now.
(from self)

You look mad!
I'm here to help.

I'm not afraid of your anger.
It's OK with me
if you feel angry.

Listen and accept;
don't change the
subject until I'm
through talking!
(from spouse)

It's OK to feel mad, but
I won't let you
hurt Mike!

You can think about what you feel.
When you are angry,
you don't need to
be immobilized.
Think!

I'm scared, too.
Let's think about
what we can do.
(from child's teacher)

You don't have to take care of me by thinking for me.

Act smart when
you feel like it —
I'm proud of you
all the time.

You don't have to
get good grades to
make your parents
look good.

Your success and
my self-esteem
are separate.
(from spouse)

You can be sure about what you need and want and think.

Let me know
what you need.

Think about what
you need and tell me.

I can learn the
new skills that I
need even if other
people think it's
unnecessary.
(from self)

(I'm glad you're here, and I see that you are doing things, and I expect you to start learning about cause-and-effect thinking.)

Affirmations for Thinking

Follow the **Directions for Others** or the **Directions for Self** below and fill in this worksheet

Directions for Others

1. Think of a person you want to send affirmations to. The person can be any age.
2. Write each affirmation the way you want to convey it to that person (words, touch, attention, listening).
3. Visualize the person as if he or she has already accepted your message.

Directions for Self

1. Write each affirmation the way you want to hear it.
2. Write the name of someone you want to hear it from. Name at least three different people.
3. Get the messages in a way that is constructive for you and for other people.
4. Give the messages to yourself, even if you don't believe them at first
5. Visualize yourself as if you already believe them.

I'm glad you're growing up.

I'm not afraid of your anger.

You can think about what you feel.

You don't have to take care of me by thinking for me.

You can be sure about what you need and want and think.

People who hear a message and consistently observe opposite behavior can feel confused or crazy. Send only the messages that you believe.

Sampler: Affirmations for Thinking—
Deciding It's OK to Think

To two-year-old Nate

"You're a big boy! I'm glad to see that you are growing up. You are taking care of yourself in new ways. I'm proud of all the things you can do. There are new things for you to learn to do. When you're not doing them, I'll tell you. I'll say something like 'You must play on the sidewalk and not on the street.' Sometimes you get mad. I'm glad to see that you know when you are mad. You can be mad and not hurt yourself or others. You can be mad and think what to do at the same time. You are a very smart kid. Remember that just because you are getting so much smarter does not mean that you have to take care of me. I can take care of myself. And you can tell me what you need."

To fifteen-year-old Jeryn

"Wow, are you ever a nifty-looking person! You certainly are growing up! I understand you're anxious to drive. That's great. I bet your folks can hardly wait to have you do some of the driving. I see that you get angry sometimes. There are lots of things to be angry about. I know that you watch a lot of television, and I know that TV programs often show anger and violence as a way to solve problems. I trust you to think about that and sort that through and use your anger as a positive force in your life. I have seen you be both mad and scared and still do good problem solving. I admire that. After all, when you are mad or scared is the time when it is most important to think clearly. I have a problem I would like to discuss with you, but I won't ask you to take responsibility for it. It's my problem. I see you trying out lots of different things and ideas now. That is great. You can try things and figure out what you want and need and still take care of yourself at the same time."

To an adult

"I see that you are working through some things that are particular to the age and stage you are in right now. I'm glad that you are doing that. Sometimes you are angry. When you are, I'll listen to what you are angry about and I'll decide if I need to do something about that. But I'll not be responsible for your bad feelings, nor will I blame you for them. You can be angry and think at the same time; you can be sad or scared and take care of yourself at the same time. So can I. You don't have to take care of me when I'm angry. I can be mad and think at the same time. Let yourself know what you really need. You don't have to settle for only the things other people think you need. You can trust your feelings to help you know what you want. You can use cause-and-effect thinking to help you get what you want and need. You're a good thinker!"

To myself

"I'm glad that I'm learning and growing. I'm glad to know how and when to be angry. I think clearly about my feelings. I know what I want and need and think. I allow other people to think for themselves."

5

Who Do We Catch Them Being?
Who Do We Tell Them They Are?[1]

Marcy and Cliff Hagen first thought of taking a foster child into their home when they saw a television program urging people to share homes with children who needed them. The Hagens discussed it for weeks. Their apartment could accommodate another child; the family had enough love to share; Marcy planned to be home full time until Matthew was in school, and Barbara had already adjusted happily to school life. The Hagens asked their children how they felt about sharing their home with a foster child. Four-year-old Matthew said he'd like a new guy to play with as long as he brought his own toys. Barbara thought it was a good idea on some days but on other days she wasn't sure. It seemed to Marcy and Cliff that this would be the ideal time to help a needy child. Five-year-old Rose has arrived, and taken over, and suddenly it is the Hagens who are needy.

Rose is an attractive and pleasant enough child, and in a way, she seems eager to please. When they talk to her, she listens to them with her wide-eyed, innocent look and nods her head up and down. Then, somehow, things end up going Rose's way, and although nothing bad has happened, the Hagens feel disconcerted and uncomfortable. They are straightforward, trusting people, and they don't quite know what to do with this new force in their midst.

Let's Help a Child!

In many ways the Hagens had thought carefully about having a foster child. They expected that they would experience some invasion of privacy, and they knew that caring for a third child would take extra energy. They had thought the financial part through carefully. They knew that taking a foster child would have an impact and somehow change life for each of the family members. Marcy and Cliff had discussed how nice it would be for Barbara, who seemed so grown-up for her eight years, to have a lively little sister to play with. Having another child might help Matthew to be a little less self-centered, to learn to share. Marcy and Cliff would have the pleasure of helping another child, of teaching her their values, and of showing their parents and neighbors that they could, in fact, gracefully incorporate another child into their family.

Now they are faced with the problem of setting limits for a child who does not seem to defy their rules, but keeps them all in turmoil![2] Barbara is irritated because Rose promises to play dolls and then accidentally walks through Barbara's dollhouse arrangement and knocks it over. Matthew steadfastly refuses to share *any* of his toys with Rose and wants a lock for his toy box to keep her out. Rose won't stay in the five-year-old room during Sunday School. And Cliff's parents are saying, "I told you so. What did you expect, taking a child like that into your home?"

Rose was placed in the Hagen home for nine months, and Cliff and Marcy have recurring feelings of concern. "What if we can't make it?" they ask each other. "What if, with all of our good intentions, we can't help this child? What if our children, instead of finding fostering a worthwhile, expanding experience, are worse off for it?"

There Must Be a Way!

Marcy and Cliff took their discomfort, went out, and had a long talk. They thought about the foster parents' orientation class they had taken before they got Rose. The situations described in class weren't exactly like theirs, but the instructor had encouraged parents to resolve or get help with any foster care problem while it was a problem instead of waiting until it became a burden. He talked about discounting—making things less important than they are—and suggested a four-step system for identifying levels of discounting.

> *Psychological discounting is the process of making something less in some way. Discounting is important to remember when you are working to build positive* **self-esteem**[3] *because discounting makes people less important or it invites people to have negative self-esteem.*
>
> *There are three things that people discount: other people, themselves, or the situation. (Although all discounts ultimately discount self.) The following items are examples of discounts to others, self, and the situation:*
>
>> *There is lots of thunder and lightning and I continue to play golf. (situation)*
>> *My kids are out of control and there is nothing I can do. (self)*
>> *My boss is so closed minded that there is no point in telling him my ideas. (other)*
>> *I can't accept a compliment unless I am positive the person who gave it is sincere. (other)*
>> *I don't need* **strokes**—*I'm tough. (self)*

116

*There aren't many good strokes in my life right now, but
there is nothing I can do about it. (self)*

*Don't expect Paul to be good in school. After all, he's a foster
child. (other)*

*To seven-year-old Wendy, someone says, "I know your
mother is an alcoholic, but you should ignore that and
go ahead with your life exactly the same as you would
if she didn't drink." (situation)*

When I get scared, I can't think. (self)

*Discounting can be done on four different levels. A first-level dis-
count denies the existence of the problem—"The problem does not
exist." The second level of discounting minimizes the seriousness
of a problem—"The problem is not serious, so I don't have to do
anything about it." A third-level discount assumes that there is no
solution—"There is nothing anybody can do about this problem so I
can't do anything about it." A person discounting at the fourth level
assumes that he is incapable of finding a solution—"I see that
there is a serious problem that can be solved, but there is nothing I
can do."*

*All four levels of discounting are equally potent for not solving prob-
lems. If a person has a problem and discounts on any level, he
doesn't do anything about the problem.*

Marcy and Cliff checked to see if they were doing any discounting. "Do we
really have a problem with Rose?" they asked themselves. "Yes," they had
to admit, "the whole family is upset."

"Is it a serious problem?" they wondered. "Yes," they concluded, "serious
enough that taking Rose may have been a mistake."

"Is there anything that can be done about it?" Cliff asked.

"Well, yes," Marcy responded, "Matt may be jealous of Rose, and we learned
about that with Barbara when Matt was born. We can do something about
that. Barbara is irritated with Rose, but I will say Barb is speaking up,
being more assertive than she was. That gets in my way sometimes, but I
think it's better for Barb than to be as quiet as she was."

Cliff agreed and added, "There must be a way to teach Rose to ask for what
she wants, to say yes or no and mean it, and for us not to end up repeatedly saying, 'Now what happened? This was not how I thought it was
going to be.'"

What should they do? Marcy and Cliff felt stuck at first. Barbara is such an easy child to manage. When Marcy says, "Barbara, I get upset when you do that," Barbara stops right away. Matthew isn't quite as quick to comply, but he usually comes around. But when Marcy and Cliff say to Rose, "We get upset when you do that," she looks at them with her big eyes and says, "Oh?" Then, instead of doing what they want, sometime during the next couple of days she does more of what they don't want.

Marcy said, "Cliff, remember when the social worker said not to keep doing something over and over if it isn't working? That's what we've been doing. When we tell Rose that we're upset with what she is doing and that doesn't work, we just say it louder, and it still doesn't work!"

Cliff responded with some despair in his voice, "You're so right!" Then he changed tone. "Let's talk about what we really want for Rose and then how to go about getting it."

Marcy and Cliff discussed at length their original feelings about wanting a foster child—their wish to be helpful, their willingness to share what they have, and their naive assumption that a foster child would be eager to learn their kind, loving values and would be grateful to them. Rose isn't grateful to them—she makes fools out of them, and Marcy and Cliff have alternately felt disappointed in themselves for not doing well enough and irritated with Rose for not accepting what they offer.

Marcy and Cliff reluctantly gave up their dreams of rescuing a needy child and focused on reality with Rose. Cliff summed up their conversation: "Looks like we thought we could change her, make her be like us, and we were wrong. What we can do is to offer ourselves and our home—it's up to her what she does with it."

Cliff and Marcy remembered that their social worker had said, "Foster parents offer love, structure, challenges, and models. Children decide what to do with those."

Cliff and Marcy planned specific ways to offer each to Rose. The love will be warm and unconditional. The structure will be a few rules, clearly set with rewards and punishments identified ahead of time. If the Hagens need help identifying suitable rewards or punishments, they will get it. The challenge will be to get Rose to grow and to stretch. They will try out different methods, not repeat something that isn't working. The models will be the Hagens and their way of life which Rose can experience as an alternative to her biological home, the one she will return to in just a few short months. The rest will be up to Rose, and neither Marcy nor Cliff can guess what she will decide to do. They are excited about their new plan, and they realize they have shifted from wondering if they could tolerate the remaining months with Rose, to looking nervously at the short period of time they will have her with them.

Who Is in Charge of What?

Marcy and Cliff Hagen have survived Rose's confrontation of their values and child-rearing methods and have come out more powerful than when they started. They will be openly in charge of themselves and their family, rather than continuing to respond to Rose's manipulative power plays. They will offer their values to Rose, and if she doesn't accept them, Marcy and Cliff's values will not be diminished. If the Hagens need help on how to handle Rose and themselves, they will get it, and that will make them more powerful. It will not be a sign of weakness.

In a sense, "family" is a state of mind, and Cliff and Marcy have changed their **frame of reference**. They no longer view themselves as Rose's "temporary" family or "substitute" family. They are her "now" family. Their job is to take care of the quality of that "now" experience rather than to spend their energy blaming her past or worrying about how she will be when she is seventeen.

They will start by changing the way they reward Rose's behavior. Marcy said, "Cliff, remember that poster that says 'What you stroke is what you get'? We have scolded Rose for taking Matt's toys. We have talked to her about kicking Barb's dolls. We have been on the alert to catch her manipulating us. And then when we think it's time to say something nice, the easiest thing to do is to tell her she has pretty eyes."

Cliff pondered, "So you think we have been reinforcing the very behavior we want her to change?"

"Could be," Marcy responded with some discouragement in her voice.

Cliff said, "Let's change that. We can make it a point to find some way each day that she helps someone, that she solves a problem, and that she is creative or fun. And we can compliment her in each of those areas. That will encourage her to nurture others, to think, and to be spontaneous and creative."[4]

> Sometimes parents get a foster child with disfunctional rules about getting along with people. These rules may be generally anti-social (It's OK to steal, just don't get caught) or they may be hard on other people (Biting and kicking is a good way to get what you want) or they may obstruct the child from taking care of himself (I won't ask for what I need because I wouldn't get it anyway). The foster parents can be so busy attempting to get the kid to accept new,

healthy rules that they may forget to encourage problem-solving thinking and spontaneity. Stroking nurturing and structuring, stroking data collection and problem solving, and stroking the spontaneous and the appropriately adaptive parts of people's behavior encourages people to develop well-balanced personalities.[5]

Learning Who We Are

Perhaps the most important value that parents of three to six year olds have to consider is whether they have a mold their children must fit or whether it is OK for the children to start figuring out who they are and practicing their own uniqueness. The assertive "Me do it!" two year olds have become three to six year olds figuring out who they are in relation to other people. They need time and space to explore themselves, other people, and the world. They like to use their imagination and to test their power. Envision adults who are caring for three to six year olds as sailors on the deck of a diving ship. The adults hold the oxygen lines, watch the gauges to be sure the exploring divers get adequate support, watch the lifelines for distress signals, and haul divers who are beyond their depth or in trouble back to the safety of the ship. This care is different from the kind given during the first three years when the adults were completely responsible for the young children's welfare. Now, when the child is about three, the adults start to let out the lifelines, to set clear rules and limits, and to expect each child to take some responsibility for safety and socially appropriate behavior.

Keep the Oxygen Coming

The steady flow of unconditional love that adults send to children from birth to three years continues. The I love you; you have every right to be here *messages are important.*

Cliff and Marcy think of many ways to express acceptance to Rose: *"I like you, Rose. . . . I'm glad you're here. . . . I'm glad that I'm getting to know you, Rose. . . . I'm willing to take care of you."*

Another part of the unconditional love that adults send children is the willingness with which the adults meet the needs of children. One of the needs of three- to six-year-old children is to start to separate fantasy from reality.

One way Marcy and Cliff help Rose separate fantasy and reality is by their matter-of-fact treatment of her fears. Rose sometimes cries in the night because she has had a bad dream. Marcy turns on the light, wakes Rose, reassures her, and asks her to identify several objects. Marcy says, "You are all right, Rose. I am here with you. You are here with us in your bedroom. What is this, Rose?"

"I don't know," Rose sobs.

"Yes, you do," Marcy insists. "Tell me what it is."

"It's Raggedy Ann. Why?" Rose demands irritably.

"I want to be sure that you are awake and that you know you are here," Marcy replies.

> *Separate reality from fantasy. If something isn't there, it isn't there. Don't try to prove something that is a fact. To look in the closet and say the ghost is not there could be interpreted by the child as evidence that there is a ghost and that it may have moved behind the chest or under the bed. Part of adult power is being sure about what is reality and what is fantasy and calmly maintaining that sureness while allowing children to gradually move toward it.*

Matthew spent several weeks being two dogs. Some days he was Spot, and some days he was Rover; but he insisted that he was not a boy and that he was a dog. He crawled instead of ran, and he called crackers "dog biscuits." On the days that he absolutely insisted that Marcy call him Rover, she did. Then she affirmed his boyness and his imagination by saying to another person in front of him, "Excuse me while I speak to my son Matthew. He has a wonderful imagination, and I am playing his dog game with him today. I'm calling him Rover." When he reprimanded her and insisted that he really was Rover, she hugged him and said, "You let me know how long I am to call you Rover, Rover," and then she winked, giving him a nonverbal signal that her words were going along with the fantasy but that her mind knew it was pretend.

Later Matthew abandoned being a dog and became a dinosaur. Marcy praised his imagination and got picture books about dinosaurs to feed his knowledge. In his hearing, to other people, she said things like, "I am learning lots about dinosaurs. It is much more fun for me than having Matthew pretend he was a dog. I already know about dogs. Life with Matthew is very interesting."

> *Giving children aged three to six straight answers helps them to separate reality from fantasy. This means no teasing at this age! Teasing often encourages confusion between reality and fantasy. It frustrates children when they are attempting to acquire information. Think of one part of the child as shelves and shelves of empty*

'how-to" and "what-it-is" tapes. The three to six year old is busy filling these tapes in order to function well later on. Teasing not only denies the sought-for information, but it may also encourage the child not to seek further information.

One afternoon Marcy's Aunt Elsie entertained three-year-old Jeannie, Marcy's niece. Elsie prepared a delightful tea party, tiny sandwiches cut like half moons, little cakes the size of thimbles, and pink lemonade tea. The table was the size and shape of Aunt Elsie's small footstool, but it was covered with a snowy linen tablecloth that fit exactly and reached to the floor. Jeannie ate her sandwiches and cakes and talked about how good the tea was.

When she finished, she thanked her aunt for the tea party. Then she said, "Aunt Elsie, is this really a table?"

"Yes," her aunt replied.

"I think it is your stool," Jeannie insisted.

"No, it is a table," Elsie said.

"Is this a napkin?" Jeannie asked.

"No, it is the tablecloth for this little table," Elsie replied.

"I have never seen it here before. Let me lift up the cloth and look," Jeannie pleaded.

"Don't touch it," Elsie warned. "You'll break the dishes."

"Where did you get it?" Jeannie asked.

"The fairies brought it," her aunt said.

"Where is your little stool?" Jeannie demanded.

"The fairies took that away during the party," Elsie explained.

"Did they really? There are no fairies! Tell, me, I know it is the stool. Is it a napkin? I want to know!"

Elsie laughed loudly at Jeannie's frustration and said, "I told you the fairies brought it. Now run along and wash your hands before you get frosting on my good upholstery."

When Jeannie returned with damp hands, the fairies had magically removed the dishes, the table, and the cloth. The footstool was back in its place. Little Jeannie, who needed to touch the stool and laugh about the tablecloth that was really a napkin, learned that when she wanted to know something, it was no use asking Aunt Elsie. But she still wasn't a hundred percent sure about the fairies. When Jeannie told her mother, Mom said, "Fairies are pretend in storybooks and on television. They do not bring tiny tablecloths to tea parties by magic. I think it was the stool and a napkin, and Elsie should have told you so. Little girls deserve to have their questions answered. Find people who will answer your questions, Jeannie. Sounds like there's no point in asking Elsie."

One way to help children separate reality and fantasy is to refrain from manipulating children's behavior and/or feelings by distracting them in a way that discounts their feelings or their observations. When a child falls and hurts himself and an adult says, "Did you hurt the floor?" the adult discounts both the child's ability to think and his feelings. Being clear about what is possible and what is not possible is another important part of separating reality from fantasy.

Three-year-old Andy, the Hagens' neighbor, wanted a baby sister or brother. His mother said, "No. Since your father and I are divorced, there won't be any more babies unless I get married again."

Andy fussed and fumed and then announced, "OK, if you won't have a baby, I will. I'll let my tummy get big, and I'll pop the baby right out my penis."

Mom said, "Hey, Andy, you really want a baby, don't you? I do too sometimes, but you can't pop a baby out of your penis, no matter how much you might want to."

That was a straight answer without a discount and with no put-down like "Ha, ha, you absurd little boy." There was no invitation to magic like "You let me know when you are ready to do that!" No teasing means no destructive name calling, no tone-of-voice implications that a person is dumb or unwanted, and no denying of information.

Adults can encourage imagination and help children separate reality and fantasy by identifying the adults' own fantasies.

For example: Matthew was waiting for his father. Cliff walked out of the bathroom and Matt said, "Hey, Dad, how come you took so long?"

Cliff looked up seriously and said, "I couldn't help it. There was an elephant in the bathtub with me, and he used up most of the water."

Matt giggled and said, "I bet!"

Cliff winked at Rose and said in an exaggeratedly hurt tone of voice, "Matt, I think you don't believe me!"

Matt returned the tone and said, "Sure, Dad, I believe you." Then he switched to a patronizing tone. "Now come on, let's go! I know there wasn't any elephant in your bathtub. He's really in the car!"

Cliff laughed and rumpled Matt's hair. "You have a great imagination, Matt!"

At four, Matthew Hagen needs clear messages about what is expected. When Matthew was afraid to try the new swing, Barbara sing-songed, "Matthew is a scaredy-cat; Matthew is a scaredy-cat!"

Cliff called out, "Hey, Barb, I want Matthew to be afraid of fast cars on the street but not of that safe swing. We didn't tease you when you were four, and we expect you not to tease him. Teasing doesn't help four year olds. Show him how to use the swing, or come and tease me. But make it fun, if you please."

Barb teased her Daddy. She hid his belongings and then looked on innocently while he searched, and just before he became exasperated, she rescued him and revealed the "lost" item. Cliff chased her and pretended to scold her. Matthew stoutly insisted that he was old enough to be teased and Barbara mostly remembered not to tease him. But now Rose is here with her incessant teasing, and Matthew doesn't like it a bit. Rose watches to see which toy he is playing with and then snatches and hides it when he isn't looking. Matt responds with recriminating howls. Marcy and Cliff tried handling Rose's teasing the way they handled Barbara's. Cliff said, "Hey, Rose, teasing doesn't help Matthew. Tease me instead." Rose responded with increased teasing—irritating, worrisome, nagging, fatiguing teasing—for everyone. In fact, Rose teased anytime she wanted some attention.

Stop Doing Things That Don't Work, and Catch Them Being Competent

Cliff and Marcy had agreed to stop doing things that didn't work. When they asked Rose to stop teasing, she didn't stop; she escalated. Marcy and Cliff thought of alternative ways to approach the teasing problem. Marcy wanted to shake Rose—hard. They decided against that. Rose's behavior improved when they stopped rewarding the teasing by talking to Rose about it. They didn't give her any attention for teasing. Instead, they set expectations for her by talking about the teasing in front of her. When Matthew howled, Marcy comforted him and ignored Rose. Or when Rose's teasing nagged, Cliff looked at Marcy and said, "Well, Marcy, I hear that Rose hasn't figured out how to make her teasing fun yet." They did not mention Rose's teasing directly to her until the day that she first teased Barb in a funny way and Barb laughed. Marcy praised Rose and called Cliff and asked him to bring home treats for everyone so they could celebrate having another fun teaser in the house.

> *Marcy and Cliff practiced the fine art of catching them being who they are and behaving in competent ways: using socially appropriate behavior, finding alternatives, thinking, and solving problems. Catching them is a way of focusing on a child's intelligence and OKness. It is a way of saying to the child, "You are an OK person; you can succeed; you are likeable; you can solve problems." Catching children being who they are and behaving competently raises self-esteem by stroking positive qualities.*

Marcy and Cliff caught Barb making her own decisions. Barbara learned her lines carefully for the Education Week Program for parents. The third grade was presenting a history program and each child had a section to recite. Barbara was excited and scared. She had never used a microphone before. Marcy and Cliff sat in the second row, waited, and sent supportive thoughts in Barbara's direction. Suddenly another child was at the microphone, saying the paragraph that Barbara had memorized. Barb's face showed surprise and then dismay, and her lip quivered. Then she straightened her body, shifted her weight, and regained her composure. The program was over. On the way home, Cliff asked Barb how she had felt.

"Awful, Daddy, just awful!" Barbara said, "I felt like crying!"

Marcy and Cliff congratulated her on making her own decision about crying during the program and suggested that she cry on the way home, in the shower, or on her pillow if her body still had some tears. They told her how great it is to have a daughter who knows her feelings, who can be upset and think at the same time, and who is learning where and when to behave in certain ways. They caught Barbara being competent.

Sometimes Marcy catches herself being competent. Matthew knows how to tie his shoes, but most mornings he stalls until Marcy gets tired of waiting for him and quickly does it for him. She fusses and declares that tomorrow he is to put on and tie his shoes before breakfast. Tomorrow's breakfast finds Matthew on his stool in his stocking feet. And Rose, who previously had dressed herself completely, is sitting on her stool swinging her feet—without shoes.

Marcy remembers that she and Cliff have agreed to discontinue doing things that don't work. Surely what she has been doing with Matthew and the shoes isn't working. The issue is not that Matthew doesn't tie shoes, it is that Marcy *does* tie them. How can she keep from getting into a hurry and forgetting: She fills the sink with hot water and starts to wash the breakfast dishes.

"As soon as I finish these dishes I am going out to the store. Will both of you be ready to go with me?" Marcy asks.

"OK, but why are you washing the dishes? Is the dishwasher broken?" Matt asks.

"No," Marcy replies.

"Then why?" Rose pushes

"I am going to hand wash the dishes for a few mornings. I decided to try it for awhile."

"Oh," Matt said. Then he commands, "Mom, tie my shoes."

"Can't, Matthew, my hands are wet," Marcy replies.

> *People can help themselves approach problems in a new way by providing new structure for themselves.*

Marcy thought of a way to keep her hands busy while she changed her words. She said nothing about the shoes until after they were tied. Then she said, "You kids certainly did a good job of getting ready to go to the store." Marcy continued to hand wash breakfast dishes for about a week until she was sure she wouldn't forget and tie shoes for capable young shoe tiers. She did continue to remark about how well Rose and Matt were doing. She remembered, "What you stroke is what you get." And she complimented herself—"I did a good job with the shoe tying." Marcy had caught herself solving a problem.

Sometimes Adults Can Catch Kids Being Smart

After Marcy learned about catching kids being smart, she gave her niece, three-year-old Jeannie, her first puzzle. Marcy sat down on the floor and said, "First you find the four corners, then you fill in the sides."

Jeannie disagreed. "I'll start in the middle," she said. She did and she finished the whole puzzle.

Marcy said, "Jeannie, you are a smart kid. You figured out your own way to do a puzzle."

A Few Clear Rules

A few clear rules are easier for three to six year olds to follow than a lot of vague rules. Rewards and punishments should be made clear ahead of time.

When Marcy and Cliff examined their rules, they found a lot of big, general rules, many of which were not clearly stated but were vaguely defined in terms of being good. "No wonder Barbara is so afraid of making mistakes," Marcy said.

"And Matthew sometimes seems reluctant to try new things," Cliff added.

Marcy identified one way she was being vague. Sometimes she asked a question instead of saying what she wanted. In a parking lot she called to Matt and Rose, "If you want to run, why don't you run on the sidewalk?" The children stopped, looked at her, acted confused, and then walked on through the parking lot. Marcy had not intended to tell them to walk instead of run. She wanted them to move to the sidewalk.

The Four Ways of Parenting

*The **four ways of parenting** method of differentiating parenting styles labels the process of telling children they are lovable as **nurturing** and labels telling them how to take care of themselves as **structuring and protecting**. Refusing to give clear messages can leave a child feeling confused and unprotected. That unclear method of soft, gooey parenting is called **marshmallowing**. Some adults marshmallow because they are lazy or they don't feel powerful enough to give assertive directions.*

Other adults, like Marcy, are high energy people who care about children and feel competent to make decisions and set guidelines, but they get caught in the "nice" trap. They have an idea that it is rude or critical to say directly what they want. So they ask questions instead of giving directions, or they say, "I prefer that you don't" when they mean "Don't!" While this manner of speaking can be effective with adults, it is often confusing to children. Children need clear guidelines about what to do and what not to do. Then they can either follow the guidelines or disobey and experience the consequences. Children need to spend their precious energy on growing and collecting knowledge, not on guessing what their caring adults want. Neglecting to provide children with adequate structuring and protecting messages is one way of abandoning them.[6]

Marcy replaced her question with a clear direction. "Don't run in the parking lot because it is dangerous. Run on the sidewalk instead." After a few weeks of using that direction, Marcy shortened it to "Matthew and Rose, use the sidewalk" as a reminder. After the rule about not running in the street or the parking lot had been around a long time, if the kids didn't comply, Marcy physically stopped them and said, "What is the rule about running?"

They answered, "Don't run in the parking lot or in the street."

"Correct!" Marcy said as she caught them being smart. If they went directly to the sidewalk, Marcy caught them being good and sent a smile.

Clear, concise rules tell what to do rather than how to be. Examples: "Do not run into the street; run on the sidewalk" rather than "Be careful about the street." "Wipe your hands on your napkin" rather than "Be neat." "Keep all of your food on your plate" rather than "Don't play with your food." "Hold the baby gently" rather than "Stop being such a roughneck."

How many rules are a few? Enough to insure safety and to start teaching socially appropriate behavior. What does that mean for a three year old? Here is an example. "Don't hit the baby, hit the pillow instead" is a safety rule that is consistently enforced. "Say 'thank you'" is a social behavior rule that is started in a limited way, perhaps in relation to gifts. A clear rule with clear rewards and punishments is "People say 'thank you' for birthday presents. You may play with your presents as soon as you have thanked. If you don't thank, you can't play with it until tomorrow." Punishment is directly related to the performance it is punishing and is non-punitive, that is, not a verbal or a physical hit. It is treated routinely. The rest of the time, politeness in three year olds is reinforced by catching them saying thanks.

Adults should demonstrate a firm commitment to rules. Enforcing a rule one day and not the next leaves the child without adequate structure in his life. If a rule is suspended, make clear to the child the reason and the duration. Besides considering the number and clarity of rules, adults should make sure that rules fit the development level of the child who is being asked to abide by them.

Matt did not follow the family's general rule about sharing. Cliff said, "You should share your toys with Rose." Marcy said, "Nice boys share." Matt refused! Cliff looked up the developmental information about sharing at the library[7] and found that several sources stressed that children need to *own* before they can *share*. Young children will give up objects to get parental approval, but true sharing cannot be expected to start before five or six years. Matt is too young for the sharing rule. Marcy and Cliff openly talked about the idea of owning and sharing in front of the children and asked five-year-old Rose if she had any things that she was sure enough about owning that she might start sharing them soon. Rose looked, with her big eyes, and said nothing. Later she told Barbara that Marcy and Cliff were dumb. She said, "Nothing in this old house is mine. When I leave I got to leave it all here." Marcy overheard and ordered cloth name tags. She sewed and glued ROSE tags on things that Rose could take with her, that were Rose's to keep. Rose didn't start to share, but she did glue a ROSE tag on Old Cat. Old Cat had been around a long time, and the Hagens were not ready to part with her. But Cliff said he would find out if Rose could take a cat home with her. If she could, they would get her a kitty which would be her very own.

Affirmations

Marcy and Cliff learned about **affirmations** in an adult class at their church. They had been affirming themselves and the children for some time. When they tried it with Rose, their efforts met with silent disbelief. They started the **affirmations for being**—*"You have every right to be here, Rose, and your needs are OK with us."* Rose looked at them and backed off, as if to say, "What is the matter with you? Are you crazy or something?" So Marcy and Cliff thought of indirect ways to offer Rose the messages. They affirmed Matthew and Barbara in front of Rose. Gradually they started to add "And Rose, too" after some of the messages. Sometimes Rose would come and stand very close to Cliff while he was affirming Barbara or Matthew.

One day Shirley, a friend from church, was visiting with five-year-old Jessica. Shirley told Marcy how much Jessie liked to hear the being affirmations at bedtime. Shirley called Jessie over. "I've been telling Mrs. Hagen how much you like the affirmations. Do you?"

"Yeh," Jessie replied.

"Tell her when is your favorite time to hear them," Shirley said.

"Right now," was Jessie's prompt response.

Shirley looked surprised, grinned, and asked, "Which one?"

"All of them," Jessie declared.

Shirley laughed, pulled Jessie up on her lap and whispered the being affirmations in Jessie's ear: *"I love you; I'm glad you are here; I'm glad you are a girl; and let me know if you need anything."* Jessie listened, smiled, and then ran off to play with Rose and Matthew.

Rose seldom displayed anger openly so Marcy and Cliff have been saying the **affirmations for thinking** to each other in front of her. Marcy says, "Cliff, I see that you are mad. *That doesn't scare me.* Want to talk about it? *We can both think about it, and you can decide what you need when you are ready to."*

And Cliff, who often buries his anger, says, "No, I'm not mad." Then he says, "Well, yes, I am mad—there were tricycles in the driveway again today. Rose and Matt, go put your tricycles in the garage."

> *The learning who we are affirmations or affirmations for separating start at age three and are important for three- to-six-year-old children to internalize:*
>   *You can be powerful and still have needs.*
>   *You don't have to act scary, sick, sad, or mad to get taken care of.*
>   *You can express your feelings straight.*[8]

Marcy and Cliff had already thought through the meaning of these messages for Matthew, for Barbara, and for each other. But now with Rose in the house, these affirmations take on a new importance. They could be a key to helping her trust herself and others. Rose doesn't express her feelings straight, and Marcy is not always sharp on picking up on that because Marcy often masks her own feelings. What Marcy and Cliff are aware of is that Rose has a lot of power in her quiet, manipulative way but that she does not seem to be happy with it. How can they get her to express her feelings straight? How can they get her to ask for what she needs instead of behaving in her secretive way and tricking them and keeping them guessing? Keeping them guessing is the clue Marcy and Cliff are working from. They do not "guess" what Rose needs. They ask her directly. If she doesn't respond, they say, "You are not saying what you want, we will just have to guess." Then they guess incorrectly, and Rose usually responds by telling what she wants in a clear, very loud voice! "Powerful, Rose, you are a powerful kid! You know how to ask for what you want," they say admiringly.

130

Matthew, meanwhile, seems to have decided that he has to win at everything. He howls if he doesn't win a game, get the bigger cookie, or get to the door first. In all things, Matthew wants Matthew's to be bigger. Otherwise he acts mad. Cliff hunches that Matt may be resenting all of the attention that Rose gets. Marcy and Cliff believe that the best way to deal with jealousy or sibling rivalry is to give more attention so they are directing more nurturing toward Matt. Marcy affirms him in the morning; Cliff affirms at night. Each arranges to spend some time, high quality focus time, however short, with him daily. In this way, they act out the *You don't have to act scary, or sick, or mad to get taken care of* affirmation. Each time he acts mad, they say, "*You are good at letting us know when you're mad. It's OK to feel mad, but you are not to hurt a person or Old Cat. Feelings don't control your behavior, you do.* The spanking stool is there if you want to hit."

Marcy learned about the spanking stool from her friend, Trice. Trice keeps a low stool in the kitchen with a ruler near by. If she feels like hitting one of her three busy boys, she grabs the ruler and gives the stool a whack.[9] If one of the boys starts to hit another, he is sent to hit the spanking stool. The person hitting the stool can say anything he wants to while he is hitting it—"I'm so mad at him, I want to hit him, like this and this and this, but I won't hit him, but I want to, he is so mean, he took my truck and he broke my car and I'm not gonna let him play with my stuff any more until he gives me one of his cars for the one he broke!" The boys are acting on the *You can express your feelings straight, and you control your behavior* affirmation.

Besides hearing Matthew's anger and channeling the hitting to the stool, Marcy and Cliff are making a special effort to catch him solving problems and to reward him for that. Marcy and Cliff are dealing with Matthew's anxiety about winning by offering extra time, attention, and love. They also make it a point to discuss between themselves in front of Matt the fact that sometimes they win and sometimes they don't and both are OK. Cliff says, "I played three games of handball today and lost all three. That Dave is one sharp handball partner. I'm tired, but wow, does my body ever feel relaxed and good!" And Marcy and Cliff hope that Matt will internalize enough positive self-esteem so he won't be upset every time he doesn't "beat."

Marcy and Cliff say that **visualizing** helps them, especially at times when they feel angry or embarrassed because they allowed themselves to be caught in one of Rose's manipulations. Marcy and Cliff are spending more time and energy thinking of ways to invite Rose to be truthful and straightforward and less time worrying about whether Rose will, in fact, accept their values. They are enjoying the foster parent experience much more than they did the first few weeks. They care about Rose as a person, and they do not get as tired and discouraged as they did.

The Hagen parents are using their experiences with Rose as an impetus to make improvements in their own relationship. Adults who are encouraging three to six year olds to know and ask for what they need can use that period to improve the ways in which they identify their own needs and express their feelings directly. Marcy and Cliff are learning to ask each other for the **strokes** they don't have to earn.

When they began, they both felt awkward. They started with the being affirmations. Cliff said they felt **plastic**. It was hard for both of them to ask, especially if they were tired or hurting. That turned out to be a clue—If you can't ask when you hurt, ask when you feel good. Early morning they usually both have high energy and feel good, so instead of waiting until evening and then not having the courage to ask, Marcy and Cliff have an agreement to ask each other for strokes every morning while they are getting up. Sometimes they ask for specific things. When Marcy hesitates, she tells herself, "I will go into a department store and say that I want some brown gloves, size six, leather. So why not tell my husband what I want from him?" Then she says, "Tell me if you think I handled Matthew's anger well last night" or "Tell me that I'm important to you." And sometimes she says, "Go through the affirmations until I hear one I especially need today." It is surprising how often she stops Cliff with, "That one—that's the one I want today—*I can think and feel at the same time*" or "*I can be powerful and still ask you to help me.*"[10]

A **stroke rule** that they are changing is "If you can't say something nice, don't say anything at all." Three to six year olds and adults need clear **negative messages** sometimes—"Don't do that" is as necessary as "Do that" for the youngster who is just starting to learn social behavior. Marcy and Cliff still aren't comfortable saying, "Don't do that, because . . . do this instead" to each other—but they don't have to change all at once. They can change a little bit, one day at a time.

Another way that Cliff and Marcy are taking care of themselves and each other is with an agreement to take time to nurture each other with careful **separation of sex and nurturing**. They make sure that their own **stroke levels** are high before a Sunday when Rose is going to visit with her **family of origin**. They start early in the week because about Thursday Rose gets grouchy, picks fights, finds fault, and generally lets them all know how "yucky" they are. When she gets back on Sunday night, she lets them all know again how inadequate they are. Marcy and Cliff were very much disturbed by this behavior until they learned at one of their foster parents' meetings that a child who likes a "new family" will sometimes be angry at them for not being her "all-of-the-time family," so she will discount and play sour grapes.

Now when Rose starts to needle, Marcy and Cliff just listen and nod. And they say to Matt and Barb, "Rose has a right to her feelings, and Monday morning we will have muffins for breakfast."

Rose says, "I hate muffins, I won't eat any."

Marcy says, "OK. But I am going to make them anyway and I am going to eat some."

Marcy and Cliff have thought a lot about power since they decided to claim their parent power and take charge of their family, including Rose.[11] Marcy says she feels more sure of her power to be a good parent since she is learning to be more direct with the children, to give up marshmallowing. Sometimes she slips back into her old ways of giving vague messages, and then when the children don't do what she wants, she feels frustrated or angry.

Marcy says that the only time she feels like hitting is when she doesn't feel powerful. She wonders if adults who batter children feel powerless in their world, or if men who beat women feel more powerful while they are beating than they do at other times. Marcy feels more powerful after she gets nurturing from Cliff and she thinks about whether nurturing—good, solid, positive nurturing—helps people feel powerful and helps them find solutions other than hitting.

Visualization

Marcy and Cliff are visualizing themselves daily as important, powerful people who are challenging an eight year old to think through her rules and are keeping strong, flexible lifelines out for two young, healthy explorers who are out looking for clues and trying out ideas about who they are. The adults also see themselves as people who ask for and get positive strokes and warm nurturing from each other.

The Results

Marcy and Cliff first thought of offering a home to a foster child so they could help some needy youngster. They saw themselves as altruistic people who could help a deprived child. Now they see themselves as loving, capable people who are offering love, structure, challenges, and modeling to an important child. She may or may not accept their offerings, but whether she does or whether she doesn't, they and she are still important, worthwhile people.

The whole family has walked through the door from the **nuclear family** experience into the **foster family** experience. Each of them as individuals and the family as a unit are irreversibly changed. Marcy and Cliff are stronger for having faced the scare they had about Rose's impact on their family and for having decided to change what they were offering to her and to Matt and Barb. They have also changed themselves.

The knowledge that parents recycle the tasks that their children are doing helped Marcy and Cliff identify the changes they are making. They are more powerful; they know better how to get what they need and how to express their feelings straight than they did before. They have a clear concept of their own identity. They are focusing on Rose's needs and their own needs, and they have stopped worrying about whether they are pleasing their parents or the neighbors. Marcy and Cliff are continuing to get support for their family from their church, and they are also meeting regularly with a group of foster parents where they practice alternative parenting skills and have fun.

They have replaced some of their manipulative handling of Barbara and Matthew with direct, clear rules. Instead of "Matt, that makes Mommy uncomfortable," Marcy now says, "Matt, will you do it this way?" They have learned to say "no" and "don't" as clearly and lovingly as "yes" and "do." They have examined and reaffirmed their own values and believe that they can be OK with being who they are without making a foster child be like them.

They know that when Rose leaves, she will probably fight with them, just as she has before each visit to her origin family. They know that they will experience the pain of wanting to keep her and they may also experience relief when she leaves, and that will be all right too. If Rose decides not to choose their values, they will not feel guilty. They have stopped thinking of Rose as a "needy" child and now think of her as an "important" child who is lucky to have them. They know that they are lucky to have her too. They have improved their positive self-esteem and they hope that she will have improved hers. Matt has not learned to share, and Barbara is not as well mannered as before Rose came, but both Matt and Barb are more straight and open, and Marcy and Cliff are pleased with the change.

Marcy and Cliff believe that if they take another foster child after Rose leaves, their family will experience more changes and growth, and that it will be positive. If they get a child with whom they cannot work out a nurturing relationship, they will cancel the foster care agreement and still be OK people. With or without more foster children, Cliff and Marcy plan to continue to improve the quality of the **stroke buffet** that they offer for their children and themselves.

134

Notes

1. Thanks to Ray McGee for permitting the use of the title of his book for this chapter

2. See the Parenting Tips for Raising the Three- to Six-Year-Old Child on pages 136-137.

3. Words which have a special definition as presented in this book are set in boldface the first time they are used in this chapter. The definition of these words is given in the Glossary.

4. See the What You Stroke Is What You Get worksheet on page 140 for examples of ways the Hagens stroke Rose to encourage her ability to nurture, to think, to express her feelings, and to adapt positively. On page 141, write the name of someone you wish to encourage to grow in a balanced way and write strokes to give that person in all the three personality areas.

5. For additional reading, see Muriel James and Dorothy Jongeward, *Transactional Analysis for Moms and Dads: What Do You Do with Them Now That You've Got Them?* (Reading, Mass.: Addison-Wesley, 1975), Ch. 2.

6. See the Four Ways of Parenting exercises on pages 138-139.

7. See Bibliography.

8. Pam Levin, *Becoming the Way We Are: A Transactional Guide to Personal Development* (Berkeley, Calif.: Transactional Publications, 1974), p. 42.

9. See the Things to Do Instead of Hitting worksheet on page 145.

10. See the Affirmations for Identity worksheets on pages 142-143 and the Affirmations for Identity sampler on page 144.

11. See *Recycling* in Glossary. Parents of three to six year olds may recycle and resolve old power problems.

Parenting Tips for Raising
the Three- to Six-Year-Old Child

I. The job of the three to six year old is learning who he is. Matt is focusing on himself in relationship to other people and to his world.

   A. He needs to establish his identity in relationship to other people.

   B. He needs to expand his imagination and differentiate between reality and fantasy.

   C. He needs to acquire information about the world, himself, his body, his sex role.

   D. He needs to start to practice socially appropriate behavior.

II. The job of the adults caring for the three to six year old is to provide a support system that will continue to nurture him while it allows him to explore his expanding world of people, things, ideas, and feelings. The energy and trust that adults expend during this period of "Why? How? What for?" is an investment in Matt's self-confidence and positive personal power.

   A. Adults will help him establish his identity.

      1. They will continue to give positive strokes for being. (Example: "I love you!") They will continue to provide loving nurturing.

      2. They will encourage him to enjoy being male while insisting that females are also OK.

      3. They will expect him to make connections between thoughts and feelings and to say how he feels. (Example: When he says, "That big dog doesn't scare me. Boys don't get scared," the adult responds, "All people get scared sometimes. Scared feelings tell you to think how to take care of yourself.")

      4. They will put limits on his behavior that will allow him to explore his relationship with other people without fear. (Example: When he says, "Mommy, I love you. I'm going to lock out your boyfriend and marry you," the adult responds, "I love you too, Matt! But if I marry, it will be to someone my own age. And I'll still love you and take care of you. And I will not let you lock Jim out.")

B. Adults will encourage his imagination.
   1. They will encourage his fantasies and separate fantasy and reality. (Example: When he says, "I am going to be a nurse when I grow up," the adult replies, "Nurses do important work. That's great." Or, when he insists, "I am a nurse now," the adult responds, "I like watching you pretend to be a nurse.")
   2. They will provide him with fantasy props—a huge cardboard box makes a great spaceship, boat, house, store, car, and encourages imagination while a commercial toy spaceship makes money for the toy manufacturer.
C. Adults will help him acquire information.
   1. They will provide safe surroundings that continue to invite him to explore, touch, manipulate.
   2. They will provide lots of information about his environment and will correct any misinformation he has as many times as necessary.
   3. They will continue to require him to think about cause and effect.
   4. They will give answers to his questions—no teasing or ridiculing at this age.
D. Adults will expect and reward socially appropriate behavior.
   1. They will compliment him when he behaves appropriately.
   2. They will give negative strokes for inappropriate behavior with reasons and expectations. (Example: "Don't do this, because, do this instead.")
   3. They will give clear behavior requests. (Example: "Pick up your blocks" rather than "Be a good boy." "Finish eating" rather than "Don't play with your mashed potatoes.")
E. Adults will affirm Matt's learning to know who he is in the ways practiced earlier in this section and will visualize him as if he had already accepted the affirmations.

III. The job of the adults is to take care of themselves.
   A. They will keep their own stroke levels high.
   B. They will resolve any of their own identity problems that bubble up as they watch Matt grow.
   C. They will remember that some days it is hard for the adults to keep their WHY buckets filled and that adults need to go out and play by themselves for a while.

Remember that your parents did the best they could. You have done the best that you could. If you want to use these new tools, it is never too late to start.

Four Ways of Parenting*

For any situation that requires parenting—advising and supporting—there are four possible ways of responding. Nurturing and structuring and protecting ways encourage positive self-esteem. Marshmallowing and criticizing ways tear down self-esteem. Below are situations. Each situation has a response given by a nurturing, a structuring and protecting, a marshmallowing, and a criticizing parent.

Read each of the four responses to each situation. Allow yourself to hear the positive and the negative implications of each. Rewrite each answer to fit your own value system where needed.

Parent Messages

Nurturing

This message is gentle, supportive, caring. It invites the person to get his or her needs met. It offers to help. It gives permission to succeed and affirms.

Marshmallowing

This message sounds supportive, but it invites dependence, suggests person will fail, and negates.

Structuring and Protecting

This message sets limits, protects, asserts, demands, advocates ethics and traditions. It tells ways to succeed and affirms.

Criticizing

This message ridicules, tears down, tells ways to fail, and negates.

Situation: Three-year-old child says, "There is a monster under my bed."

Nurturing

No, there is no monster under your bed. (Said softly.) There are no monsters here, sweet baby, so go to sleep.

Marshmallowing

Oh, how awful to be so scared! Look dear, I'll look under your bed and prove to you there is no monster!

Structuring and Protecting

No, there is no monster under your bed (Said firmly.) Time to go to sleep now.

Criticizing

Listen, if you weren't such a fraidycat, you wouldn't worry about monsters. If you don't shut up, I hope it gets you!

*See Glossary, pages 269-270, for further information.

Situation: Parent says, "My four year old runs into the street, and I'm afraid he will get hurt."

Nurturing

I'm glad you're concerned about your child's safety.

Marshmallowing

It's really tough to have to spend all your time running after your four year old.

Structuring and Protecting

A four year old is too young to make his own rules. You make the rules and enforce them. Say to your four year old, "Don't run across the street. You might get hurt. Ask me to walk across with you."

Criticizing

For heaven's sakes. He could be killed. You just have to watch him every minute.

Situation: Four-year-old says, "I run into the street."

Nurturing

I'll walk across with you.

Marshmallowing

Oh, it's really hard not to cross the street when you want to.

Structuring and Protecting

Come and get me when you want to cross the street. I will go with you and help you learn how to cross the street safely.

Criticizing

I'm sick and tired of you bugging me about crossing the street. You're too little, so just forget it!

Situation: Adult says, "My spouse wants me to go on canoe trips. I don't want to but I think I should."

Nurturing

Both of your needs are important.

Marshmallowing

You'd better go. It'll only last a few days. It's important to please your spouse. Marriage involves give-and-take, you know, so give.

Structuring and Protecting

Talk with your spouse. Say what you want. Listen to what he/she wants. Find a way for you both to have enjoyable vacations.

Criticizing

Of course you should go. Your spouse works hard all year and deserves to have you along on vacation.

What You Stroke Is What You Get

name ___Rose___   age _5 years_   time _Thurs. aft._

To encourage people to become whole and well balanced, compliment all aspects of their personalities.

Encourage nurturing: structuring and protecting, having and using morals and ethics, and doing things for self and others.

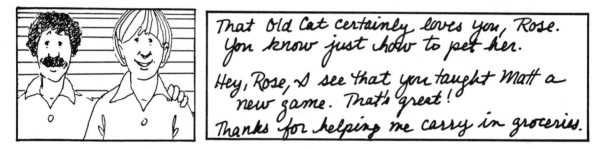

That Old Cat certainly loves you, Rose. You know just how to pet her.

Hey, Rose, I see that you taught Matt a new game. That's great!

Thanks for helping me carry in groceries.

Encourage dealing with current reality, gathering facts, estimating probability, and solving problems.

You watch and listen and figure out how to buy people very well— you're a smart kid.

Will you watch and listen to Matt and figure out what he would like as a surprise for his birthday?

Encourage feeling and acting naturally and adaptively. *

You have beautiful eyes!
I love you.
You say no very well.
Thank you for cooperating.

*See page 51 for more examples of what to stroke and how to stroke.

140

What You Stroke Is What You Get

name ———————————————— **age** ——————— **time** ———————

To encourage people to become whole and well balanced, compliment all aspects of their personalities.

Encourage nurturing, structuring and protecting, having and using morals and ethics, and doing things for self and others.

 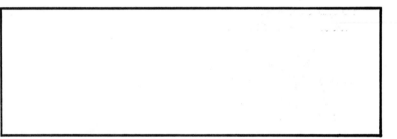

Encourage dealing with current reality, gathering facts, estimating probability, and solving problems.

Encourage feeling and acting naturally and adaptively. *

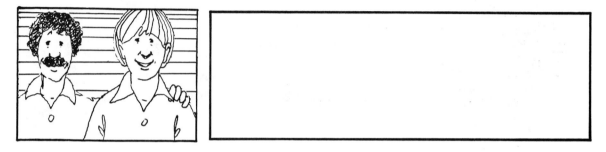

*See page 51 for more examples of what to stroke and how to stroke.

Affirmations for Identity—Learning Who We Are:
Three to Six Years

These affirmations for learning who we are have special importance for children who are three to six years old, for teenagers, for people who are owning their power to be who they are and to ask straight for what they need, for people who are giving up old and inadequate ways of dealing with life or who are giving up crutches and are incorporating healthier ways, and for everyone else.

You can be powerful and still have needs.

To BECKY- 4 years old

I see you're trying out lots of new things. I'm here whenever you need me.

TO ALAN- 15 years old

Asking for what you need makes you more independent; not less.

To ME- adult

I can be competitive on the job, and still ask to be pampered sometimes.
(from self)

You don't have to act scary (or sick or sad or mad) to get taken care of.

When you stop whining and tell me what you need, I'll help you. You don't have to be bored to get my attention.

Today is your big game, and you are sick, again. You can find a better way to be noticed than to get sick.

I can know when I am tired and get rest before I get sick!
(from self)

You can express your feelings straight.

You can tell me just how you feel. It's OK to be angry. What do you think? How do you feel?

I would rather hear what you are feeling than watch you sulk.

Tell me how you feel; I won't be shocked.
(from friend)

(I'm glad you're here, I see you are doing things, I expect you to continue learning about cause and effect, and I expect you to start differentiating feelings and actions and to ask for your needs to be met straight.)

Affirmations for Identity

Follow the **Directions for Others** or the **Directions for Self** below and fill in this worksheet.

Directions for Others

1. Think of a person you want to send affirmations to. The person can be any age.
2. Write each affirmation the way you want to convey it to that person (words, touch, attention, listening).
3. Visualize the person as if he or she has already accepted your message.

Directions for Self

1. Write each affirmation the way you want to hear it.
2. Write the name of someone you want to hear it from. Name at least three different people.
3. Get the messages in a way that is constructive for you and for other people.
4. Give the messages to yourself, even if you don't believe them at first.
5. Visualize yourself as if you already believe them.

You can be powerful and still have needs.

You don't have to act scary (or sick or sad or mad) to get taken care of.

You can express your feelings straight.

People who hear a message and consistently observe opposite behavior can feel confused or crazy. Send only the messages that you believe.

Sampler: Affirmations for Identity— Learning Who We Are

To five-year-old Claudia

"You are big enough to walk to your friend's house alone, but you can still want me to go with you sometimes. Even though you are big enough to do many new things for yourself, we still expect to take care of you. I like it that you tell me when you're mad or scared or sad or glad! I will not tease you."

To sixteen-year-old Brad

"When you plan your party you don't have to do it alone. You can ask for ideas and use them or not. You don't have to plan your party the way I would. I appreciate it when you tell me how you feel. I will be glad to help you. You do not have to get sick or mad or act incompetent to get me to help you."

To an adult

"You can be powerful and not overpowering in solving your problems. Say what you want and how you feel. Making other people guess what you are feeling is a set-up to get hurt. You don't have to get a headache to get me to take care of you. I will nurture you because you are you."

To myself

"I can write a book and ask for help in doing it. I will ask for help before I get tired or overworked. I will say when I am sad, when I am discouraged, and when I am proud."

Things to Do Instead of Hitting

Some ways that parents of young children can express anger straight without harming their children or anyone else—by Colleen Shaskin, the mother of Jessie, eleven months, and David, twenty-six months.

A. Take time to ask yourself what you want and/or need.
B. Rip up old newspapers or magazines and throw them about. (Keep a supply handy for this purpose.)
C. Stomp out of the house and walk briskly until your anger dissipates. (Do this only if someone else is in the house so your babies are not left alone.)
D. Punch a bean bag chair.
E. Say, "I'm going to scream for X number of minutes." Then do it. Make angry sounds but eliminate words that might hurt others.
F. Open the linen closet door, whip the towels out and throw them across the room. (Don't throw them at anybody.)
G. Or do same with dirty laundry and eliminate having to fold the clothes again.
H. Go outside and throw a basketball against the house.
I. Take a towel and beat on the bathtub with it.
J. Shout, "I'm so angry, and I expect you to stop what you're doing now!"
K. Count to ten loudly and in an angry voice. (Go to twenty if you need to.)
L. Do an angry dance.
M. Throw snowballs at a tree.
N. Whip marshmallows into the sink and yell a karate type yell as you throw.
O. Take a shower to calm down. Let the water wash the negative feelings away. (An alternative is a hot bath.)
P. Pile up pillows or inflated inner tubes and smash them with a tennis racket using your whole body. Keep knees bent.
Q. Pound on a mattress.

R. Kick into pillows piled against a wall.
S. Blow into a paper bag and then pop the bag.
T. Play angry notes on a piano.
U. Pull weeds with vigor saying "I'm so mad!" with each pull.
V. Throw rocks into a lake or river. (Don't throw at anything.)
W. Take a bucket of water and a big brush. Pretend the water is paint, and paint the car with huge brush strokes.
X. Give up the anger as inappropriate to the situation.
Y. Decide to think. Resolve the issues about which you are angry.
Z. Get physical, pleasurable strokes yourself to prevent your anger.

Write your own ways to express or dissipate anger without hurting another person or yourself.

6

Rules and Tools and Woulds and Shoulds, or Who Is Responsible?

For Elaine Knutson, the pang of sadness at seeing Danny, her youngest child, go off to kindergarten lasted about five minutes. It isn't that Elaine doesn't like her children, she does. But she had some things that she wanted to do. She restored a chest, hung some wallpaper, worked on the church bazaar and took a few classes. Elaine has always wanted to finish school. She also thought about getting a job.

Then her father got cancer. The family experienced long months of illness, pain, death, and mourning. Elaine cared for her father and helped her mother through her grief. Now, Danny is in third grade, and Lucy is in sixth. And Enid Fredrickson, Elaine's mother, is settled into the east bedroom with her own furniture and some cheer. Enid Fredrickson enjoys the children, and she and Elaine share a lot of interests. But Elaine needs some time to herself, and there isn't enough work in their house to keep two active women busy.

Elaine and Rolf have started talking about whether she should get a part-time job or go back to school. Grandma Fredrickson would be willing to look after the children if Elaine had late afternoon classes or was delayed at work. Grandma and the children have always been so close; it seems like a perfect arrangement.

Grandma Fredrickson likes to visit Rosemary Coleman, Elaine's divorced sister, to help with her three boys. But Grandma could go there on weekends or days that Elaine was home. Otherwise, the children could go from school to Rolf's Aunt Sally's house and Elaine could pick them up on her way home.

Elaine would be more comfortable if she could get over that uneasy feeling about the way Grandma reacts to her eleven-year-old granddaughter Lucy's heavy eye-makeup. Elaine feels sure that Lucy is experimenting and won't wear that heavy goop all of her life, but Grandma is so upset about it! Also, Elaine and Rolf are concerned about Grandma Fredrickson's open dislike toward some of Danny's friends.[1]

The boys have a club house in Cecil Bishop's back yard. Elaine doesn't think they do anything wrong, but Grandma insists that her spot flashlight disappeared on a day the boys were in and out between the kitchen and the club house. Grandma has declared that Danny will not be allowed to play with those boys on any day that she is responsible for the children.

Expectations

When Elaine's father died, she, Rolf, and the children decided to ask Grandma Fredrickson to come and live with them. They talked about all of the benefits of having Grandma with them. She could have the guest bedroom; she would have privacy, but she wouldn't be alone. The children would enjoy spending time with her. She would live closer to Rosemary and she could make short visits to Rosemary's crowded apartment. She was skilled with a needle, and she could take over the laundry and the sewing.

The Knutsons did not talk about difficulties that might arise because Grandma was living with them. Oh, Elaine worried some about how her mother and Rolf would get along on a daily basis. But Enid and Rolf get along well, and it's Elaine who feels the pressure of constantly having someone with her. She was accustomed to privacy while the children were in school. Elaine doesn't complain about feeling pushed. Her mother has to live somewhere, and Mrs. Fredrickson is making a real effort to fit into the Knutson family without getting in the way. However, sometimes Elaine is short with Rolf. She answers him sharply or sets her jaw in a hard line when he doesn't do something she wants him to. One day he said, "Hey Elaine, whatever it is—don't take it out on me!" and went out to the garage and cleaned the work bench. It was great to have a clean work bench, but Elaine didn't like the distance she felt between them that evening.

The next morning before he went to work, Rolf said, "Elaine, you better get out of the house some."

Elaine thought, "He's right, and not just for the morning. I do have time enough to go back to school now, but I worry about the friction between Mother and the kids. If only Lucy would wash her face and Danny would come down out of that tree!"

Extended Family

Danny Knutson lives near relatives. He plays with his Coleman cousins, his great Aunt Sally lives near his school, and his grandmother lives in the same house with him. Danny lives in an **extended family**.[2] He can ask Aunt Sally about his father's boyhood. His grandmother often tells stories about how life was before television and airplanes and what his Mommy did when she was his age. Danny feels a sense of continuity, something that children like Jason Banner, growing up in **nuclear families**, are not as likely to experience. From his kin, Danny can learn about major changes in life-styles and values. He can see that people adjust and survive. He can also experience the conflicts that come from changing values and from intergenerational pressures and expectations.

Some days Danny wishes that Grandma Fredrickson would live with Aunt Rosemary and his Coleman cousins. Then she'd stop complaining about the guys in the clubhouse. Grandma thinks they stole her spot flashlight. And they didn't. Danny thinks, "It just happened that her old spot flashlight disappeared about the same time they got one like it in the clubhouse. It's a brand name spot! There must be millions of them all over the city. I saw one in Cecil Bishop's house. Larry Revel's folks wouldn't care if Larry took three spot flashlights for the clubhouse. They even gave him a piece of carpet for the house."

The guys are always telling Danny that he should get more stuff from his house. But Danny's mom says, "No, you boys are supposed to build things for a clubhouse, not take good things out of your homes." Still, Danny would like to take a few things.

Danny told Elaine, "Mom, one of the guys says I could get some neat stuff from Aunt Sally's back porch and she'd never miss it. I wouldn't do that, but the Bishops and the Revels let their kids have stuff for the clubhouse. Sometimes I want to take things from here and forget to tell you."

Elaine said, "Danny, I expect you to have more **self-esteem** than to let the other kids make up your mind for you."

How Can We Build Positive Self-Esteem in Kids Who Are at Somebody Else's House?

> *"I thought the parents were supposed to control the children," a parent once said, "and it turned out that the children have to learn to control themselves." Parenting a child who is at school most of the day and spends the rest of her time playing with friends or checking out their parents so she can come home and say "But none of the other parents make their kids do that!" can be frustrating.*

Rosemary and her boys are visiting the Knutsons. Danny and his cousins are in the tree house. "Where is Lucy?" Rosemary asks.

"At Jenny's house, where else?" Grandma retorts. "That child only comes home to eat and sleep. It seems to me that she is always at Jenny's house. And when she does come home we get a full report on how things are done at Jenny's house. Jenny's mother grocery shops every Tuesday and Friday. Jenny's father doesn't fertilize their lawn, so he doesn't have to mow it every week. So why does Rolf fertilize? Jenny's mother sews beautiful clothes for Jenny. Jenny's mother's family goes to the lake every July no matter what else happens during the year. Jenny's father hangs his tools on the garage wall instead of junking them into drawers. Jenny's father doesn't care how much eye-makeup she wears! And Jenny keeps a journal, and Lucy thinks that probably everyone should keep a journal, especially me! It would keep me busy she says!" Grandma gives a disgusted little sigh and continues, "When Lucy does come home she usually brings Jenny with her. Those girls spend so much time at each other's houses you wouldn't believe it. Why, the other day Jenny helped me bake cookies while Lucy was helping Jenny's mother plant petunias. It's unbelievable."

Rosemary and Elaine laughed and Rosemary said, "Mother, I have the feeling I've heard this all before. Do you remember Paula Smith? She practically lived at our house when Elaine was Lucy's age. Why, those girls were inseparable. Elaine, do you ever hear from Paula?"

"I get a birthday card from her every year," Elaine replied. Then, turning to her mother, she asked, "You really liked Paula, didn't you Mother?"

"Yes, she was a sweet girl. I did like her, and I was glad you had a friend you liked so much. But sometimes I got lonesome for you—I wanted to have you to myself for a while."

Rosemary said, "Mother, do you wish Lucy would spend some time with you without Jenny?"

Mrs. Fredrickson pursed her lips and thought for a moment. "Well, yes, Rosemary, I guess I do. She is my only granddaughter and she is very special to me."

> *One of the jobs of the six- to twelve-year-old child is to check out family rules. Children often do this by observing other families and making comparisons. The six to twelve year old may sound very critical as she goes through the necessary process of sorting through which customs are strictly her family's and which are generally shared by the community.*
>
> *The six to twelve year old often has lots of rules. She may not follow them herself, but she howls when someone else breaks them! She doesn't have the skills and tools to do some of the simplest*

jobs, but she can cruelly tease another child for a similar lack. And still she can be lovable, engaging, companionable, and entertaining. So what are parents to do?

*Four ways adults can encourage six- to twelve-year-old children to develop positive self-esteem and responsibility are first, by affirming their efforts to learn to do things their own way; second, by giving them lots of positive **strokes**;[3] third, by challenging their behavior and decisions; and fourth, by **visualizing** them as if they are already self-confident, independent, and responsible for their own behavior.*

Affirmations for Learning to Do Things Their Own Way

*The **affirmations** that a child between six and twelve years of age needs to hear are the learning to do things my own way ones:*
> You can think before you make that rule your own.
> You can trust your feelings to help you know.
> You can do it your way. It's OK to disagree.
> You don't have to suffer to get what you need.[4]

*Support the child in her journey toward independence and responsibility. The separation that she started at about eight months and the independence she asserted at about two years are now followed by her push to become responsible for her own behavior. Her job during these middle years is to find her own way of doing things—her own **frame of reference**—and to put strong enough rules in her head so that she learns to protect and take care of herself. This process is gradual. In these six years she will find her own methods of doing things, and then she will internalize some rules she previously followed just to please her parents. For example, stealing in a first-grade classroom would be treated seriously but would not be viewed seriously. Stealing in a sixth-grade classroom would be both treated and viewed as serious. The first grader may not have internalized a rule against stealing; the sixth grader should have that rule.*

When Elaine discussed her concerns about Danny and the spot flashlight with her sister, Rosemary suggested that Elaine challenge Danny's values and behavior more often and that she use affirmations. Elaine knew what Rosemary meant by challenge. Rosemary goes round and round with her kids doing what she calls **healthy hassling**. Elaine is uncomfortable listening to it, but she has to admit that her nephews are very self-sufficient kids. Rosemary is doing a good job of parenting. Rosemary gave Elaine a copy of all of the affirmations and told her to figure out how to say the learning to do things our own way set in a way that her kids could hear.

Elaine read them aloud: "*You can think before you make that rule your own. You can trust your feelings to help you know. You can do it your way. It's OK to disagree. You don't have to suffer to get what you need.*" She took them home and asked Rolf to help her think of ways to say them.

Rolf said, "How about the times the kids throw things on the bus and Danny says he does it because all the guys do. Instead of scolding him, we can give him the *You can think before you make that rule your own* affirmation by saying, 'Hey, Danny, when all the guys are doing something, you can decide if it's a good thing for you to do.'" Rolf said he didn't think the *You can do it your way* affirmation was such a good idea for kids. He said, "We can't let them do things any way they want to; we might lose control." But then Rolf thought of the clubhouse. "We really don't have a lot of control over what goes on in the clubhouse, so let's think how to let Danny know he can do things his own way without being overly influenced by the other guys."

Elaine decided that *You can do it your way* doesn't mean to let children do things that are dangerous and it doesn't mean to let kids run over parents. It means to encourage children to develop their own way of doing things, their own style. Elaine said, "I can stop complaining when Lucy moves the furniture in her bedroom. It doesn't look nearly as nice to me as the way I had it arranged, but I will tell Lucy that it is her bedroom and I am glad she is moving her furniture in a way that pleases her."

Rolf didn't like the *It's OK to disagree* affirmation. He said, "Oh, no! Not with me it isn't! I'll start with some of the others, but I won't go along with that one. Not yet, anyway."

Elaine said, "OK. Don't say it till you mean it. If we say something we don't mean, that's not an affirmation for positive self-esteem, that's a lie."

Elaine thought that the *You don't have to suffer to get what you need* affirmation was ridiculous. She asked Rolf, "Who would suffer to get what they need?"

Rolf thought about it and replied, "Well, it could mean you don't have to be tired or sick before you ask me to help you with something. Danny has stomachaches that go away mighty fast when his friends call. I wonder if he's using his stomach to get attention." Rolf decided that he would say, "Danny, when you want some time just with me, say so and I'll spend time with you. Or if I can't right then, I'll make a date with you. You don't have to have a stomachache to get attention."

Elaine and Rolf showed Grandma the four sets of affirmations that Lucy and Danny need, and she suggested that although Lucy is in the same age group as Danny and is definitely testing rules, she may need the **affirmations for being** too.

"Reread that first set," Grandma said, "I think they might help Lucy. She seems so resentful of Danny."

Rolf read: *"You have every right to be here. Your needs are OK with me. I'm glad you're a girl. You don't have to hurry. I like to hold you."*

"Yes," Grandma said. "I think we should try those." She recounted a conversation she had had with Lucy on Tuesday. "Danny and Lucy were squabbling," Grandma said. "Lucy accused, and Danny defended. Then Danny accused, and Lucy pouted. Lucy said, 'Danny is always in the way. Whenever I want to do something, I can't, because of Danny.' I said, 'Lucy, how can Danny "always" be in your way when he spends most of his time in Cecil Bishop's tree?' 'Grandma,' Lucy wailed, 'He doesn't do things the way I tell him to, and when Jenny is here, he bugs us all the time!' I said, 'Well, Lucy, I suppose it seems that way. That's just the way your mother used to feel about her little brother Dick. It seemed to me that he and his dog were always off somewhere, but Elaine thought he was always interfering with her and her friends.' Lucy stormed, 'Well, if everybody wasn't so interested in his old tree house. . . .'"

> *At age eleven Lucy is practicing her sex role by watching her mother and her grandmother, spending lots of time with her girl friends, and pushing her brother away. In addition, Lucy may be **recycling** some early feelings she had several years ago before her baby brother was born.*

Before Danny was born, Rolf and Elaine told Lucy that she would soon be having a little sister or brother. Three-year-old Lucy was alternately excited and pensive. She called the baby Bunrock. Lucy asked lots of questions about when she was as little as Bunrock. She snuggled in Elaine's lap and demanded that Elaine repeat to her again and again the story about when she was born—"After being married for four years, your father and I still didn't have a baby, and then Lucy Elaine Knutson was born. We were so happy, and we enjoyed her so much! She changed our lives, and we liked it. It was so wonderful. You are that baby girl, Lucy Elaine Knutson, and I love you!"

One day, after she had heard that loving story for the twentieth time, she slid off her mother's lap, placed her sturdy three-year-old body squarely in front of her mother and said, "Why are you and Daddy having Bunrock?"

Elaine answered, "Because you have made us so happy and life is so wonderful having you in the family. And because we think you will enjoy the new baby too."

Lucy glared at her mother with disbelief and contempt, turned on her small heel, and walked out of the room. Elaine was shaken.[5] How could Lucy doubt her?

Children make the best sense they can out of what they perceive, and young Lucy perceived that she was about to be replaced. Not an uncommon way for a child to feel. Parents can increase their understanding of the child's position by putting themselves in her place. Suppose that Rolf had come home from work one night and said, "Big news, Elaine. I'm going to bring home another wife soon."

Elaine is shocked and perplexed. She asks, "Why, Rolf, why?"

Rolf assures her, "Well, Elaine, I like you so much, and life is so much better for me and happier for me since I married you that I thought it would be nice to have another wife to enjoy and love. It doesn't mean that I'll love you any less—things will be just the same between you and me. Besides, I think you will like her. She can help you with the housework, and you and she can have lots of fun together."

Children who are faced with the arrival of another child make some decisions. Adults cannot make or control those decisions. What adults can do is to continue to extend love, care, and attention to the older children. Adults can accept the children's feelings in a matter-of-fact way.

Grandma, Rolf, and Elaine decided that they will each offer Lucy more personal time and attention each day—time when Danny is not mentioned and attention that has nothing to do with Danny or his activities. They will find many ways to offer the being affirmations to Lucy.

Grandma Fredrickson was clever with crafts. She fashioned some brightly colored cardboard blocks and lettered the affirmations on the sides. Sometimes she tossed a block at Lucy as Lucy entered her grandmother's room. Lucy would catch the block, turn it over in her hands, read the words, and hand it back to her grandmother with the message Lucy wanted read aloud on the top surface of the block. Dan liked the **affirmation blocks** too. He tossed them back and forth with his dad and they read whichever message surfaced to each other.

Grandma cut small circles of different colors and wrote the affirmations on them. Lucy sorted and arranged the circles and read them aloud. Grandma called them **affirmation cymbals** because she said, "I want you to hear these messages loud and clear, Lucy, like clanging cymbals."[6]

Hugs, Howls, and Hassles

> *Children between the ages of six and twelve continue to need strokes for being, like I love you; you are important to me. Hug, hug. They also need clear rewards for doing well, rewards that focus on behavior. Say "Thank you for sweeping the floor. It looks clean!" instead of "You are a good kid and you do a good job." General compliments are all right, but they are not enough. Negative strokes should also be explicit. Instead of saying, "You watch too much TV," say "Turn the volume down on the television; the noise hurts my ear" or "Turn the television off or find another program. That program is showing violence as if it were OK, and I don't want you to put that message into your system." Limit-setting messages build positive self-esteem when they offer protection and structure. Negative messages that name call or suggest that the child will fail tear down self-esteem."*[7]

Healthy Hassling

Rosemary had suggested to Elaine that she could help Danny reflect on his behavior and ideas by challenging him in a friendly way, by doing what Rosemary calls "healthy hassling."[8]

Rolf's Aunt Sally is a natural-born healthy hassler. She challenges the children whenever she sees them. She chooses the topic, starts the hassle, and keeps a nurturing quality in it. The kids don't seem to mind. Elaine and Rolf have watched both Rosemary and Aunt Sally challenge the children and have decided that healthy hassling is a way to encourage children *to think before they make a rule their own*. It is different from arguing. It is done to nurture rather than to win the point. In fact, Aunt Sally told Rolf and Elaine not to hassle something the kids don't have any choice about. "That isn't fair," she said, "And don't hassle when you don't feel nurturing." She cautioned, "In good hassling, sometimes adults win and sometimes the kids win. And sometimes they both win. The point of hassling is to get the children to consider alternatives."

Elaine listens to Aunt Sally do healthy hassling to focus Lucy's attention on her behavior without criticizing her. Sally fires a barrage of friendly questions at Lucy—"Lucy, I hear you calling your friend a queer. Tell me what a queer looks like? Is she tall and pale and thin?"

Lucy replied, "No, Aunt Sally, she doesn't look like that at all."

"What does she look like then?" Aunt Sally asked.

"Well, she looks like a queer, that's what." Lucy aimost seemed at a loss for words.

Sally pushed her, "I've never seen one, Lucy, help me out."

"She looks like my friend. That's what." Lucy said evasively.

"Tell me, how does it work for you to call names?" Aunt Sally asked.

"What do you mean, Aunt Sally?" Lucy looked puzzled.

"Does it help you keep the friends you really want?"

"Oh, Aunt Sally," Lucy said, "It's no big deal. Everybody calls her queer!"

Sally studied Lucy's face briefly. "Lucy, how would you feel if I called you queer?"

"I wouldn't mind, Aunt Sally," Lucy said, biting her lip.

"Well," Aunt Sally replied, "I'm not going to do it. I like you too much to call you derogatory names, dear niece. Tell me, what other names could you call your friend?"

"Oh, Aunt Sally, I can't think of any now."

"You spoof your old Aunt Sally; I know you are smart enough to think of names. Come, child, pass that bowl of fruit around and see if anyone wants a piece." Aunt Sally ended the hassling on a positive note.

> *Children may be irritated by hassling or may view it as an affectionate interchange. Adults are responsible for keeping hassling nurturing. They shouldn't let themselves get lured into put-down arguments or into expressing bad feelings. Destructive teasing hits a vulnerable spot, digs in, and should always be avoided. Enjoyable teasing is done for fun. Hassling is different from teasing. Hassling keeps saying "How come?" and ends with a compliment like "You did a good job thinking during that round" or "I don't agree with your conclusion, but it takes a sharp mind to think as quickly as you did."*

Elaine decided that her discomfort with hassling came from her own fear that it would turn into teasing. When she realized that she could prevent that, she felt better. Grandma Fredrickson was upset with Elaine's decision to hassle and objected strongly at first. Elaine asked her mother to keep score on the effects of the hassling, so Grandma counted how many alternatives each hassle produced. If there were none at the time of the hassle, Grandma listened for evidence that Lucy or Danny had done more thinking later. Grandma also kept track of the number of times Elaine ended the hassle with a compliment. Grandma approved of that part and soon she was making suggestions to Elaine on how to improve her compliments.

Grandma Fredrickson still insists that Danny shouldn't be allowed to go to the clubhouse. "Rolf," she says, "Those boys are not good for Danny. They put him up to things he would never think of by himself."

Lucy adds, "Yes, Dad, those boys are so mean! I don't know how Danny can stand them. And he's getting to be just like them."

Rolf says, "I don't believe in blaming peers for a kid's behavior. I believe that kids and adults choose their own peer pressure when they choose people they spend time with." He asks Elaine and Grandma to help him think of ways to challenge Danny to think about three ideas: I am responsible for what I do. People cannot control me, but I can allow them to. I cannot control people, but they can allow me to.

Elaine and Grandma agree to help but Lucy says, "That will never work with Danny. He's hopeless."

That night Danny says he is late for dinner because he was at Larry Revel's house and the Revels eat late. Elaine says, "Danny, you know that we eat between 6:00 and 6:30."

Danny replies, "Yes, but we weren't through with our game. And the guys would be mad if I left early and busted up the game."

Rolf asks, "Danny, was there someone else there who could have taken your place in the game?"

Danny thought for a second, "Well, Larry's sister was there, but she's a girl." Lucy shot him a nasty look.

Elaine lets the remark pass and asks, "Was it a game in which one person could have played two parts?"

Danny replies grudgingly, "Well, I guess so, but the guys told me to stay."

Rolf says, "Think of a way you could have left."

Danny ponders and comes up with, "Well, I could have said we were having pizza—nobody expects a guy to be late for dinner if they're having pizza!"

Everyone laughs and Rolf says, "Tricky thinking, Dan. How else could you have done it?"

Danny thinks again, "Well, I guess I could have said I have to go. I could have asked the guys to come here tomorrow after school for another game." Danny shot a glance at his grandmother. He wonders if she'd want the guys at their house.

Grandma looks at Danny thoughtfully and then tells how she got his Uncle Dick to come home for supper when he was Danny's age and wanted to play ball until sundown. Grandma relates, "Uncle Dick had a dog, a big Irish setter, and on days when Uncle Dick was playing ball, I would keep the dog in the house until just before supper. Then I'd open the door and say, 'Red, go get Dick.' Red would streak toward the sandlot where the kids played ball. Red loved to play ball! The first kid to see Red approaching would yell, 'Get the ball, it's Red; go home Dick, and take your dog.' And somebody would grab the ball while everybody yelled, 'Hurry up and get your dog, Dick! Go home, Dick, so we can finish our game.' If Red got the ball there would be a long, long chase and probably no more ball game that evening."

Danny and Lucy laughed a lot, and Grandma said that, at the time, she had thought it was a very good arrangement. But now as she thinks back on it, she says, "I can see that it kept Uncle Dick from figuring out ways to get himself home. And I see that Danny doesn't need a dog to help him do that."

> *The adults choose the areas of responsibility to hassle a child about. They choose topics they want the child to think about. Some children will start an argument about anything and everything. The adults can turn that into a healthy hassle, or if the topic is not negotiable or they're not feeling like hassling, they can refuse to argue.*

Lucy said, "The Benson kids don't have to make their beds!"

Rolf said, "In our family, people make their own beds, Lucy."

Lucy countered with, "Grandma could do it."

Rolf wasn't going to be moved. "She could. She makes her own bed, you make yours."

Lucy said, "I don't want to."

Rolf wasn't going to hassle. "This is a rule in our family that everybody is expected to follow, even when they don't want to. That includes you, Lucy."

Lucy said furiously, "I hate you!"

Rolf replied calmly, "That may be, but make your bed anyway."

> *In this case, Rolf could have parented [9] by critically saying, "Well, stop worrying about the Bensons and do what I tell you. You pay more attention to them than to us. If you think those Bensons are so wonderful, why don't you go live with them?" Or he could have parented with a patronizing marshmallowy, "Poor Lucy, you don't want to make your bed, do you? Well, honey, I'll talk with your mother about another way of getting it made. Let me handle it."*

> *Criticizing and marshmallowing are both potentially harmful offerings for children. **Criticism** tears down self-esteem with harsh words. **Marshmallowing** erodes self-esteem by indicating that the adult does not believe the child is capable. [10] Healthy hassling can be used to show children ways to update rules and methods.*

Danny said, "The guys say it's OK with their folks to bring things to the clubhouse from home without asking."

Elaine said, "You may take fruit or crackers without asking."

"No, Mom, I mean things like pillows and hammers."

"That may be OK in your friends' homes," Elaine said. "But in our house the rule is that you ask before you take things other than food or your own belongings."

"The guys say that's dumb."

"Their saying it's dumb doesn't change the rule," his mother insisted. "If you want that rule changed, you can ask the whole family to talk about it, and maybe we will change the rule and maybe we won't, but until it is changed, you ask."

> *Elaine provided firm structure without criticizing and refused to argue about a subject that was not negotiable.*

Visualization

Grandma Fredrickson understands hassling now and tolerates it fairly well when Elaine and Rolf do it. But she doesn't enjoy it and doesn't plan to do any of it herself. When she gasps at the sight of little Lucy wearing heavy green eye shadow and mascara, one of the things that Grandma can do instead of hassling Lucy is to visualize Lucy as she will be when she has learned to use makeup artfully. Grandma closes her eyes and sees Lucy at eighteen wearing skillfully applied makeup, doing things her own way, thinking before she makes a fashion rule her own.

> *When Elaine and Rolf and Grandma and Aunt Sally have af-*
> *firmed, stroked, hassled, and visualized, will Danny and Lucy be*
> *independent, responsible youngsters with high self-esteem? That*
> *decision can only be made by Danny and Lucy.*[11]

Even the Best Hasslers Get Tired, or Good Moms and Good Dads Need Nurturing, Too

> *Meanwhile, back in the parents' corner, while Mom and Dad have*
> *been loving and encouraging and challenging their six- to twelve-*
> *year-old children, the children have been testing every rule and*
> *challenging their folks. Children need to challenge; it's the way*
> *they find out which rules are important at their house, and it's the*
> *way they incorporate their own rules and methods. They may*
> *spend long hours at their friends' houses, busily checking things*
> *out, and only come home long enough to eat and report on which*
> *rules the neighbors have and do not have. Those rules are fre-*
> *quently presented as far superior to the home rules. Parents can*
> *get very tired of this.*

Sometimes Rolf and Elaine get tired—especially Rolf—when Danny disagrees with him. Rolf has a rule in his head that said "Good fathers are smart enough and competent enough so that their children admire them and never disagree with them."[12] And Elaine feels especially tired when she has allowed Dan and Lucy to do things their own way, to disagree with her. Then she may slip into fretting about how Grandma will feel. Sometimes Elaine is sharp with Rolf, and they go to bed with that hurtful, silent distance between them. It's hard to identify exactly what is wrong, and they are both too tired to talk about it. Anyway, Elaine is afraid if they do start to talk that she will burst into tears and say some things about her mother that she really doesn't mean.

> *Parents like Elaine and Rolf who have nursed their children*
> *through infancy, survived the creeper exploration stages, weath-*
> *ered the independence of the two year olds, and answered the*
> *questions of the preschoolers deserve a rest! Like Elaine, many*
> *parents are anxious to focus some time away from their children.*
> *It's not that they don't care about the children. Most of the parents*

160

of grade-schoolers are deeply concerned about the growth and welfare of their children. They don't expect the school to be totally responsible for their children. In fact, most parents are willing to invest a lot of time and energy in the growth and development of children from six to twelve. Parents may not always feel sure about what to do, but they do care!

*So, where can parents who are busy **nurturing** their children and their own parents get some nurturing for themselves? At no time is it more important for parents to carefully and visibly nurture themselves and each other than while their children are putting independent nurturing methods into their own heads. Also, this is a good time for parents to practice looking at each other as people rather than as parents and to start preparing themselves for the separation from children that will take place when kids are teenagers.*

Elaine decided to focus on the positive kinds of nurturing that she gets from her mother and to ask Rolf to nurture her more. Elaine had learned about **separating sex and nurturing** from Julia Banner. She and Rolf decided that would be a good thing to practice before Lucy and Danny reached puberty. Elaine remembered that when she entered adolescence her family stopped touching her. Just at a time when she needed reassurance! Maybe they thought acne was contagious? Elaine and Rolf thought of a way to improve the quality of nurturing that they do for each other. Each made lists of things they would like to do during the week. This was special, extra nurturing. It didn't have to be earned. This was nurturing for Elaine and Rolf just because they are important people!

Psychiatrist Carl Whitaker once said that all American adults have unresolved dependency needs.[13] Each of us may have some spot in ourselves that was not taken care of well enough when we were young. The dependency doesn't need to interfere with our adult lives or our parenting unless we continue the deprivation. Fortunately, adult couples, friends, and relatives can nurture each other unless—We get so busy that we forget; we pretend we are so tough we don't need it; or we forget to swap nurturing and end up with one dependent adult and one depleted adult. It is important for adults to arrange to get their nurturing from several sources. (Some people get therapy to help them accept nurturing.)

Single parents need support. Since they have no spouse to turn to, most of them are forced to build a network of support people. Support networks are important for married people as well. But wanting total support from a spouse puts a heavy burden on that person and leaves one vulnerable when that person is tired or ill or angry or gone.

Elaine's sister, Rosemary Coleman, is a single parent. She is busy working and taking care of her three boys. It is not easy for her to get nurturing. But, when she doesn't take time for herself, she gets depressed. She and Elaine are supporting each other. They get together once a week, even if only for one hour, to have fun, to appreciate themselves and each other, and to take a rest from hassling—time out for themselves, not talk about raising children.

> *Adults who are living with six to twelve year olds may find this a good time to recycle some of their own needs to be independent and to do things their own way. The learning to do things our own way affirmations will be helpful for them too:*
>> You can think before you make that rule your own.
>> You can trust your feelings to help you know.
>> You can do it your way.
>> It's OK to disagree.
>> You don't have to suffer to get what you need.

> *Mrs. Fredrickson has many adjustments to make in moving from her role of mother and grandmother. In a way, she is recycling what Lucy is going through—finding new identity and new rules for herself as a woman. Life in an extended family can offer support and continuity, but it is important for individuals to maintain their identity and not to be defined solely in terms of their relationships.*

Elaine asked Grandma Fredrickson if she wanted to go to Rosemary's for the afternoon. Grandma said, "Well, yes, I guess I better."

Elaine said, "Mother, you don't sound very enthusiastic. Do the boys get on your nerves?"

Her mother said, "Well, sometimes, but I'm lucky to live near my grandchildren. I'll go."

Elaine persevered. "Mother, is there something you would rather do instead?"

Grandma answered, "Well, Elaine, I hate to ask. You and Rolf do so much for me, and I hate to impose any more driving on you."

"Mother," Elaine said, "What is it you want to do?"

"Well," her mother hesitates, "my friend Jolly Hayward is in town, and I would like to see her."

"Good," Elaine said, "We will ask her to lunch." Grandma looked disappointed. Elaine paused. "Mother, if you could do whatever you wanted to do today, what would it be?"

Grandma brightened, "You won't be hurt if I tell you?"

"No," Elaine assured her.

"I would like to go out to lunch with my friends. I would like to spend the whole afternoon with people who call me Enid."

Elaine said, "Oh. I see." And she thought, "I'm not the only one who needs to get out. I hadn't even thought that Mother might be needing time away also."

Grandma said, "Oh, Elaine, don't get me wrong. I love you and the children and Rolf, and I like living here, but sometimes I almost forget who I am. Everyone calls me Grandma."

Elaine said slowly, "I see. Mother, what would you like us to call you?"

"Well, I like to have you call me Mother, but I wish Jenny Benson would call me Mrs. Fredrickson, and I think that Cecil Bishop and Larry Revel should call me that too. And it would be all right if Rolf called me Enid now and then. I do need to hear my own name."

Elaine looked at her mother, smiled, and said gently, "All right, Enid Fredrickson," and kissed her mother on the cheek. Elaine thought, "And I better get busy finding out who I am instead of hissing at Rolf when I feel weighted down."

Affirmations

Elaine, Rolf, and Mrs. Fredrickson have been affirming Lucy. Following their conversation about names, Elaine asked her mother to read through the list of affirmations and think about them for Enid.

Rolf and Elaine are using the affirmations for themselves now.[14] They read them to each other each night, think about them, and discuss them. The *You can think before you make that rule your own* affirmation helps Elaine to remember that each time Aunt Sally or Rosemary or her mother offers her ways to "improve" the children, Elaine can think about the idea and decide if it is something she believes in before she does anything about it.

Rolf doesn't think *Trust your feelings to help you know* is a very helpful affirmation for him because he likes to think things through unemotionally. In fact, sometimes it is hard for him to know how he feels. Lots of times he isn't angry or sad or happy, he just thinks about things. But he is discovering that when he feels his neck muscles knotting it is a signal that he is under stress, and he can decide what to do about the stressful situation.

The *You can do it your way* affirmation encourages Elaine to stop reading her new book about sex and invite Rolf to play!

The affirmation *It's OK to disagree* is harder. Rolf and Elaine are revising their old rule that they should always agree on how to raise the kids. For example, Rolf thinks that school is important and if the kids miss the bus the parents should take them to school. Elaine thinks that kids should be responsible for themselves and that that is more important than missing a day of school. So, if Lucy misses the bus before Rolf leaves for work, Rolf takes her to school because school is important. If Lucy misses the bus and only Elaine is home, Lucy has to find a way to get to school. Or she can spend the school hours in her room with her books and without television because being responsible for yourself is important. Elaine and Rolf respect each other's position and talk with the children about their difference in a matter-of-fact way.

The *You don't have to suffer to get what you need* affirmation translates into *You can ask for a backrub just because you want one. You don't have to have a stiff neck to deserve one.* Rolf enjoys that.

The Knutsons also invited Rosemary to ask them for what she needs *before* she gets depressed, with the understanding that if they can't or don't want to comply, they will say so. This is much easier than worrying about Rosemary and wondering what she needs. In the past, when Rosemary looked especially tired, the Knutsons have taken all three boys for an overnight to give Rosemary some time for herself. Rosemary let the boys come because she thought Elaine and Rolf wanted all three of them together. She would have preferred to have two of the boys visit the Knutsons while she had a chance for one-on-one time with the third. Rosemary said, "I'll ask for help the next time I feel myself starting toward Fatiguesville!"

> When people improve their ability to nurture well and to accept nurturing, they improve their own self-esteem. It is important for people to protect themselves from other adults who absorb nurturing and give nothing in return. That kind of nurturing should be reserved for little children.

Visualization

One way to improve your ability to take care of yourself and others is to think how you will look and act as an expert nurturer! Visualize yourself caring for another person or visualize yourself caring for yourself.

Elaine wrote a letter to herself describing how she, Elaine, would like to be taken care of. Then she visualized herself as a person who does those things. In her visualization, she saw herself taking better care of her own health, spending more time reading, and getting more exercise.

Where Is the Self-Esteem of the Knutson-Fredrickson Extended Family Today?

Rising. Enid Fredrickson still misses her husband, but she is seeing her friends regularly, and she is insisting that her grandchildren's friends call her Mrs. Fredrickson.

Rolf and Elaine are spending less time in silent distance and more time having fun together. They have changed their unimportant "you shoulds" for the children to "will you's." And sometimes the children say they will and sometimes they say they won't. Lucy is wearing blue eye shadow instead of green, which, according to Enid, is no improvement. But Lucy says she is learning about options. Lucy and Danny still squabble, but their fights are more out in the open and shorter lived than they used to be. Rolf is thinking more often about feelings and the knot in his neck muscles. Elaine has decided to go back to school and let her mother and Danny settle their own differences about Danny's friends. Mrs. Fredrickson found her spot flashlight behind some books in her room last week, and she is sewing a beanbag chair for Danny and thinking that she just might let him take it to the clubhouse. And Enid Fredrickson has also announced that she is going to stay with an old friend while the rest of the family go on vacation!

Notes

1. See the Parenting Tips for Raising Six- to Twelve-Year-Old Children on pages 167-168.

2. Words which have a special definition as presented in this book are set in boldface the first time they are used in this chapter. The definition of these words is given in the Glossary.

3. See the What You Stroke Is What You Get worksheet on page 174 for examples of ways the Knutson-Fredrickson family can stroke Danny to encourage his ability to nurture, to be responsible, to think, to express his feelings, and to adapt positively. On page 175, list strokes you can give to a specific person to help him or her grow in all personality areas.

4. Pam Levin, *Becoming the Way We Are: A Transactional Guide to Personal Development* (Berkeley, Calif.: Transactional Publications, 1974), p. 48.

5. Thanks to Claudia, Larry, and Brendon Lanpher for the Bunrock story.

6. Thanks to Chuckie Pattie for creating the affirmation blocks and cymbals.

7. For further examples, see *Four Ways of Parenting Description: The Criticizing Parent* in the Glossary.

8. Hassling has a negative connotation when it is used to describe behavior that blocks, aggravates, impedes, or criticizes. "Healthy hassling" is challenging in a nurturing way. This concept is taken from Sally Dierks' unpublished paper, "Creative Hassling."

9. See the *Four Ways of Parenting Description* and the *Four Ways of Parenting Exercise* in the Glossary.

10. See the Four Ways of Parenting exercises on pages 169-170.

11. See the Stroke Rules and Self-Esteem worksheet on pages 176-177.

12. See A Good Father list on page 24.

13. Carl Whitaker, "The ABC's of Family Therapy and Consultation" (Lecture delivered at Minneapolis, Minn., March 18, 1977).

14. See the Affirmations for Structure worksheets on pages 171-172 and the Affirmations for Structure sampler on page 173.

Parenting Tips for Raising
the Six- to Twelve-Year-Old Child

I. The job of the six- to twelve-year-old Lucy is to do things in her own way. Lucy needs an environment in which she is free to test rules, in which her worth is affirmed, and in which the rules and structure she is incorporating are constantly challenged. In order to decide upon her own way of doing things she needs to do several things.

    A. She needs to explore rules—what they are for, how they are made, how to get around them, the consequences of disobeying them, and how her family rules differ from the rules of other families.

    B. She needs to try out her own values and ways of doing things to get her own needs met.

    C. She needs to incorporate her own rules into her own head solidly enough to enable her to take care of herself.

    D. She needs to disagree with others and find out that they won't go away.

    E. She needs to separate reality from fantasy.

II. The job of the adult who cares for Lucy is to continue to care for the child while she internalizes her own rules. The energy that adults spend explaining, defending, and challenging rules is an investment in Lucy's independence and responsibility. Since Lucy needs to test rules, the adults will do the following:

    A. They will provide a firm and loving environment in which Lucy can test rules. They will listen to her, expect her to think, and explain their own values to her. They will make clear which family values and rules are not negotiable. They will react to her challenges with both thoughts and feelings.

    B. They will help Lucy find her own values and ways of taking care of herself.

        1. They will hassle and argue with Lucy in order to get her to use adult thinking about how her new rules are related to her wants and needs. (Example: She may say, "I am never going to wear rain boots." The adult could respond with "Is that so? Why do you plan never to wear rain boots? What will you do if they are required for your Girl Scout camp-out?")

        2. They will stroke her for thinking logically and creatively and for arguing well. (Example: "You thought of lots of good reasons during that argument.")

        3. They will offer Lucy problem-solving rules.

        4. They will expose Lucy to many new experiences and encourage her to acquire many new skills, and they will not compete with her or dominate her activity.

    C. They will help Lucy incorporate her own rules and ways of doing things. They will support her, continue to expect cause-and-effect thinking, and allow her to experience any nonhazardous natural consequences for her ways of doing things.

    D. They will continue positive strokes for being and give assurances to Lucy that they will continue to care for her even when she disagrees with them.

E. They will help Lucy separate reality from fantasy by encouraging her to report accurately, and they will do the kind of teasing that requires her to separate fact from fiction and that leads to positive strokes.

F. They will affirm Lucy in the ways practiced earlier in this section and will visualize her as if she has already accepted the affirmations.

III. The job of the caring adults is to care for themselves.

A. They will keep their own stroke levels high so that they will have the energy to maintain their own good humor while Lucy tests and while they hassle her new rules.

B. They will use the hassle time with Lucy to rethink some long un-examined rules and ways of doing things.

C. They will start their own separation from Lucy, and then will nurture the parts of their lives that are separate from her.

D. They will not discount their own needs while over-providing for Lucy

Remember that your parents did the best they could. You have done the best that you could. If you want to use these new tools it is never too late to start.

Four Ways of Parenting*

For any situation that requires parenting—advising and supporting—there are four possible ways of responding. Nurturing and structuring and protecting ways encourage positive self-esteem. Marshmallowing and criticizing ways tear down self-esteem. Below are situations. Each situation has a response given by a nurturing, a structuring and protecting, a marshmallowing, and a criticizing parent.

Read each of the four responses to each situation. Allow yourself to hear the positive and the negative implications of each. Rewrite each answer to fit your own value system where needed.

Parent Messages

Nurturing

This message is gentle, supportive, caring. It invites the person to get his or her needs met. It offers to help. It gives permission to succeed and affirms.

Marshmallowing

This message sounds supportive, but it invites dependence, suggests person will fail, and negates.

Structuring and Protecting

This message sets limits, protects, asserts, demands, advocates ethics and traditions. It tells ways to succeed and affirms.

Criticizing

This message ridicules, tears down, tells ways to fail, and negates.

Situation: Father says, "I feel left out. All my wife ever thinks about is the baby."

Nurturing

I understand the way you feel. It's rough when you don't get the attention you're used too.

Marshmallowing

That's just the way things are. There isn't anything she can do to change the fact that the baby is only one month old and needs a lot of care.

Structuring and Protecting

Sit down with her. Make a list of things the two of you like to do together. Decide which one on the list you can do first. Do that.

Criticizing

You should take care of yourself. Work a little harder, and you won't notice your loneliness. Or get out and have some fun with someone who is more interested in you.

*See Glossary, pages 269-270, for further information.

Situation: Thirteen year old says, "I'm going on a rock climbing expedition, and I'm scared."

Nurturing

You're my favorite mountain goat.

Marshmallowing

You worry me. You're too careless to climb those rocks.

Structuring and Protecting

Trust your feet. Be realistic about what you know, make safe decisions, and ask for help before you need it.

Criticizing

You'd better be careful. One false step and you'll break your neck.

Situation: Parent says, "My eight year old deliberately hurt a child on the school bus."

Nurturing

I'm sorry to hear that. I know that you care about your child and don't want him/her to be a bully.

Marshmallowing

Kids will be kids! If only the bus drivers would take some responsibility! Well, don't think about it, and maybe it will go away.

Structuring and Protecting

OK, I'm glad you heard about it. Bullying is a serious call for help. Find out what your child needs to feel better about himself and help him get it.

Criticizing

Good thing. You have to learn to dish it out in this world. Too bad about the other kid, but he should learn to watch out for himself.

Situation: Six year old says, "I took gum from the store without paying."

Nurturing

I care about you, and I see that you need some rules about how to get gum. I'll help with those

Marshmallowing

You worry me, you might get caught! Here, give me that piece, and I'll get you a whole box of gum, so you'll have what you want.

Structuring and Protecting

These are the rules (morals, ethics) in which I believe. I expect you to follow them. I'll go with you to the store to return the gum right now.

Criticizing

Where did you get that gum, you little thief? Don't you ever listen to me? Why do you think I take you to church? You're a disgrace to the family. You'd better take that gum back. The next thing I know you'll be stealing money

Affirmations for Structure—Learning to Do Things Our Own Way: Six to Twelve Years

The structure affirmations are particularly important for six- to twelve-year-old children, people in the late teens and early twenties, for people of all ages who are entering new social settings (such as organizations, businesses, recreation groups, families, and retirement), and everyone else.

You can think before you make that rule your own.

TO KAREN—
  11 year old

It's OK to decide whether you agree with your teacher. Follow his rules at school, but you don't have to carry them with you.

TO JOE — 17 year old

Be your own person! See if others' values are comfortable for you.

TO ME—adult

I don't have to agree with my spouse. I can disagree without trying to change him/her.
(from self)

You can trust your feelings to help you know.

When you're not sure what to do, check your feelings.

Sleep on it— you'll know what is the best thing for you to do.

You've tried using logic. Now trust your feelings.
(from self)

You can do it your way.

I'm glad that you have your own special way of writing.

I like your style!

Here it is— get the job done!
(from boss)

It's OK to disagree.

I'm glad to hear your opinion. We don't always have to agree.

You and I see that differently.

Let's collect lots of opinions before we decide.
(from family)

You don't have to suffer to get what you need.

I'll make you some pudding just for fun. You don't have to be sick to get me to cook for you.

You can find new friends. You don't have to absorb the insults for the few good things that person gives you.

You don't have to work all the time to please us. We like you any way you are.
(from family)

(I'm glad you're here, I see you're doing things, and I expect you to continue learning about cause and effect. I expect you to differentiate between feelings and actions and to ask to get your needs met straight. I also see that you are trying out, thinking about, altering, and claiming your own way of looking at things and doing things in order to take care of yourself.)

171

Affirmations for Structure

Follow the **Directions for Others** or the **Directions for Self** below and fill in this worksheet.

Directions for Others

1. Think of a person you want to send affirmations to. The person can be any age.
2. Write each affirmation the way you want to convey it to that person (words, touch, attention, listening).
3. Visualize the person as if he or she has already accepted your message.

Directions for Self

1. Write each affirmation the way you want to hear it.
2. Write the name of someone you want to hear it from. Name at least three different people.
3. Get the messages in a way that is constructive for you and for other people.
4. Give the messages to yourself, even if you don't believe them at first.
5. Visualize yourself as if you already believe them.

You can think before you make that rule your own.

You can trust your feelings to help you know.

You can do it your way.

You don't have to suffer to get what you need.

It's OK to disagree.

People who hear a message and consistently observe opposite behavior can feel confused or crazy. Send only the messages that you believe.

Sampler: Affirmations for Structure—
Learning to Do Things Our Own Way

Seven-year-old Diane

"Yes, I understand that you've been at your friend's house checking out how things are done there. And I understand that your peers put a lot of pressure on you to do things certain ways. You can think things through before you decide on your own rules. Sometimes you get lots of conflicting messages about what you should do. You can think, and you can trust your feelings to help you decide. I see that you're trying things out and trying different ways of doing things. You can figure out the way that's best for you, and you can do things that way. Sometimes you will disagree with other people. It's OK for you to disagree and work things out. You can develop rules in your own head that are strong enough to help you get what you need. It's OK for you to have needs, and you don't have to act sick or scared or sad or mad to get taken care of. You can ask straight for what you need."

Late teenage Kyra

"I see that you're making choices about life-styles and priorities. Some of those don't agree with some of mine. It's OK to disagree, and it's OK to do things your own way. If you're not clear about any of my values, I will discuss them with you, and I expect you to respect me and my values. You can trust your feelings to help you know what you need to do, and you can think before you make any rule your own—whether that rule came from me, TV, your friends, or Mr. Moon. I see that you're trying things out, thinking about things, altering and claiming your own way of looking at things, and doing things in your own way in order to take care of yourself. I trust you to make decisions that are not harmful to you or other people."

Adult

"I see that you are starting something new (a marriage, a job, a business, a church, a play group). You can go into that situation, figure out the rules, and think before you incorporate them into your own life. You can trust your feelings to help you know if you are doing the right thing for you. You can find out how to do things in your own way. It's OK to disagree, and you can find ways to get what you need straight—without inviting someone else to be responsible for your feelings by using sadness, anger, or sickness to get taken care of. You can know your own needs and get them met."

To myself

(Read the adult message above to myself.)

What You Stroke Is What You Get

name ___Danny___   age _8 years_   time _Sat. morning_

To encourage people to become whole and well balanced, compliment all aspects of their personalities.

Encourage nurturing, structuring and protecting, having and using morals and ethics, and doing things for self and others

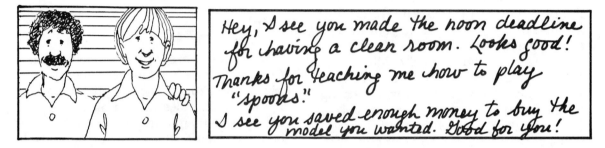

Hey, I see you made the noon deadline for having a clean room. Looks good!
Thanks for teaching me how to play "spoons."
I see you saved enough money to buy the model you wanted. Good for you!

Encourage dealing with current reality, gathering facts, estimating probability, and solving problems .

Danny, I'm impressed with the way you figured out how to build the window in your club house.

Encourage feeling and acting naturally and adaptively . *

I like to play "spoons" with you.
Thank you for being quiet when I ask you to be quiet.
Please follow your grandmother's rules when you are in her room.

*See page 51 for more examples of what to stroke and how to stroke.

What You Stroke Is What You Get

name ———————————————— **age** ——————— **time** ———————

To encourage people to become whole and well balanced, compliment all aspects of their personalities.

Encourage nurturing, structuring and protecting, having and using morals and ethics, and doing things for self and others.

Encourage dealing with current reality, gathering facts, estimating probability, and solving problems.

Encourage feeling and acting naturally and adaptively . *

*See page 51 for more examples of what to stroke and how to stroke.

Stroke Rules and Self-Esteem*

*Thanks to Hogie Wycoff for suggesting these items.

In the left-hand column on this page is an example of how people who have low self-esteem act and what they believe. In the right-hand column on the next page is an example of how people who have high self-esteem act and what they believe. Think about your own self-esteem; then fill in the center columns. Celebrate the things you like about your columns. Make any changes in your actions or beliefs that you need to make.

Low Self-Esteem
(helpless and hopeless)

act	believe		act
Don't ask for what they want.	OH, WELL, I'll LIVE...		
Don't accept positive strokes.	I DON'T NEED THEM.		
Don't give the strokes they have.	OTHERS DON'T WANT MY STROKES.		
Don't reject toxic strokes.	I HAVE TO TAKE THEM.		
Don't love themselves.	IT'S CONCEITED.		

High Self-Esteem
(lovable and capable)

believe	act	believe
	Ask for what they want.	I SHOULD ASK.
	Accept positive strokes.	I NEED AND DESERVE THEM.
	Give the strokes they have.	MY STROKES ARE WORTHWHILE.
	Reject toxic strokes.	I AM RESPONSIBLE FOR MY OWN HEALTH.
	Love selves.	I AM LOVABLE.

7

His, Hers, Theirs, Whose?
Will the Blended Families That Work
Please Stand Up?

Stephen Blakeborough's feet scuffed the leaves and kicked a small stone off the trail, but he didn't see the curling leaves or hear the skittering pebbles. His mind was on Kathryn, and he felt numb, except for the part of him that felt hollow. He had been so sure Kathryn would agree to marry him. He had watched her love for him grow as he had become more committed to her. He knew Kathryn was lonely, as he had been, as he was now with a new rush of aloneness, and they had talked about living together, about combining their families, many times. And they had good times together!

True, his Bryan and her Kimberly don't get along too well. But her kids need a father! And his Bryan and Becky like Kathryn. Stephen knows that sixteen-year-old Karla and thirteen-year-old Kimberly Muer like him. He is certain that Kathryn loves him, and he knows he wants her.

Stephen still couldn't believe that Kathryn had said no. Well, she hadn't said no exactly, but she got a terrified look in her eyes, a look that he had not seen before, and she said she would have to have time to think. "Think about what?" he wondered.

Kathryn Muer's husband, Barry, died three years ago. She and the kids have recovered from their grief and built a strong family unit. Kathryn has become accustomed to managing alone. Now her oldest son, Nathan, is nineteen and about to leave home.

Stephen is divorced and his children, Bryan and Becky, live with him. Although their mother visits the children and helps with child support, Steve is openly looking for a full-time mother for the kids, as well as a wife for himself. He talks about his own wishes for intimacy and the kids' need for mothering about equally. That's part of the scare for Kathryn.

To say that Stephen's fourteen-year-old Bryan and Kathryn's Kimberly don't get along well is an understatement.[1] Headstrong, awkward, mercurial Kimberly currently spends a lot of time telling people what they should do, and she frequently offers Bryan reams of unsolicited advice on his behavior, mixed with pungent comments about his person. He responds with a dismal assessment of her intelligence level, the bleakness of her future, and the current state of her acne. They could collaborate on a handbook of derogatory adjectives. Kathryn remembers that Karla and Nathan were bossy at thirteen and got over it. But right now she isn't sure that Kimberly and Bryan will ever be friends. "How could they live in the same house?" she wonders.

Kathryn also has misgivings about Becky. Becky is ten, just the age Kimberly was when her dad died. But Becky is so different from Kimberly—so boisterous, so athletic, so, well, self-sufficient. "How do you mother an independent ten-year-old girl who already has a mother?" Kathryn wonders. Kathryn would be the stepmother. All those children's stories came flooding back—Cinderella, Hansel and Gretel, Snow White. Who wants to be a stepmother? Not Kathryn. She's thought a lot lately about sharing life with Steve, but when she heard the word *marry* she felt a wave of apprehension about listening to Kimberly and Bruce daily, about living with Becky. Still, Kathryn's girls and Becky are friends, and Becky is an engaging person, like her father. And there Kathryn is, thinking about Steve again.

Maybe she and Steve can make it work. The two of them get along well, but how can they be sure about blending families, and how will they know if they are doing it successfully?

> *Blended families come in different sizes, ages, and mixes. The important issue for a merging family is to find a way to blend, to become a new, whole family. Blending does not mean making an exclusive family, one that keeps other people out, it means making a family in which all of the members belong, care, and have allegiance to each other. It's a family in which people are accepted and honored for being who they are without being compared to someone else.*

Steve and Kathryn sorted through the blended families they know to see how those families had gone about their mergers.

The Ghosts of Parents Past—A Family That's Unblended

Kathryn told Steve about her neighbor, Neil Hiesler. Kathryn helped Neil pick up the pieces after his wife, Elizabeth, suddenly died, leaving him with four young children and an infant. Kathryn hoped that Neil would remarry soon. He was lonely and he needed help with his children. That round-cheeked baby needed steadier mothering than she could get from the succession of housekeepers who came and left. Kathryn said that Neil dated as often as he could find the time and had found several women he liked. But when Kathryn asked him about them, he said that none of them compared to Elizabeth. Neil seemed determined that his children, having been born to the angelic Elizabeth, should not have to settle for second best in a second mother. Kathryn said, "Sometimes I think that Elizabeth gets more angelic as the months go by." Steve said she sounded like a nice ordinary woman whose increasingly unordinary ghost was being used to keep her children from having a second mother.

Kathryn didn't mention it to Steve, but she decided to do some serious thinking about her first husband, Barry. "Am I willing to let him be a good first dad who is now dead? Or am I, too, creating a superghost?" Kathryn wondered.

"You have to say old goodbyes before you can say new hellos." This saying probably holds more truth for blended families than for anyone else. The woman who hangs onto sadness for a dead husband throws a separating ingredient into the new blend. So does the man who keeps his anger toward an ex-wife. The child who persists in a romantic fantasy of the family that could have been if only Mommy and Daddy had stayed married can also keep the blend from jelling. It is important for people in blending families to count their past wins and enjoy them, recognize their losses and let them go, and then stay squarely in the here and now, in the new family. Let the ghosts of other family configurations stay peacefully in the corner; keep them out of the middle of the action.[2]

Kids Need Real Live Folks— A Family That Is Blended and Functioning

Sixteen-year-old Karla Muer and Jennifer McBain are close friends. They talk on the phone for hours, study together, sleep at each other's houses, and discuss boys and who likes whom this week. Jennifer told Karla she hoped that Mrs. Muer would get married again, that her mom remarried, and that Mrs. Muer could talk with Connie McBain about it.

Kathryn was surprised. She'd known the McBains several years, but she didn't know that Jennifer's twenty-two-year-old brother was six years old when Connie and John McBain were married. When Kathryn and Steve bumped into Connie and John after the movies, the four of them went to the ice-cream shop for dessert and conversation. Kathryn told the McBains about Jennifer's offer, and they said they would be glad to talk, but they didn't have much to tell.

Connie explained: "Jeff's dad and I were divorced when Jeff was two. His father died shortly before John and I got married. John adopted Jeff, and when Jennifer and Eric were born, nobody talked about half brothers or sisters. We just raised our family."

John said they hadn't talked a lot about how they had done it, "I wanted to be Jeff's dad, and Connie let Jeff's first dad be a memory. So there wasn't much to discuss."

Connie said that Jeff had come home from school one day and told John that the kids at school said John was not his real dad. She recalled that John said, "Yes, I am your real dad. I am your dad. Those kids have not been dads yet so they don't know what it means to be a real dad. I know because I am one. Yours."

And they also recalled the time that the other preschoolers on the block were playing house and Jennifer and Eric taught them the game about geting a new mom or dad. Some of the mothers called Connie to find out what was going on. Connie asked little Jennifer and Eric about the game and they said, "Jeff told us not to worry, Mom, that if you lose your mom or your dad, the one that's left has to find you a new one." Connie said, "I don't know what the other mothers thought, but I think it was a great game!"

Kathryn and Stephen wondered how many other blended families like the McBains have just decided to be families. Nobody knows or cares if they are blended. Maybe lots. "Maybe you hear most about blended families when they don't work," Kathryn mused.

When Jeff McBain came home for a holiday, Kathryn asked him how it had been for him growing up with John McBain. He said, "It was OK, except that sometimes I'm mad at Dad for not being my dad from the beginning, like he's been for Jennifer and Eric."

Jeff's insight was helpful for Kathryn. It might explain why, even now before they've become a blended family, little Becky who is usually eager to see Kathryn, sometimes becomes suddenly withdrawn and sullen. Kathryn decided that this kind of resentment from kids is natural and understandable and second parents can expect it and not take it personally. She calls it an occupational hazard of being a second mother. But she still isn't sure she wants to take the job and join her family with Steve's. "We can't meld a family the way Connie and John did," she reminded Stephen. "Our children are older. And your first wife, Esther, is still in the family picture."

> It is important for new parents to relate well with the new children for the welfare of the children as persons and for the strength of the new family. But the better the new parent does his or her job, the more the kids will resent it from time to time. This is a significant piece of information for second parents to remember.

Some Blends Don't Take—A Blended Family That Separated

Steve works with Roger Hillstrom. Roger and his first wife have three children, who live with their mother. Roger seemed to be delighted about his second wife. Now Steve has heard that Roger is in the midst of a second divorce. Steve really doesn't want to know what happened. He would rather think about how much fun it is to go sailing with Kathryn. But he and Kathryn had agreed to talk to as many people as they could. Besides Roger wanted to talk and had invited him to lunch.

"What happened, Roger?" Stephen asked.

"Well, it didn't turn out like I expected," Roger explained. "Liz has four teenagers, and they seemed to get along well with my kids. I thought we would have these great big family holidays and vacations."

"And?" Stephen inquired.

"And it didn't fly! My kids were willing, but I couldn't work things out with her family."

"Why not? What happened?" Steve asked cautiously.

"Steve, you know about closed systems at work, the way all the units interlock in a rigid pattern? Well, that family was a closed system. I love that woman, and I like each one of those kids. But they have a tight family thing going, and they don't open up the system and let me in. I never did figure out how to break in. It's too lonely always being on the outside, so I'm getting out completely."

That evening Kathryn and Steve talked about Roger and how tough it would be to have that happen to them. Kathryn realized that she was beginning to think that she and Steve *could* build a family. Steve admitted that it looked harder than he first thought. After talking with Roger Hillstrom, Steve decided he could use some help.

Shortly after Barry died, Kathryn attended a series of lectures on **self-esteem**[3] at Kimberly's junior high school. She learned about **affirmations** and **visualizations** and **positive stroking** and has been using those self-esteem building tools with both of her children and Stephen's. Now Bryan's junior high is offering the same lecture series, and Steve is attending.

All of Ours

Henry North goes to the lectures with Steve, and he invited Steve to his home after a class to meet his wife, Mona, and to eat hot apple turnovers.

When Henry and Mona Kopecky married, he had two boys and she had one. Now Henry and Mona's daughter has started school. "Looks like a stable, vital family," Steve thinks. Both Henry and Mona say they have lots of problems. But they also say that's part of life, and they didn't expect anything else.

"Doesn't everyone have some problems?" Mona asks, as she looks evenly at Steve.

"How was it when you were first married?" Steve asks.

"Well," Henry pauses, "We had problems during the first couple of years while we worked out the visiting arrangements with Mona's first husband and established who was responsible for what."

"How did you do it?" probed Steve, his thoughts flickering back to the difficult months after his separation from Esther.

"The arrangement that we finally settled on was that whichever adult was with the kids at the time was responsible for behavior. No 'What does your mother usually let you do?' and no complaining afterwards."

Mona added, "Henry and I arranged time with each kid individually and that seemed to help us as much as them." She recalled the times they were so busy being good parents that they forgot to take care of themselves, and she ended up in the hospital for an enforced rest. "After that we made sure we found time for ourselves as individuals and as a couple."

Steve said, "Certainly looks like you've made it!"

"Thanks, Steve, but you notice I'm at the school lectures with you." Henry finished his apple turnover. "We've got two teenagers and two who soon will be, and I'm feeling the pressure. For one thing, I want more information about the **recycling** idea we heard about tonight."

Recycling

"Honey," Steve told Kathryn later, "Henry and Mona are a couple who go after the problems before they get big. Let's do that! I've heard you mention that Karla and Nathan were recycling some things. I didn't understand it before. Now I'm beginning to!"

The idea that people recycle early developmental tasks at a later age in a more sophisticated way and have another chance to solve old problems implies not only that adults are responsible for their own behavior and attitudes, but also that it is always possible that people will choose to make their own lives better. This process can be seen in a youngster who is thirteen years old, going-on-infant.

Pam Levin in Becoming the Way We Are *says: "At around 13, we begin a rebirth. We begin to recycle through our previous stages as we finalize growing up. We begin all of the stages of development over again. We eat all the time, we want to be fed, taken care of, thought for. We have high stroking needs. We are concerned about money as an energy supply, and we spend a lot of time talking about sex. We have an incredibly short attention span and are overcome by waves of energy filled with strange, unfamiliar urges—erotic, exciting, and scarey. We have supply needs from others. We need to have our external supply needs met—we need to be fed and taken care of in a loving way."*[4]

Steve thought about Kimberly. At thirteen, Kim is not easy to get along with. Kathryn says Kim has been a delightful child, but right now that isn't what Steve sees. She is a smart, competent kid, and yet suddenly she will want Kathryn to take care of her in babyish ways. Steve recalled a conversation he overheard when he stopped at the Muer home early one morning. Kim had just come into the kitchen and was talking with her mom.

"Hi, Mom."

"Hi, sweet girl!"

"Mom, will you fix my lunch today?"

"Kim, I expected you to eat at school today, and I don't have time to fix your lunch this morning, but you may pack a lunch if you want to."

"I don't know how."

"Kimberly, you've packed your own lunch many times!"

"Oh, Mom!"

"Tell you what, Kim, I can't help you this morning. But I'm going grocery shopping tomorrow after school. You come with me, and we'll get food that you especially like. You can plan the menu for Friday night, and I'll cook whatever you like." Kathryn gave Kimberly a hug.

"Oh, Mom, do you mean it? Really? Hey, thanks, Mom!"

Later Steve asked Kathryn about it, and she said that she and Kim did indeed go grocery shopping and have a special dinner. "But it doesn't always work out that way," she laughed. "For example, last week Kimberly, who is usually very independent about her clothing, didn't know what to wear. She couldn't find any clothes she liked, didn't know if things went together. I said, 'Kim do you want me to help you with your clothes?' Kim squealed, 'Mom, would you, really?' Kim was delighted. I said, 'Yes, Saturday morning I will go through your closet with you and we will see what you need.' On Saturday morning Kim rushed in and said, 'Mom, will you be terribly disappointed if we don't go through my closet? I know I promised, but I want to see Vicki before band practice, OK, Mom?'"

Kathryn shook her head and smiled. Then she continued, "It's fix her food, find her clothes, think for her one minute. The next minute she is chattering on and on about boys and wanting extra allowance for cosmetics and high heeled shoes."

Steve said, "It does sound as if she is recycling being an infant in some ways. The hormone changes must add the sexual element that sounds so incongruous to me. But the idea of recycling helps me make sense of it."

> Sometimes the thirteen-year-old-going-on-infant stays in a dependent place for quite a while. Other times he seems to brush past it. He will demand absurd-sounding care. If he gets the assurance that his nurturing adults are willing to care for him and are not demanding that he hurry and grow up, he may quickly move on to other activities.

Steve thought about the **affirmations for being**—the messages infants need to hear.
>You have every right to be here.
>Your needs are OK with me.
>I'm glad you're a (boy, girl).
>You don't have to hurry.
>I like to hold you.[5]

"Kathryn hit every one of them in the pack-my-lunch exchange," Steve concluded.

Then he thought about the **affirmations for doing**, the toddler messages:
>You don't have to do tricks to get approval.
>It's OK to do things and get support at the same time.[6]

186

"Yes, Kathryn does give Kim approval without demanding that Kim earn it by being cute or smart or sick or whatever," Steve thought. "And Kathryn does support Kim's activities without critical remarks like, 'Anyone who is big enough to play the French horn in the band is big enough to decide what to wear without bothering her mother!' Both of those sets of affirmations certainly seem to fit for Kimberly," Steve concluded. He is anxious for Kimberly to grow past the criticizing that she does so continuously. She will, he guesses. Bryan criticized a lot last year. And he has eased off, except when Kimberly is around.

> *A thirteen year old frequently has rules in his head that he doesn't follow a good deal of the time. But he often uses a very loud voice to tell everyone else to follow those same rules all the time.*
>
> *Fourteen year olds often recycle two-year-old developmental stages. Pam Levin says, "At around 14 we may be stubborn, negativistic, compliant or rebellious (depending on our mood), and messy. We say 'I forgot . . .' as the bathtub overflows into the downstairs. We are testing control and establishing a thinking position in a social world."*[7]

Bryan acts like fourteen-going-on-two sometimes. Last Saturday, he and Steve had finished the weekend housework, and they were doing some electrical repairs when Bryan's mother called. She wanted to see him the next afternoon. His explosion was out of proportion to her request. "You don't care about me or you would have called earlier in the week. You think you can call me any time and I can rearrange my schedule to please you. I can't and I won't!" he insisted. "And furthermore you are always unreasonable with me."

After Bryan hung up the phone and cooled down, Steve asked what Bryan had planned for that Sunday afternoon. "Nothing," Bryan said. "Why?"

"How come the big explosion at your mother?" Steve prodded.

"She bugs me when she does that. I don't know why. I felt like saying no, that's all," Bryan replied defensively.

"You don't usually object to seeing her," Steve observed.

"Ya, right, Dad, but I just felt like saying no today." Bryan opened the refrigerator door and surveyed the contents. Steve thought, "Teenage separation—sounding like a two year old just starting to declare to the world that he will become independent."

Steve silently recited the **affirmations for thinking**—the messages needed by two year olds:

> I'm glad you're growing up.
> I'm not afraid of your anger.
> You can think about what you feel.
> You don't have to take care of me by thinking for me.
> You can be sure about what you need and want and think.[8]

He wrapped them all up in the easy acceptance of his voice, "OK, Bryan, I hear you." Steve mused, "Maybe those negative explosions of Bryan's have something to do with his not getting along with Kimberly."

Steve recalled a typical exchange between Bryan and Kim: "Here comes sloppy Bryan! Did you find your way home all by yourself?" Kim opened.

"Look who's talking. You wouldn't know sloppy if you saw it in Saran wrap," Bryan answered with a calculated, casual tone.

"Turkey!" Kim jabbed.

"Listen, Blotch Face, when I want your opinion, I'll ask for it. I'll send the letter to the funny farm," Bryan jeered.

The tone reminded Steve of a toddler and a two year old quarreling over one block when there were nineteen more blocks two feet away. Steve thought, "Recycling, reworking all of the earlier tasks with sexuality added—maybe that's what some of the noise is about!"

> *What about age fifteen-going-on-three? Pam Levin says: "When we are 15 we want to argue and hassle. We try to figure out ways that we can't do something the way others want us to. We are getting ready for a friendly divorce from our guardians."* [9]

Henry North's son Jim was fifteen last year. Henry said Jim was always arguing and hassling. If Henry wanted Jim to do something one way, Jim insisted upon doing it another way. He seemed to be saying, "If I am going to grow up and be me and be separate from you, I have to have my own ways of doing things."

When Jim wanted to take a girl out or go to a party, transportation became a major problem. Jim wanted a motorcycle; Henry said no but offered to drive Jim and the girl. Sometimes Jim argued until it was too late to call the girl, and then he accused his parents of causing him to miss the fun.

Steve thought about the **affirmations for learning who we are— separating**, first used between ages three and six:

You can be powerful and still have needs.

You don't have to act scary (or sick or sad or mad) to get taken care of.

You can express your feelings straight.[10]

"Yes, the first would fit the ambivalence Henry described," he thought. "One moment Jim acted grown-up and independent; the next moment he was dependent, and he didn't quite know how to handle the swings. The second and third affirmations fit too: *You don't have to act scary or sick or sad or mad to get taken care of* and *You can express your feelings straight.* It's difficult for some fifteen year olds to admit their dependence, to ask straight out for comfort when they're scared."

> *In the continuing effort to become mature, independent adults, six-teen to nineteen year olds recycle the birth-to-twelve-years developmental stages all over again. Pam Levin says: "At 16 we want to emerge as separate, complete and whole. We want to relate to our guardians as two whole people. We still may need protection, and we still have needs, but we are ready to get those needs met from the larger world. We have assumed responsibility for our own needs, our own feelings, and our own behavior as a grown-up person in the world."* [11]

"This year at sixteen Jim is more reasonable," Henry tells Stephen. "The arguments between us have subsided and now the hassle is usually playful. That's the way we talk to each other." Both Jim North and Kathryn's Karla are mature-acting sixteen year olds most of the time. And yet, every so often, they act like little kids. Usually reasonable Karla suddenly decided that she had to go to Europe for the summer. Kathryn should pay for the trip, and furthermore, the decision had to be made within two days. Kathryn said, "No."

Karla raged! "All of my friends are going, and this summer, right now, is the time for me to go!"

Kathryn said, "No, we don't have the money set aside for that."

Karla slammed the door and went to her room to pout. Steve thought about the **affirmations for learning to do things our own way—building our own structure:**

You can think before you make that rule your own.

You can trust your feelings to help you know.

You can do it your way.

It's OK to disagree.

You don't have to suffer to get what you need.[12]

189

Kathryn expects Karla, at sixteen, to think before she makes a rule her own, whether the rule comes from her family or from her peers. Kathryn says, "I know what your friends want and do is importrant to you." But Karla remembers that when Nathan and his friends destroyed some property, Kathryn held Nathan fully responsible and said, "Think about your friends. What will people who do what they are doing now probably be doing in ten years? If you don't feel good about that, this may be the time for you to choose some new friends. You decide."

Steve had heard Kathryn say the same thing to Kimberly and Bryan when they talked about the drug scene at the junior high. "But Kimberly and Bryan are not sixteen, should they be recycling the *You can think before you make that rule your own* issue?" Steve wonders.

> *Recycling refers to the process of reexperiencing earlier developmental tasks at a new level and in a more sophisticated way. Although there are general ages at which people appear to recycle certain tasks, this is not a tight schedule, and there can be a great deal of fluctuation. In addition, it is important to remember that once the age for any set of affirmations has been reached, those affirmations are applicable, in some form, for the rest of the person's life.*

Steve thought, "OK, I've gone through the recycling affirmations for teen-agers. Now what about the new ones that Bryan needs, the **affirmations for sexuality**. Those are

You can be a sexual person and still have needs.

It's OK to know who you are.

You're welcome to come home again.

I love you.[13]

"*I love you*," Steve thought. "For sure. The kids know that I love them." Steve never stopped saying that, and their mother didn't either. "*You can be a sexual person and still have needs.* Yes, indeed," Steve mused. He resolved that he must tell Bryan that. Having sexual impulses does not mean you are so grown up that you never need to be taken care of. Ever. Steve can vouch for that! And it does not mean that when you have sexy feelings you have to do anything about them. "How am I going to start?" Steve questioned himself. "Maybe I can find the right time and way to say, 'I'm glad you're going to the dance' or 'Your shoulders get broader every week' or 'You can have some boys and girls over Friday night if you want to.' And when Bryan looks depressed, I'll say, 'Tell me what you need, son.'"

"The *It's OK to know who you are* affirmation is harder," Steve thinks. "Bryan has so many areas in which he doesn't agree with me." Bryan handles monely differently, and according to Stephen's standards, Bryan's taste in music is atrocious. Steve thinks, "We do share a love of nature, but he may never appreciate the old, the historical, in the way that I do. That affirmation must mean it's OK to know who you are as a sexual person, too."

Stephen said, "Bryan, sometimes I think it must be tough on kids your age, growing up in a time of changing sex roles. You can't just look at your dad and see how to be a man. Other times I think it is great because you have more options than I did. I'll be interested to see how you work that out, and I trust that you will find a way that works for you."

Bryan looked surprised and then said, "Thanks, Dad."

Steve practiced other things he could say to Bryan when the timing was appropriate. "Bryan, I don't like listening to your music, but I sure do enjoy your enthusiasm for it." Or "Bryan, how can we work it out this evening so I can listen to the music I like and you can listen to yours?" Another thing Steve could say is "Bryan, I'm uncomfortable with the amount of money you spend on photography. I guess it's hard for me partly because I didn't have that kind of money when I was your age. I do like some of your pictures though. That one of the power lines and the clouds is really great."

Steve thought that saying the affirmations still felt awkward, but he resolved to say them because he knew the importance of letting Bryan be Bryan and not trying to make him into Steve the Second. And that may be the clue for the next affirmation.

You are welcome to come home again is an affirmation that sounded trite to Steve until he pondered it for a while. Since teenagers need to separate, to become independent, and to leave their families emotionally in order to be welcome to come home again as equal adults, they must know they will be welcomed for who they are, not for being a carbon copy of their parents. Steve thought more about coming home again. He knows a family, the Dunnavaus, who have two kids in their twenties who have come back home to live. The girl has a divorce, and the boy won't keep a steady job. And what about the unmarried teenage girls who bring a baby home to raise? "I wonder if they are welcome? I wonder if they are home again, or if they never really left, never became separate. That could be part of the problem," Steve thought. "How would I feel if Kathryn and I were married, and Nathan decided to come home and freeload? Well, Nathan wouldn't do that, but what if? Would we let him? I don't think so."

Separation

For every young adult who comes home, not as an equal adult, but as a dependent adult, there is at least one parent who is willing to be imposed upon. One of the developmental tasks of the sixteen to nineteen year old is to separate–become a separate, adult being. This task started in earnest about age two with "No," "I won't," and "You can't make me!"

From three to six, the child separated himself further by finding out more about who he was in relationship to other people. From six to twelve, he started to separate himself from the family rules by incorporating his own rules. At twelve and thirteen, he was declaring his independence even more loudly as he criticized the way other people did things. At fourteen he sounded like a two year old again–"No," "I won't," and "You can't make me!" The volume and intensity of the fourteen-year-old push may be inversely related to the success of the separation at earlier ages–the healthier the separation achieved during the earlier pushes, the smoother fourteen will be.

Sometime between sixteen and nineteen, many young people leave home abruptly. They go away to work or to school or to the armed services or to get married. They have completed their emotional separation, and they return as adults. Other young people leave home gradually. They go off for a while, then are back for a time, forth and back, in and out. Some young people complete their emotional separation while they are still living at home. They gradually assume equal, adult roles. Other young people leave by doing the thing their parents won't tolerate, thus accomplishing their separation by forcing their parents to force them out. Some young people set up fights to help themselves leave. They fight about drugs, hours, money, table manners, music, or who used all of the hot water. When they finally go, they are relieved to be out, and their parents are relieved to have them gone. Parents who did not successfully complete their own separations and have buried the problem will likely find it bubbling up to the surface when their children start pushing away. It is advantageous for the parent to do whatever growth or therapy is necessary to complete that separation before the problem reverberates through the separation attempt of the teenager.

Steve knew it could be touchy with Nathan because he seems to resent Stephen for replacing his dad. When Steve said, "Nathan, how are you going about choosing a college?" Nathan gave Steve a cool look and said, "I've asked you to call me Nate!" Barry's death when Nathan was sixteen could have hurried his separation. "He seems so grown up," Steve thought. "I wonder if he had time enough to be a teenager. I hope he has a good time next year in college. I'll think of him as Nate Muer, the young man who is Kathryn's son, and I'll avoid the advising role."

Ambivalence

Kathryn and Stephen have decided to marry. Since it is Kathryn and Stephen who are forming a long-term merger, they decided it is not necessary for the children to be ecstatic about combining the families. When Kathryn and Steve told the children, they got mixed responses. Nathan was cool to Steve, told his mom he wants her to be happy, and then sat forlornly on the front steps, pondering how he would feel not to have a home to come to. He assumed, without asking, that the Muers would move out of their present house and that when he left in the fall there would no longer be a room for him.

Karla's empathy for her mother showed in her obvious delight with her mother's sparkle, but she looked at Steve in a new, distant way. Her remaining years at home would be different with this handsome man in the house. Sometimes Steve's presence seemed to Karla to fill the room, and she wasn't sure how she would deal with this intrusion into her life.

Kimberly squealed, "Oh, Mother, how could you? I can't possibly live in the same house with Bryan!!" And then she started to chatter excitedly about the wedding.

Bryan was quiet. He thought about Kathryn and knew he would enjoy hassling her on a regular basis, but she is so different from his own mother, and he wondered how his mother would feel about this new arrangement. Also, Bryan wondered what was in it for him in sharing his life with three more kids. Bryan thought, "I've always been the oldest one. Wonder if Nate will try to edge me out. And Kimberly, yuk, how will I put up with gruesome Kimberly?"

Only Becky shouted with joy. "Yeah! I've been the only woman in the house long enough! Now there will be more girls than boys." Becky hugged Karla and said, "I'll have my very own sisters!" Then she stopped suddenly, looked pensively at Kathryn and said, "But don't you ever think you will be my mother, because you won't."

> *Children need parents, and when one or both are missing for any reason, children need other adults to nurture them. If a new nurturing adult takes the job with the clear knowledge and complete acceptance of the child's ambivalence, and if the new parent takes*

the job because it needs to be done and hopefully because he en-joys that particular child, the way is clear. If the adult takes the job with the idea that the child will love him and appreciate his willingness to be the new parent, he is setting himself up for dis-appointment. The better the job he does, the more the child will, at times, resent him for not having been there all of her life.

*Certainly hostile stepparents can invite low self-esteem in chil-dren. And hostile stepchildren can have a powerful impact on the self-esteem of adults who are hoping to fill their **stroke banks** with love and appreciation from stepchildren.*

Kathryn's and Stephen's teenagers have two to four more years at home. Kathryn has decided that she will love and nurture Becky. If in some future year, Becky and her mother decide to live together, Kathryn will not view that as a reflection on her parenting.

New Rules for New Families

Kathryn and Steve have agreed on a few rules for their new blend. The first is that the parents will keep their own stroke banks filled high with posi-tive strokes and will invite the kids to do the same. The second is that the parents will focus on developing their own relationship in a positive, open way and trust the kids to work out the relationships between them with the clear understanding that it is up to them to decide if they will be friends.

Third, Kathryn and Steve will not interfere with each other's handling of the children. Bryan pushed Kathryn really hard the other day. Kathryn and Becky had been doing some friendly hassling about what to order from the Chinese Food Carry-Out Shop. As they finished, Bryan interjected himself into the conversation. He wanted butterfly shrimp. Kathryn told him she and Becky had already completed the order.

"I want shrimp," Bryan raised his voice.

Kathryn said, "This is a special meal I promised Becky that she and I would plan."

Bryan roared, "I want some butterfly shrimp!"

Kathryn's voice remained even. "Becky and I planned this meal. You may choose another day." Steve looked up from across the room.

"Today!" Bryan shouted.

Kathryn did not raise her voice, "No, another day."

Tall Bryan stood over her angrily, "Becky always gets to choose—I want shrimp today!"

Kathryn straightened her body but remained loose. "No, Bryan."

Bryan barked, "I want shrimp today!" Steve didn't move.

Kathryn looked Bryan evenly in the eyes. Her voice got slightly softer, more sure. "No, Bryan."

Suddenly Bryan flushed, backed away, and said, "Well, whatever you got, I won't like it."

Kathryn said, "OK, Bryan." Later she thanked Steve for staying out of it.

Steve inquired, "How did you feel?"

"OK," Kathryn said thoughtfully. "I knew I was going to stand my ground, so Bryan didn't have a choice."

Steve said, "You did well, Kathryn O' Mine. But I'll be glad when Bryan finishes recycling two-year-old stuff."

For a fourth rule, the parents agreed to disagree sometimes. Since the Blakeboroughs and the Muers are bringing two sets of family rules into one house, Steve and Kathryn have some things they will disagree on. For example, Steve believes that breakfast is important and that it is a parent's responsibility to see that children eat an adequate breakfast. Kathryn believes that her children should be responsible for being aware of their health and changing their eating patterns if they do not feel well. Steve will continue to see that Becky and Bryan eat breakfast and Kathryn will continue to expect Kimberly, Karla, and Nathan to manage their own eating habits. Steve and Kathryn will make it clear that they don't have to agree with each other's rules in order to respect each other's rules.

Fifth, since **discounting** invites low self-esteem, Kathryn and Steve will use a no-put-down rule, and invite the kids to observe it also. They will continue to use affirmations. The parents will say how they are feeling about themselves and the blending process and will not engage in quiet brooding.[14]

Secrets

Quiet brooding often leads to secrets. When parents decide not to tell children what is going on (Dad lost his job; mother is hooked on drugs; brother is in trouble with the law; sister is pregnant) the children know that something is going on—that there is a secret. Not knowing what the secret is can be more scary than being told what the problem is, with the calm assurance that the family can and will cope and that they will get whatever help is needed.

Lots of Strokes from Lots of Folks

*In order to develop or maintain positive self-esteem, teenage people need tons of good strokes, just like people of all ages. They need good strokes from lots of folks—from their parents, from themselves, from peers, and since they are separating from their parents, they need good strokes and friendships with adults other than their parents. They need to become responsible for their own **stroke economy**, for knowing what good strokes they need and for getting them.*

A dad in Steve's self-esteem meetings asked for suggestions about strokes. "Sometimes when my sixteen year old seems to want strokes, she won't take them. She acts like a little girl and cuddles up beside me, and then suddenly she says, 'I don't need you,' and she pushes away."

The group offered the following suggestions: "Tell her she is important, and you are glad you know her. . . . Ask her for a hug; tell her dads need hugs sometimes and you want one now. . . . Let her decide to talk and then talk about something fun. . . . Talk about something serious. . . . Listen to her. . . . Say you want to spend three dollars on her right now and ask how you can have the most fun with the money in the next half hour. Then do whatever it is. . . . Rub her back while she is reading. . . . Give her a little present because you want her to know you love her. . . . Ask her opinion and honor it. . . . Tell her how she takes good care of herself, how she solved a problem well, and two ways she is fun to be with."

A sixteen year old may respond to any of these strokes positively, or she may respond negatively. It is up to her to take what she needs at the time. It is also her job to start moving away, to become independent. It isn't surprising that sometimes her response to her parents is "I don't need you."

What You Stroke Is What You Get

Stephen has considered and resisted the idea that what you stroke is what you get. He recognizes that complimenting a behavior encourages a child to continue it, but he wants to reject the idea that scolding can also invite a child to continue doing the very thing he is being scolded for. "Still," he thinks, "Scolding is one form of attention, and I have noticed that when I ignore Becky too long she does something that bugs me. Instead of scolding her I could give her a hug, or chase her playfully, or say, 'Becky, have I been ignoring you? When you want attention from me, ask for it. You don't have to whine.' I wonder if that would discourage whining."

It is helpful for Steve to realize that stroking a child's weak areas helps strengthen them, but it is not immediately obvious to Steve how to do that. Life would be more pleasant if Bryan and Kimberly were kind to each other. They aren't, so how can Steve tell them they are?

> Dividing desirable qualities and behaviors into three general categories makes the task of strengthening the personality easier.
>
> The first category is the nurturing, protecting, moral, and ethical part. That is the part that helps take care of self and others—"You take good care of your pets" or "Thank you for helping me" or "I admire your stand on that issue."
>
> The second category is the thinking, data collecting, probability estimating, and problem solving part—"She understands the concepts behind her algebra problems" or "Ask Emil, he is good at thinking of alternative solutions to problems" or "You find practical ways to do things."
>
> The third category is the appealing, creative, spontaneous, fun loving, rebellious part of us and our adaptations to those spontaneous feelings—"I love your laugh" or "You giggle when I want to, but I don't dare!" or "You surely make a lot of noise when someone steps on you!" or "I heard what you wanted to do and I appreciate your willingness to compromise."[15]

Steve thinks about Karla. She is pretty and helpful and gets compliments on her appearance and kindness. It is easy to say, "Thanks for helping me" and "You look great today; I like your new outfit." She doesn't get a lot of strokes for thinking well. Steve decides to let her know she is smart. He is surprised at how easily his tongue slides into the familiar pattern and how awkward he feels telling her she is smart.

Karla found a summer job. She did it without asking for help from anyone She didn't even tell Kathryn about it until she came home and said, "Guess what! I have a job for the summer selling cosmetics in Rich's Department Store. I start training next Thursday."

Steve said, "Great, Karla—you'll be a good advertisement for cosmetics! I'd like to buy cologne from you." Then he thought, "OK, that tells Karla she is pretty and knows how to wear makeup." He said, "Karla, I'm glad to see you earning some money for yourself. That helps your mom out too." He thought, "That tells her she is taking good care of herself and other people. I still haven't told her she is a good thinker." Steve fumbled with words and finally said, "Karla, however you went about finding that job you must have done some good problem solving."

Karla looked sideways at him, thought awhile, and then said, "Yes, I did. I tried a whole bunch of things that didn't work. Everyone else acts as if it just happened. I really did solve several problems." She flashed him a smile and said, "Thanks for noticing, Stephen."

Steve thought, "Wow, she needed that—glad I said it even though I didn't feel comfortable doing it."

> When an adult has an established habit pattern for stroking another person, changing the pattern may feel awkward. Strokes should be sincere. Sometimes people back off from changing stroking patterns because they confuse "awkward" with "insincere." Insincere strokes are destructive when accepted. Awkward strokes may annoy the sender, but they are a way of saying to the receiver, "You are so important to me that I am willing to make changes in myself for your benefit." That is a powerful gift.

Stephen is watching the way he strokes Becky and is irritated to observe that he is using the same pattern with her that he does with Karla. "Be helpful and attractive" is the message. Steve wants Becky to be smart, think clearly, and problem solve well, but it is easy to fall into the cultural pattern of stroking girls for beauty and nurturing.

Steve finds it easy to compliment Bryan on his problem solving. Bryan has been clever at thinking of ways to solve problems since he was a tiny boy. Steve thinks, "I wonder how much I've influenced Bryan's smartness by noticing it, enjoying it, and telling other people about it. Maybe a lot. Bryan doesn't take as good care of property or people as Becky does. Becky has learned a lot of that since Esther left. I wonder how much I've promoted that by expecting it and rewarding it. It's harder for me to thank Bryan for cleaning the kitchen or cooking. It's automatic to expect Becky to help and to thank her." Steve told Kathryn that the person doing the self-esteem lectures believes that we shortchange our kids and our families when we mostly stroke girls for being pretty and nurturing and mostly stroke boys for thinking. Kathryn was silent for a while and then she said, "I do find it easier to compliment Nathan for finding here-and-now solutions to problems and Karla for being considerate than the other way around."

Kathryn and Steve are making a conscious effort to stroke each of their family members in all three areas. Steve is helping himself break old patterns by writing down some ways he can offer all three to Becky and to Bryan.[16]

> When adults change the ways they have been rewarding children by continuing the positive rewards they had been giving and adding other areas to stroke, children respond differently. Some, like Karla, accept the unfamiliar rewards with pleasure. Other children resist the change. They look suspicious and walk away. Or they say, "Why do you say that? I don't believe it."
>
> Joanne was a normal, bright, busy explorer at eighteen months. In grade school and junior high, her teachers complained that she was a low achiever. Joanne's parents recognized that they had been ignoring her intelligence and stroking her for her beauty and her loving ways. They continued to tell her she was pretty and to thank her for her considerate acts, but they also watched for clear thinking, complimented her for it and told her she was smart. It was two years after they started stroking her for thinking before Joanne responded to one of her mother's "You can think clearly" comments by saying, "I'm starting to believe that I'm smart. I'll study, and I'll do a good job on my test."
>
> Adults offer, and children decide what to internalize and how to act upon that. Adults cannot make children be any certain way. What adults can do is to enrich the **stroke buffet** that they offer children by stroking each child in sincere ways in each of the three areas regularly. They can also teach children to recognize and get strokes in all three areas.

Strokes for Older Folks—Outside Sources

Steve and Kathryn talked seriously about their stroke economy as a couple. One of the reasons Steve's first marriage ended in divorce was that he and Esther had both believed the golden **stroke rule**. Each of them expected to get almost all of their good strokes from the other. They ignored strokes from outside and from themselves. Whenever one was ill, depressed, or tired, the other automatically went into pain from lack of strokes. Then there was no one to take care of either of them. They spent so much time competing about who was going to be taken care of that they didn't have much time for fun.

Kathryn had decided after Barry died that she would never again expect any one person to fulfill so many of her needs. It felt too risky and it really didn't seem fair to either person.

Kathryn and Steve have decided that they will depend on each other for only twenty or twenty-five per cent of their strokes. They will get another twenty or twenty-five percent from themselves and will extend their **stroke bases** to get the rest from outside sources—from their children, from colleagues, from friends and neighbors, from relatives, from church, clubs, organizations, volunteer activities, and from sports and hobby companions. This economy will leave them sufficient energy to have fun together and will enable them to bring the energy and love that flows from high stroke banks to the process of blending the families. It would be easy to depend heavily on each other now but hazardous to the marriage and the blend on any day that both Steve and Kathryn are feeling low.

Steve listened carefully in his self-esteem meeting when people talked about finding lots of places to get good strokes. Jill had a rigid golden stroke rule that insisted "Husband strokes are necessary and others don't count!" She said she couldn't think of workable ways to extend her stroke base. She asked for help because her husband was her major source of nurturing—of caring for her. He was out of town, and she was depressed. Steve thought, "She sounds like Esther used to."

The group offered suggestions for her to consider. "Decide how many bundles of nurturing you want in a week, and divide them up among several people. . . . Ask your sister. . . . Arrange a swap with a neighbor—I mend for a neighbor, and she cooks for my freezer. . . . Ask your friends. . . . Join a small group at church, and figure out a way to get nurturing there. . . . Get a body massage. . . . Use the phone to call people who are likely to give you what you want. . . . Take a long bubble bath, and then rub lotion over your whole body. . . . Take yourself and a friend out to lunch. Let the restaurant staff do the cooking, serving, and cleaning up." Steve recalled the resistance he had felt to similar suggestions after he and Esther separated.

Outside, after the meeting, Steve overheard Jill say, "Yes, but I've tried all those things and none of them work. I really want Jack to take care of me."

Steve thought, "Jack and Jill. Incredible! The nursery rhyme couple ended up in a heap at the bottom of the hill! And so did Esther and I. I'm not going to do that to Kathryn!"

200

More Strokes for Older Folks—Self and Strokes

One of the ways that Steve and Kathryn will avoid the heap at the bottom of the hill is to get lots of their strokes from themselves. They are taking care to stroke themselves and each other in the same three general areas as they do the children. Kathryn says to herself, "I should do this. I can figure out how; I am creative." To Steve she says, "Thanks for your opinion. . . . I appreciate the information you gave me. . . . Let's go sailing!"

In return, Steve gives her a hug and says, "I want you to know that you are the prettiest, smartest, neatest first mate I ever set sail with!"

Besides complimenting themselves when they do well, both Kathryn and Steve are saying all of the sets of affirmations to themselves.[17] Kathryn won't tell what hers are; she wrote them for herself. They are what she needs to hear, and they are private. She did admit that she had spent some long moments with *You can be powerful and still have needs* and *You can be sure about what you need.* Some of her fear about marrying Steve had been related to the fact that she was doing some recycling around needs and power. Part of her said, "Hey, I just learned how to be truly independent. I can manage my house, my checkbook, and my life by myself. Why would I want to give that up and become dependent on a man again?" As she worked it through, Kathryn realized that she did not have to be stuck in an either/or position, that she did not have to give up all of her newfound independence to live with Steve. She could have intimacy without being dependent.

Ooh, Look at Them Now—Visualization

Both Steve and Kathryn are visualizing the Muer-Blakeborough family in their minds. They see each of the children in turn as competent, resourceful people who keep their own stroke banks filled with positive messages. They close their eyes and see and hear the teenagers as independent, happy, problem-solving young adults. They see themselves as pivotal persons in a family that is blended, close but open with teenagers pulling away and springing back, as they do their uneven separating act. When good strokes come from the children, Kathryn and Steven enjoy. When the children send hostile messages, Kathryn and Steve oil their feathers like ducks and let the **negatives** roll off. Kathryn and Steve—together.

Both Kathryn and Steve believe that a strong, stable, loving family is important.

> *Strong, stable, loving families come in different sizes, ages, varieties, and blends. Romantic idealization by adults or children can*

*get in the way of families, but any of the people in any of the
families can improve the quality of living experiences they offer to
each other and themselves. Parents can invite their children to
have positive self-esteem and can show their children how to
achieve it by increasing their own lovableness and capableness.*

Notes

1. See the Parenting Tips for Raising the Thirteen- to Nineteen-Year-Old Child on page 203.

2. For further discussion of family ghosts (which Satir calls shadows), see Virginia Satir, *Peoplemaking* (Palo Alto, Calif.: Science and Behavior Books, 1975), p. 188.

3. Words which have a special definition as presented in this book are set in boldface the first time they are used in this chapter. The definition of these words is given in the Glossary.

4. Pam Levin, *Becoming the Way We Are: A Transactional Guide to Personal Development* (Berkeley, Calif.: Transactional Publications, 1974), p. 50.

5. Ibid., p. 27.

6. Ibid., p. 32.

7. Ibid., p. 51.

8. Ibid., p. 36.

9. Ibid., p. 51.

10. Ibid., p. 42.

11. Ibid., p. 51.

12. Ibid., p. 48.

13. Ibid., p. 52.

14. See the Four Ways of Parenting exercise on pages 204-205 for further examples of positive structuring and protecting parenting.

15. For further reading on this way of stroking, see Muriel James, *Transactional Analysis for Moms and Dads: What Do You Do with Them Now That You've Got Them* (Reading, Mass.: Addison-Wesley, 1975), Chapter 2.

16. See the What You Stroke Is What You Get worksheet on page 210 for examples of ways Steve Blakeborough can compliment his daughter to encourage her ability to think, to nurture, and to express her natural feelings. On page 211, write ways you can stroke a child, an adult, or yourself in the three personality areas.

17. See the Affirmations for Sexuality worksheets on pages 206-207 and the Affirmations for Sexuality sampler on pages 208-209.

Parenting Tips for Raising
the Thirteen- to Nineteen-Year-Old Child

I. The job of the thirteen- to nineteen-year-old Bryan is to separate from his family. He should emerge as a separate, independent person with his own values, a person who is responsible for his own needs, feelings, and behaviors.

II. The job of the adults caring for Bryan is to allow him to rework each previous stage with the added dimension of sexuality. They will continue to give positive strokes for being and doing well and negative strokes for behavior of which they disapprove.
   A. They will remember that:
      1. Thirteen (going-on-infant) Bryan is sometimes independent and sometimes wanting to be fed and cared for.
      2. Fourteen (going-on-two) Bryan is sometimes reasonable and competent and then suddenly engaged in a rebellious outburst.
      3. Fifteen (going-on-three and hassling) Bryan is sometimes doing admirable adult reasoning and suddenly arguing every unimportant detail.
      4. Sixteen to nineteen (going-on-birth-to-twelve-years) Bryan is adult and responsible with sudden short journeys back into one of the younger behaviors.
   B. They will realize that his separation may be slow or sudden or that he may engage in the one behavior (whatever that is in his family) the adults won't tolerate so that they will force him out.
   C. They will be ready to re-engage with Bryan on an adult level.
   D. They will admire and enjoy his sexuality without being seductive toward him or allowing him to behave seductively toward them. They will remember that his developing sexuality has a special set of needs and that he will not be ready to give up all of his dependent needs.
   E. They will affirm his independence by doing the separation affirmations practiced earlier in this section. They will visualize Bryan as if he had already accepted the affirmations.

III. The job of the caring adults is to take care of themselves.
   A. They will prepare new time and stroke structures to fill the holes left by the separation.
   B. They will remember that areas where they experience the most discomfort with Bryan will indicate that the adults haven't resolved those particular issues for themselves. They can do that right now, before the nest is empty.

Remember that your parents did the best they could. You have done the best that you could. If you want to use these new tools, it is never too late to start.

Four Ways of Parenting*

For any situation that requires parenting—advising and supporting—there are four possible ways of responding. Nurturing and structuring and protecting ways encourage positive self-esteem. Marshmallowing and criticizing ways tear down self-esteem. Below are situations. Each situation has a response given by a nurturing, a structuring and protecting, a marshmallowing, and a criticizing parent.

Read each of the four responses to each situation. Allow yourself to hear the positive and the negative implications of each. Rewrite each answer to fit your own value system where needed.

Parent Messages

Nurturing

This message is gentle, supportive, caring. It invites the person to get his or her needs met. It offers to help. It gives permission to succeed and affirms.

Marshmallowing

This message sounds supportive, but it invites dependence, suggests person will fail, and negates.

Structuring and Protecting

This message sets limits, protects, asserts, demands, advocates ethics and traditions. It tells ways to succeed and affirms.

Criticizing

This message ridicules, tears down, tells ways to fail, and negates.

Situation: Parent says, "When I want my daughter to do something and I ask her if she wants to, I feel frustrated when she says no."

Nurturing

You are a smart loving person, and you are too important to spend time feeling frustrated over this. You can resolve it.

Marshmallowing

Try to teach her to be nicer.

Structuring and Protecting

When she has a choice, ask. When she doesn't have a choice, tell, and then insist that she does whatever it is, however long that takes.

Criticizing

Sounds like you don't know how to control your daughter! I wish you'd be a better parent!

*See Glossary, pages 269-270, for further information.

204

Situation: Adult says, "My spouse and I disagree on how to raise the children."

Nurturing

I see that you both care about the children but express it in different ways. Let them know how much you care about them.

Marshmallowing

Give in and make peace. Everyone knows that children get mixed up if parents don't agree!

Structuring and Protecting

I can tell that you care about your children. Kids don't have to have their parents agree on everything. They can learn that Mom does some things one way and Dad another. What's important is that you and your spouse respect each other's positions and let the children know that you expect them to learn to deal with different kinds of people.

Criticizing

You dummy! Don't you get along? How do you expect kids to know what to do if parents don't agree? It's all your fault.

Situation: Parent says, "My two and a half year old hits my seven month old. What shall I do?"

Nurturing

(With a firm, gentle hand, move the child.)

Marshmallowing

Ask him why he does that.

Structuring and Protecting

Say "Hit the spanking stool or the bean-bag chair, don't hit the baby" as you move him away from the baby.

Criticizing

Say "You are so rough! You'll kill her!" and spank him.

Situation: Parent says, "My twelve-year-old son spends most of his time at his friend's house and comes home just long enough to tell me what we do wrong."

Nurturing

So your son is out checking how other people do things. You have a smart kid, and you're letting him grow.

Marshmallowing

I suppose you are doing the very best you can. Too bad he doesn't appreciate you.

Structuring and Protecting

Love him, listen to him, challenge him to think, and then you do what *you* decide is best.

Criticizing

Well, if you were doing it better, he wouldn't be so dissatisfied.

Affirmations for Sexuality
—Working Through Old Problems
with Sexuality Added and Separating from Parents:
Thirteen to Nineteen Years

The affirmations for sexuality are important for thirteen- to nineteen-year-old human beings, for any older persons who are making relationship separations, and for everyone else.

You can be a sexual person and still have needs.

To JOANNA —
16 year old

Don't confuse sex and nurturing. I would hate to see you use sex as the only way to be physically close.

TO ME —
adult

It's OK to feel sexually excited and know I'm in charge. I can decide to act or not to act on my feelings. (from me)

It's OK to know who you are.

Joanna, I'll call you by the name you prefer. Are you willing to forgive my mistakes while I learn to use Joanna instead of Jo-Jo?

It's ok to find out what I want to do with my life next. (from me)

You're welcome to come home again.

I'm glad you are out having fun with your friends. I feel good when you come home again.

I can find new strengths and new abilities, and my family will still love me. (from family)

I love you.

I love you, and it's fun to hassle and tease you when you're in the mood. That's fun!

You are important to me and I love you. (from friends)

(I love you, and I'm glad I know you. I see you are doing things, and I expect you to continue to learn about cause and effect, to differentiate between feelings and actions, and to get your needs met straight. I see that you are trying out, thinking about, altering and claiming your own way of looking at things and doing things. I see that you are recycling, going over old needs and problems with the added dimension of sexuality. It's important to work through problems and to separate from parents and to assume responsibility for your own needs and feelings and behavior as a grown-up person in the world.)

Affirmations for Sexuality

Follow the **Directions for Others** or the **Directions for Self** below and fill in this worksheet.

Directions for Others

1. Think of a person you want to send affirmations to. The person can be any age.
2. Write each affirmation the way you want to convey it to that person (words, touch, attention, listening).
3. Visualize the person as if he or she has already accepted your message.

Directions for Self

1. Write each affirmation the way you want to hear it.
2. Write the name of someone you want to hear it from. Name at least three different people.
3. Get the messages in a way that is constructive for you and for other people.
4. Give the messages to yourself, even if you don't believe them at first.
5. Visualize yourself as if you already believe them.

You can be a sexual person and still have needs.

It's OK to know who you are.

You're welcome to come home again.

I love you.

People who hear a message and consistently observe opposite behavior can feel confused or crazy. Send only the messages that you believe.

Sampler: Affirmations for Sexuality—
Working Through Old Problems
with Sexuality Added and Separating from Parents

A letter to Wade, age 14

Dear Wade,

Sometimes I have to search for the right words when we are together, so I have decided to write this letter to you. You are the physical size of a man now, taller than I am, and I'm proud of every inch of you. You are also growing and gaining experience intellectually. You have always been a clear, perceptive thinker, particularly about knowing yourself and knowing what your own needs are.

You will be playing football this fall at school. I'm sure that you know what the locker room conversation is about with a group of teenage boys. It's OK to know who you are, to take pride in yourself, and to make your own decisions about what to say and what to laugh at.

You have a strong body and a good brain. Take care of them both. Recognize that you also have emotional needs to be met. You are becoming a sexual person, and that is normal and wonderful at the same time. It is OK and normal to have sexual feelings for a girl, and at your age it's also OK and normal not to do anything about those feelings. These are decisions that only you can make.

Remember, you are important to me, and I love you very much.

Dad

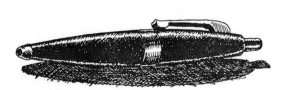

A letter to me, age 29

Dear Self,

I know who I am. I am a full-grown adult, a powerful sexual person. Just as I have emotional, physical, and intellectual power, I also have emotional, physical, and intellectual needs. It's OK to be grown-up and to have these needs. I will make my life so that my needs are met. When I choose, I can go back to those people who nurtured me as I grew. The places and the world have changed as I grew, but I can return to the people who care. Any place that I live I can create my own physical and emotional home to return to. I am lovable and capable and I can find responsible ways to live my life.

A letter to J.J., age 17

Dear J.J.,

You are a beautiful, sexy-looking girl. Your emerging sexuality adds a new aspect to your life. You still have areas in which you need and want to be dependent. It's important for you to know who you are and where you are in your own sexual development. You can feel your sexual feelings without doing anything about them. Take the time you need to explore your sexuality. You will find new ways of relating to girls, to women, to your brothers, to boys, to men, and especially to your father. You do not have to have sexual intercourse because all the kids are doing it, because a national survey says that half the girls your age have, or because someone pressures you to do it. That is yours. You can decide. Make your decision a responsible one for yourself and for others. I look forward to your separation, and I look forward to your return to our family as an equal adult. I will enjoy that very much. My heart is full of love for you. I trust you to become the strong, capable, full, wonderful woman that I see emerging now.

Love,
Mom

A letter to Marc, age 22

Dear Marc,

I love seeing you. You are so handsome, strong, smart, and sexy. You can be grown up and still ask for things. You can be grown up and still be a kid at times. If you want me to give a special party for your graduation, I will. I'd love to.

I see that you are finding out who you are in the technical world. I hope you will also explore yourself in the social, political, artistic, and psychic world. You know your intellectual and your firm self very well. It is important for you to know your feeling and your gentle self as well. I know that you are developing your sexuality and finding out who you are as a sexual person. That is an important part of your life journey at your age. I expect you to make thoughtful, joyful decisions about your sexuality and to use it to expand and affirm your own life. I expect you not to use it in a way that exploits yourself or another person, physically or emotionally.

I hope that you have a clear separation between sex and nurturing and that you do not offer sex to a person who needs nurturing or accept sex as a substitute for nurturing for yourself.

You're always welcome here. You are welcome whether I am expecting you or whether you pop in with your bag of dirty laundry on your back. Whatever your relationship with your girl friend is, when you are in our house, I expect you to follow the sexual mores that your father and I teach and follow.

Do you know that I am eager for you to complete your emotional separation from us and to be a full family member with new equal adult status? That will be so exciting and enjoyable for me that I can hardly wait. But I will, and you must do it on your time schedule, not mine.

I love you a hundredteen.

Hugs,
Mom

A letter to an adult, age 50

Dear Sally,

You are a beautiful, sexy-looking woman. The loss of your husband alters your life in many ways. Do not forget that you are still a sexual person. You can know that you are and choose how to fit that into the new life that you are building. You may rejoin your old social grouping or find new ones, but keep in close touch with the many places you are welcome to come home to.

I love you very much,
Jean

What You Stroke Is What You Get

name ___Becky___ age _10 years_ time _Fri. evening_

To encourage people to become whole and well balanced, compliment all aspects of their personalities.

Encourage nurturing, structuring and protecting, having and using morals and ethics, and doing things for self and others.

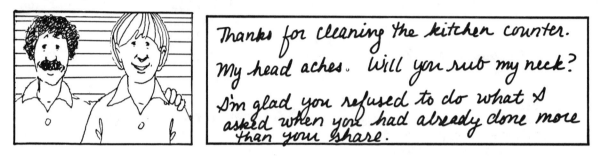

Thanks for cleaning the kitchen counter. My head aches. Will you rub my neck? I'm glad you refused to do what I asked when you had already done more than your share.

Encourage dealing with current reality, gathering facts, estimating probability, and solving problems.

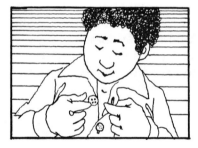

You did a good job of listing your clothes and writing down what you think you need for school this fall. Great math paper, Becky.

Encourage feeling and acting naturally and adaptively . *

Where is that clever Becky? I want to have some fun with her! Becky, where are you? So you didn't hear me! (tickle, chase, hug, kiss)

*See page 51 for more examples of what to stroke and how to stroke.

210

What You Stroke Is What You Get

name _____ age _____ time _____

To encourage people to become whole and well balanced, compliment all aspects of their personalities.

Encourage nurturing, structuring and protecting, having and using morals and ethics, and doing things for self and others.

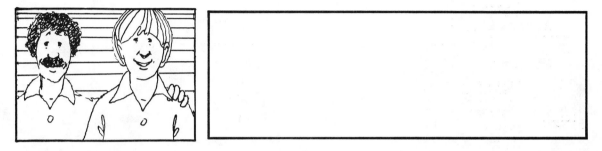

Encourage dealing with current reality, gathering facts, estimating probability, and solving problems.

Encourage feeling and acting naturally and adaptively. *

*See page 51 for more examples of what to stroke and how to stroke.

AMY SALGANIK.

8

What's a Nice Family Like Us
Doing in a Place Like This?

Leonard Walter Martinson sat motionless in his favorite chair, staring at the TV screen. With one glance his wife, Melissa, caught the hopelessness in the droop of his shoulders, the grey cast of his skin, and the fact that the TV set was not on.

"Where is Mary?" she demanded.

"Gone," Leonard sighed almost inaudibly.

"Why didn't you call me?" Melissa asked accusingly.

"I just found out," Leonard sighed again.

"What is it this time?" Melissa's voice was shaky.

"Downers," Leonard replied.

"Oh," Melissa's voice trailed off, then came back strong. "I knew we should have searched her room last night when she was out. If only you hadn't got home so late." And they were off again on another round of the months of fighting they had been having since Mary's chemicals had taken center stage in the family.

Who's to Blame?

"Look," Leonard snarled, "I'm not to blame this time. If you had stayed out of it yesterday when I was trying to lay down some rules, she would probably be here right now." Leonard and Melissa went another round in their game of who's-to-blame.

> *The first question that the family of a chemically dependent person usually asks is "Why? Why did she do it?" And the possible answers are often quickly followed by identifying the responsible person and assigning blame.*

Leonard and Melissa have been here many times before. Leonard is sure of all the things Melissa has done to cause Mary to turn to chemicals. And Melissa has identified Leonard's culpable areas.

Mary has had low self-esteem since she was a little tot. "That's Melissa's fault. Everyone knows that the mother is responsible for the first three years," Leonard thinks.

The move when Mary was in sixth grade was hard on her. She didn't want to move and couldn't make any friends in her new school. "That's Leonard's fault. If he had been satisfied with his job in Kansas City, everything would have been all right," Melissa thinks.

Mary's never been as good a student as Charlie is. Charlie's fault? No. Charlie can't help it that he is smart. Charlie is just naturally good at everything. Handsome, appealing, entertaining Charlie has always been an engaging child.

Bonnie Prince Charlie was born when Mary was fifteen months old. Too soon for Mary to be bumped out of the nest by a baby? She was still a baby herself. Melissa's fault. She forgot her contraceptives when they went for an anniversary celebration to the Clariford Inn. When Mary should have been a rebellious two-year-old, Charlie was exploring his world with the speed and energy and cuteness of a half dozen puppies. And Melissa was so busy with him that she didn't have time to listen to Mary's "I won'ts" and "You can't make me's."

Mary withdrew into a corner. Leonard's fault. If he had been making more money, Melissa could have had household help which would have freed her time to attend to Mary.

Mary felt badly about not doing as well in school or band or swimming as Charlie. Grandma's fault for making such a big deal of it. "When are you going to do as well as your brother, Mary? . . . How can you let him get ahead of you like that, Mary? . . . When are you going to buckle down to work, Mary?" Always, always, always, whenever Grandma visited, phoned, or wrote a letter.

Seventh grade was worse than sixth. Mary tried to make friends, be popular, please her peers. It didn't work. School's fault. The teachers should watch the kids more carefully and plan better school activities. The summer between seventh and eighth grade, Mary stayed in her room or watched TV almost the entire summer. She didn't have friends, and she ignored the many ways her parents tried to please her, and she did not find Charlie entertaining. Melissa's fault. She should have found ways to get Mary involved with other kids. Leonard's fault. He should have taken them on a vacation to a dude ranch where Mary could have met some new kids.

Eighth grade was the year Mary made friends—with all the other kids who did not have a group of friends. They found one thing that made them feel better. Alcohol. And another. Pot. School's fault. Schools should catch the pushers.

At last Mary had found something she could be good at—being the worst! Whatever destructive thing her gang got into, Mary did it the best, the most, and the biggest. Mary's fault. And she got no competition from Charlie. He was too busy getting good grades, playing football, going to orchestra practice and comforting his parents when they felt bad about Mary. They felt terrible!

Melissa felt sad and tried to fix everyone and everything. Leonard didn't know what he felt, but he knew he didn't like the situation. He decided that Mary had to go into therapy. Mary didn't want to and fought with him about it. Melissa tried to fix things between Mary and her father.

My Dad Has Horns and Other Despicable Characteristics, and My Mother Isn't Very Likeable Either

Leonard arranged for Mary to go to a therapy group for adolescents involved with drugs. She went only once. She announced that she would not return and that she hated the group and her father. He arranged for her to see Dr. Ferrard, a psychiatrist. Dr. Ferrard talked to Mary, Melissa, and Leonard. He thought Leonard was the family problem. Mary agreed! The doctor said Mary was just the symptom carrier, and Leonard should stop fixing Mary and fix himself. Mary agreed, terminated her relationship with Dr. Ferrard, and told her father she hated him even more.

Melissa was in physical pain over Mary; Leonard was in a daze; and Mary stayed spaced out. No matter whose problem it was, Melissa and Leonard believed it imperative to get Mary off chemicals. In order to do that they would get back to "Why?" which led to "Who is to blame?"

Leonard had to do something. He took Mary to see Dr. Hedges, a therapist who worked with chemically dependent people. Dr. Hedges insisted that Leonard and Melissa come too. Even Charlie had to attend.

It was an interesting arrangement. Dr. Hedges was interested in family systems. Melissa was interested in changing Leonard. Leonard was interested in fixing Mary. Charlie found more ways to be competent. Mary played the blame game and was determined to prove to Dr. Hedges that her dad had horns and other despicable characteristics and her mother wasn't very likeable either. Leonard couldn't understand what had happened to his little Mary. He and she were so close when she was little, and he couldn't understand why she was making him into a monster in this determined way. He was shocked and depressed; and he was also sure that Melissa was somehow to blame.

Dr. Hedges pointed out that any of the reasons for Mary's chemical abuse that the Martinsons had identified could be present in a family that did not produce an abuser. He suggested that as long as Melissa and Leonard continued to play the blame game and spend their energy fixing blame or feeling guilty, they would be helping Mary to stay in her destructive patterns.

Nobody's Guilty

Dr. Hedges told them that he would not continue to work with them if they were not willing to stop looking at the past for why and look at the present for what to do now. He said they may never know why; he said the real question was what are they willing to do to improve the situation now

Leonard and Melissa had structured so much time and spent so much energy asking why and deciding who was to blame that it was hard to bring those activities to a screeching halt.

One thing that they discovered was that they were both feeling terribly guilty and that each had been blaming the other to try to relieve the guilt. The idea that nobody is guilty is tough to accept. Leonard is not the guilty one; Melissa is not the guilty one; Dr. Hedges said that Charlie was not guilty—he was just finding a satisfactory place for himself in the system, whatever that means; and Mary is not the guilty one.

Let's Get to Work

The Martinsons discovered that they didn't know what to do instead of feeling guilty and blaming. Dr. Hedges talked about "letting go," but neither Leonard nor Melissa understood that. Leonard said, "It sounds as if we're supposed to stop caring about Mary. We can never do that."

Leonard said he didn't think Mary was hearing him, and Dr. Hedges agreed. Leonard said, "We tell Mary we love her and want to help her. She

216

thinks we are saying we want to control her. Maybe it would help if we could really hear each other and answer each other."

Dr. Hedges said, "That is the most hopeful thing I have heard since you Martinsons first walked into this clinic. Now you are talking about doing something." He said that when the Martinsons stop **redefining**[1] each other—stop changing what they heard to make it fit what they expected to hear—and start answering each other straight they will all be more aware of what is really going on in the family

Strokes—What You Send Is Not Necessarily What They Get

The Martinsons **convert strokes**. When Leonard says "Mary, do you know that I love you?" she asks, "How can you expect me to believe that?" If Melissa says, "Do you want to go to the shopping center with me?" Mary flashes, "You want to get me out of the house so Daddy can search my room. Well, there's nothing there!" When Mary says, "Daddy, you don't really care if I'm happy, do you?" Leonard says, "Mary, I want you to give up chemicals."

Dr. Hedges called the way they talk to each other redefining. He explained what redefining is and how to replace it with straight communication.

> Redefinition is a method that people use to turn or alter stimuli to fit their **frame of reference**, their preconceived notions of themselves and the world. When someone redefines you, that person switches the subject or responds to you without answering your question. Example: Betty's preconceived notion is that her mother was important because she had a beautiful voice and that Betty is not important and does not have a beautiful voice. So when someone says, "Betty, you have a beautiful voice," Betty responds with "You should have heard my mother's voice "

> Example: Gibby believes Maria is bossy and manipulative. Maria asks, "What would you like to do tonight?" Gibby responds, "What would you like to do?" He refuses to say that he wants to go sailing, goes reluctantly to the art show, and then feels sorry for himself and angry at Maria.

> Redefinition is done by switching how, what, when, where, who, and why; by switching from one what to another what, from one how to another how, and so on; or by switching from where to

217

*when, how to what, and so on. Example: "Where are your boots?"
is a where. "I won't need them until tomorrow" switches to when.*

*Remember that saying "That is a redefinition" is itself a redefini-
tion if it does not answer the question. Example: "Where are your
boots?" is a where. "I won't need them until tomorrow," switches to
when. "That is a redefinition" switches to what but does not answer the question.*

*Also remember that questioning the redefinition rather than repeat-
ing the original question is another redefinition. Example: "Where
are your boots?" is a where. "I won't need them until tomorrow,"
switches to when. "What does tomorrow have to do with your
boots?" switches to what and questions the redefinition but does
not answer the original question.*

After the Martinsons had practiced identifying a few redefinitions with Dr.
Hedges, he said, "Leonard, are you willing to stop redefining?"

Leonard replied, "Do you really think this will help Mary now?" Dr. Hedges
paused a moment. Leonard had switched from the "what" he is willing to
do to a "what" the doctor thinks.

Dr. Hedges turned to Melissa, "Are you willing to stop redefining?"

"Do you think Leonard understands how to stop it?" Dr. Hedges paused
again. Melissa had switched from "who" Melissa to "who" Leonard.

Dr. Hedges asked Charlie, "Are you willing to stop redefining?"

Charlie smiled at the doctor and said, "You did a cool job of explaining it,
Dr. Hedges." Charlie had switched "you" Charlie to "you" Dr. Hedges.

Dr. Hedges turned to Mary and said, "How about you, Mary, are you willing
to stop redefining?"

Mary said, "You don't think the rest of them will do this silly stuff, do
you?" Mary switched "what" will I do to "what" do you think.

Dr. Hedges looked squarely at Mary and said, "Mary, will you promise not
to take any chemicals between right now and the start of our next meeting?"

Mary looked away and said, "No!"

The doctor sighed, "Thank you, Mary. That was the only straight answer I
got. Before that I heard four redefinitions."

Leonard and Melissa took the sample list of redefinitions[2] that Dr. Hedges gave them and discovered that the Martinson family had great skill at redefining. It took several weeks of practice, with some fighting in between, and several sessions with Dr. Hedges before they got through the redefinitions to straight talk about what they wanted from each other and about how they really felt.[3]

Melissa and Leonard worked on what was going on or not going on between Melissa and Leonard. They learned that redefinition puts down the person who is redefined because he doesn't get what he asked for and it allows the redefiner to continue to distort reality. "In other words," Leonard said, "everytime we allow Mary to redefine us, we allow her to reinforce her old concepts about herself and us. And everytime we insist that she answer us straight, we are insisting that she respond in the here and now instead of out of some old idea."

"Right, and if you get her to think in the here and now it may not even matter what that old idea was," Dr. Hedges added.

They thought about each **affirmation**. When they said the **affirmations for being**—*You have every right to be here. . . . I like to hold you. . . . Your needs are OK with me. . . . I'm glad you're a girl. . . . You don't have to hurry*—to Mary she laughed and then went into a rage and screamed, "You don't really mean it! You're both phony!"

Melissa guessed that Mary hadn't heard the **doing affirmation**, *You don't have to do tricks to get approval*. "Mary has finally found the tricks that get approval from her friends," Melissa pointed out. "Even though what she is doing is destructive, she does get approval for it! Her friends are devoted to her, call her, emulate her, want to get high with her. Mary has found something she is good at."

Dr. Hedges talked with Melissa and Leonard and Mary about the theory of **recycling**. Leonard said, "If this theory of recycling is true, Mary was recycling six to eighteen months, the exploratory age, when she started to use drugs at thirteen. She could have lost out on some of her exploring with Charlie being born when she was fifteen months old. I'm sure sorry she decided to do her recycling of exploring by exploring chemicals." Dr. Hedges asked the Martinsons what Mary could explore besides chemicals, and Mary pouted.

There Have Been Some Changes Made!

Melissa and Leonard have done all of the good things that they as parents of a chemical abuser could think of to do. They got their daughter into therapy. The whole family went into therapy. Mary and Leonard made changes in their relationship, and they changed the way they behave toward Mary. They did less redefining, less criticizing, and gave more positive strokes.

Has Mary stopped using chemicals? No. Leonard asked her why. She said, "Because it's fun, Daddy. It's so exciting! It's much better to be high with my friends than to be around here worrying about re–de–fin–ishion!"

Leonard said, "I can't understand you, Mary; I worry about you so much!"

Mary laughed loudly, "I know it, Dad," she said. Mary was not only enjoying the excitement of the drugs, she was also enjoying watching her father and mother squirm.

"Daddy," she said, "did you know I can handle more stuff than any one else in my crowd? They think I'm cool. And if you push me, I'll run away." And she did.

A nightmare followed. Melissa and Leonard remember it in a haze. Call the police . . . worry . . . find Mary, really freaked out . . . worry . . . locked ward . . . worry . . . won't see Dr. Hedges . . . worry . . . into a hospital treatment program . . . worry . . . out of the hospital . . . relief . . . back to school . . . worry . . . with old friends . . . worry . . . drunk again . . . worry . . . run away again . . . repeat the whole thing . . . worry . . . into a different treatment center, highly confrontive   worry.

You Can't Fix the Kid

Leonard and Melissa feel as if they have been run over by a steamroller. They have blamed; they have fought; they have gone to therapy; they have changed their behavior; Charlie has sustained them throughout, but Mary is no better. Worse in fact. Leonard is depressed. "I have done everything I know to do and lots of things I never dreamed I could do. Still my daughter is a junkie, and I have no more ways to help her. Furthermore, she hates me. Melissa, what can we do?"

Melissa says, "Leonard, do you remember, the first time we ever saw Dr. Hedges, he said, 'The first thing you should know is that you cannot fix Mary. Only Mary can fix Mary.'"

Leonard said, "Yes, I remember, but I didn't believe it."

Melissa says, "Neither did I. Then. But I do now."

"I'm beginning to believe it myself." Leonard sighed, "Melissa, is this what 'letting go' is?"

220

Letting Go

Letting go was a favorite phrase with the therapy group Leonard and Melissa were in as part of Mary's hospital treatment. Leonard hated the phrase and Melissa resented it. Melissa guessed it has something to do with being responsible for other people's feelings, but Melissa's first response to the idea of letting go was sheer terror. She had been hanging on so hard and so long that letting go sounded like giving up her last hold and losing all hope—like drowning. Leonard thought it meant he was supposed to abandon Mary, and he didn't see that she needed that on top of all her other troubles.

When Leonard and Melissa finally understood that letting go meant not being responsible for what was not their responsibility, they started to make sense of it. Melissa worked through it from the feelings angle. She wanted to be able to make Mary happy but she could not. Leonard went at it in reverse. "It's not obvious to me why I should let go, so what do I do to Mary if I don't let go?" Leonard demanded. People in the therapy group told him that not letting go is crippling; it is **discounting**; it is patronizing because it implies that Mary can't think for herself. It discourages initiative; it discourages responsibility for self and others. It deprives Mary of learning experiences and the chance to experience how to manage herself in a world with other people. Trying to shelter her feelings deprives her of the chance to learn coping skills. Leonard yelled, "Stop, stop! Enough! Initiative, responsibility, coping skills—those words I understand! Why didn't you say so before? I'm ready to let go."

Deciding to let go was the start. Doing it was a long journey for both Leonard and Melissa. They had learned about **four ways of parenting** in one of the Parent Support Groups at the hospital. At first it was discouraging how easy it was for Melissa to play the **marshmallow** role and for Leonard to play the **critical** role. Melissa complained, "If either one of us were 'playing', it wouldn't be so yucky!" Melissa knew that her marshmallowing enabled Mary's chemical use, and Melissa was so busy learning how to give clear **nurturing** and **structuring and protecting** messages that she forgot to worry about Leonard. He was practicing nurturing messages, and getting better at giving them every day.[4]

Leonard asked Dr. Hedges for more help with letting go. Hedges asked Leonard how he felt about it, and Leonard replied, "I don't feel any way about it—I just want to learn to do it."

Melissa complained, "It's hard to stop being responsible for Mary."

Dr. Hedges observed, "Mary is almost eighteen. Soon she will be a legal adult. Mary has to be responsible for herself. Besides," he reiterated, "no matter how much you want to do it for her, you can't."

Leonard said, "I can't figure out how Charlie and Mary can be so different. They grew up in the same house—we raised them the same way. How can Charlie be so sure of himself and Mary have such a poor self-image?"

Hedges said it might help them understand how Mary already is responsible if they understood the four aspects of **self-esteem.**

He said, "First there is fate. Mary had no control over the fact that she was born female and had a brother when she was fifteen months old. Then there are the positive and negative messages that life has offered her. Melissa and Leonard, you have sent out a lot of healthy, loving, life-giving messages to this girl. But no parents are always positive, and you have sent some destructive messages along the way too. Mary had fate to respond to, and she had the positive and negative messages that you offered or that she perceived."

Stroke Buffet

Doctor Hedges continued to explain how Mary is responsible for her own self-esteem. "Mary, and Mary alone, decided which messages to make important, and she decided how to interpret them. Imagine Mary at age three or four walking around a buffet table[5] on which are laid out many messages. She has an empty basket in her hand, and she has to fill it from the messages on her table. She picks up several messages and decides that they are hers—that is how life will be for her. You can offer her new messages. You can tell her you think she misinterpreted messages. You can challenge her redefinitions. You can tell her what you want her to pick up, to believe, but you cannot make her change what she has in her basket. Only she can do that."[6]

Dr. Hedges gave Melissa and Leonard a list of possible early messages[7] and asked them to go home and think about what messages they had chosen when they were little. He said this might help them with letting go. At home, Leonard said, "I don't believe it. Three year olds are too little to think. She wouldn't know what she was choosing."

> When young children attempt to make sense out of their lives by making decisions about their experiences, they have to base the decisions on inadequate data. The decisions are primitive and may include magic thinking—"If I ever do that, Mommy will leave me" or "They must have had another baby because they think I'm no good" or "Mom and Dad would not be getting a divorce if it weren't for me. After all, they were married before I was born. It must be my fault" or "When I think of something to do, they get mad at me. Maybe if I don't think, they will like me."

222

Leonard is right–three-year-old children are too young to un-
derstand what they are choosing. But they are not too young to try
to make sense out of life. When Mary takes responsibility for her
own decisions, accepts that she was trying to make sense of life
and did the best that she could at the time, and takes full respon-
sibility for the need to update or amend archaic decisions or to
make some new ones, she will have started her journey into a new
way of life.

Melissa didn't buy the idea that Mary had found her destructive stuff at
their house, but Melissa was interested in the **stroke buffet** idea. She had
promised Dr. Hedges that she would think about what messages she,
Melissa, had picked up when she was a little girl—so Melissa literally set a
stroke buffet table. She wrote the messages from Dr. Hedges' list on
squares of paper and laid them out on the dining room table. Then she
walked around the table slowly, reading the messages and reaching to pick
up ones that she remembered feeling or hearing clearly as a child. She
held five paper squares in her hand and read:

> What will the neighbors think?
> If something goes wrong it must be your fault.
> Try harder.
> Anything worthwhile is worth suffering for.
> You can succeed.

The messages on the table had triggered Melissa's memory. She looked at
the collection in amazement. She took a fresh paper square and wrote:

> Be responsible for other people's feelings.

Melissa pondered the messages for a long time. Dr. Hedges had asked her
to identify a way each could be interpreted to help her support a
chemically-dependent system. She thought, "'What will the neighbors
think?' encourages me not to see the problems with Mary. If I don't see any
problems, the neighbors may not either. It also contributes to the secrecy."
Melissa recalled saying to Leonard, "Now that we know, let's not tell anybody. I especially hope my mother never finds out."

Melissa continued musing, "'If something goes wrong, it must be your
fault' explains my willingness to try to improve Leonard's behavior and to
feel responsible for all of Mary's acts. It is behind some of the marshmallow
parenting that I've done so well. That comforting let-me-do-it-for-you type
of parenting seemed kind at the time, but it has surely invited Mary to be
dependent and not to be responsible for her own life and problems.

"'Try harder' makes it difficult for me to know when to quit, when to let go
of Mary," Melissa thought. "I say to myself, 'If only I can have another
chance I can try harder and maybe I can fix Mary, and Leonard, too!'"

Melissa considered the next message. "'Anything worthwhile is worth suffering for.' Helping my daughter *is* worthwhile, and in order to help Mary, I'm willing to suffer and suffer and suffer. Think of all the times I've given up what I want in order to do something that would be good for Mary."

Looking at the next message, Melissa thought, "'You can succeed' gives me encouragement to be responsible for anything that goes wrong and to suffer well and keep on trying harder in my attempt to fix it. 'Be responsible for other people's feelings' helps me get upset when mother criticizes Mary. I try to stay between them, to placate Mother with logical explanations of Mary's behavior, and I try to protect Mary from Mother's barbs."

Melissa brought her list and her hopelessness and dejection to Dr. Hedges. "What can I do with a bunch of loser messages like these? I am a real mess," she complains. "How can I change?"

Hedges advised, "Melissa, you can decide how you want to change your behavior. Get in touch with some of your power and competence by taking another look at each of those messages to find the positive, supportive life-sustaining part of each one."

Melissa wrote a second list—"What will the neighbors think?" has helped me learn how to be sensitive and pleasant. "If something goes wrong it must be your fault" helps me be responsible for my own actions. I expect to do my part in problem resolutions. "Anything worthwhile is worth suffering for" encourages me to go on, even when the going is tough. I am not a quitter. "You can succeed"—yes, I can succeed. I can do whatever is necessary to help Mary and all of us. If I have to I can even "let go," whatever that means. "Be responsible for other people's feelings." Nothing.

Melissa took her second list to Dr. Hedges. "Look," she urged, "look at all of the positive things I have going for me!"

Hedges cheered and hugged her.

"But," Melissa complained, "I can't find *anything* positive in 'Be responsible for other people's feelings.'"

"What do you want to do with it?" Dr. Hedges watched Melissa's face.

"Well," her eyes flashed angrily, "I want to throw it away."

"All right," Hedges agreed, "as soon as you have a positive message to put in its place."

224

At home Melissa fussed at Charlie and Leonard. "I'm still not used to the idea that I'm responsible for the messages in my head. When Dr. Hedges asked me what new messages I needed, I went blank. But I'm not going to stay blank!"

Charlie said, "Hey Mom, I know you can do it!"

The following week Melissa told Dr. Hedges that she had replaced "Be responsible for other people's feelings" with "Allow and encourage other people to feel their own feelings."

Hedges congratulated Melissa, "You're letting go!"

"Let go! Let go!" Melissa and Leonard still hated the phrase, Charlie said he didn't know what to let go of; and Mary, who was home from the Confrontive Center for a Sunday afternoon, scoffed. "It's only talk! You will *never* do it! Mother won't have anything to do if she lets go. Daddy might lose his precious control, and he couldn't stand to do that, not even for one minute."

Leonard said, "Don't you talk that way, young lady! This is my family and I am going to lick this problem myself!"

Mary jeered, "See what I mean," and continued in a sing-song voice, "What are you going to lick it with, Daddy? Boxing gloves? A riding whip? Your tongue? That's it—your tongue—like you lick a stamp for a letter?" Her sing-song voice turned to scorn. "Fat chance that *you'll* ever let go!"

After Mary went back to the Confrontive Center, Leonard said, "Melissa, do you still have those cards with the stroke buffet messages? I want to take a look." Melissa found the cards, and Leonard came face to face with his "Don't be out of control" message. Not as rigid as Mary sees it, but there all right. Leonard also picked up a "Don't feel" message and caught himself saying, "Oh, I don't know, I'll have to *think* about that." Leonard got out the list of affirmations he and Melissa had been using with Mary and Charlie and gave them to himself religiously.

Responsibilize

Melissa found Leonard sitting on a kitchen stool looking at the ceiling, chewing on a pencil, and tapping his foot. "Leonard, what is it?"

Leonard turned and waved the pencil at her. "I'm making a list—come and see: Responsibility, Winner, Competent, Make It, Pride, Self-Control, Initiative, Coping, Independence, and *Cttoliaphe*."

"Leonard," Melissa was mystified, "what is it?"

"It's a list of the things that letting go encourages. I'm looking for a new word."

Melissa said, "I see. Responsibility, Winner . . . Leonard, what is *Cttoliaphe*?"

"An acronym for 'Chance to Try Out Life in a Protected Home Environment.' At the moment I lean toward 'Responsibilize.' Think back a couple of years. If someone had asked you to 'Responsibilize Mary' instead of 'Letting Go of Mary' would it have been easier for you?"

Melissa laughed. "Sure would have! Let me see the list again." Melissa thought "Responsibilize" was a little austere. "Competentize" and "Pridize' didn't quite make it either. "Capablize" wasn't too far off, but she finally settled on "Winnerize." Leonard stayed with "Responsibilize" and both Leonard and Melissa let go of letting go. Charlie liked the new words, and Mary said that they seemed to be getting the idea, finally.

I'll Do It Myself

A month later Mary took herself out of the Confrontive Treatment Center and came home. "Can I live here?" she asked.

"Of course, of course! We love you." Leonard and Melissa hugged her. Charlie was silent.

"I can't stay there any longer, Mom," Mary explained. "They're down on me. I hear what they're saying about what I've done to myself and to you, but they aren't giving me any help to build myself up again. I want to come home and prove that I can cope here, myself!"

Melissa thought, "*You can do things and get support at the same time.*" This is what that affirmation means for Mary. Out loud Melissa said, "I'm glad you're home and I'm glad you're growing up!" Maybe Mary is ready to recycle eighteen months to three years and decide it is OK to think!

How Do We Take Care of Mary and Ourselves at the Same Time?

Melissa and Leonard were exuberant and joyful and relieved! They had decided months ago that they couldn't fix Mary, that only Mary could do that. They had also decided that while they gave Mary any support they could, they also have to protect and take care of themselves. Besides putting some new rules in their heads about how to relate to their children and each other, Melissa and Leonard are affirming themselves daily. And they are **visualizing** the whole family as a loving, capable, healthy unit. Each of them is active in a support system beyond the family. Leonard meets weekly with six friends who call themselves "The Breakfast Group." The rules of the group are, "Claim your wins, no 'yes, buts,' no 'ain't it awful.'" Melissa relied on Mothers, Fathers and Others Who Care About Children, a task and support group. There were days when Melissa went to a meeting or to the home of one of the members, said, "I hurt," gave no further explanation, and got nurturing. Leonard and Melissa were not willing to go back to the old days of worry, of searching for drugs to prevent another incident, of wondering what Mary was doing when she went to her room and closed her door. They agreed on some new structure and presented it to Mary. "We love you, and we want you to live here, with us. You may do that as long as you stay straight. No alcohol, no pot, no other mood-altering chemicals."

Mary looked serious. Then she smiled at her folks and said, "Fair enough. May I drink coffee?"

Mary proved that she could make it at home. In fact, she managed very well. High school was another issue. She dared not spend time with her old friends—they were still organizing their time around highs. And she made no new straight friends. She didn't know how. She was so much older and more sophisticated in some ways. She felt beyond them. Their talk was so trivial. Yet she felt behind. Way behind. They made new friends so easily—had so much skill in idle chatter that sounded like nothing but ended up with a date. Mary realized that while the straight girls had been entering puberty and worrying about boys and acne and clothes and how to talk with upperclassmen, she had been spaced out, or in a hospital, or in treatment. She had lots of new tools for geting along, but she was more at home in a therapy group than in the high school lunch room. Her school has a support group for kids who have been through chemical dependency treatment, but Mary dropped the group after a few sessions. All of the kids in the group had been through therapy, and the group leader let them play therapist for each other. The group didn't focus on how to relate to straight kids and that is what Mary wanted and needed to learn.

Where Is She Now?

Mary found a strong Alcoholics Anonymous group with some adults and some kids she liked. With the help of the AA group and her parents, Mary figured out for herself what she needed to do. She dropped out of high school and entered a school of business. The students there were mostly two to five years older than Mary and she felt somewhat more at ease with them. She has three new friends, Lynn, Joe, and Charlotte. Mary has been living at home for six months now. Leonard and Melissa do not jump when they hear the phone or panic if Mary is not in by midnight. They never did find out for certain why Mary used drugs, but they know that if Mary has decided to stay chemically free that she can do so, one day at a time, doing what she needs to do.

Meanwhile, Leonard and Melissa are offering the full list of affirmations to Charlie, to Mary, and to themselves. Melissa asked Mary to write down the special affirmations she most needs to hear from her parents, and Leonard and Melissa find many ways of giving them to her. They are

> You can trust your feelings.
> You are capable; you can handle that.
> You figure things out well.
> We trust you to know best what will work for you.
> You are the final authority on your needs.[8]
> I love you.

Leonard calls them Mary's self-esteem package. They are the way she needs to hear *You are lovable and capable.* Leonard affirms Charlie's ability to decide what he wants to do with his life for himself. Melissa and Leonard think the thirteen- to nineteen-year-old affirmation *It's OK to know who you are* is especially important for Charlie to internalize. They hope he will be himself for himself and not assume a position in the family in response to Mary's changes. Charlie admits that sometimes he holds a sea of anger. They are assuring him, *"We are not afraid of your anger,"* but so far Charlie seems to be keeping the anger inside himself.

They are watching Charlie to see what he will do. His understanding and support throughout the worried hours sustained Melissa and Leonard, but Melissa sometimes wonders who sustained Charlie and what he has done with all of the anger he had at having a freaked-out sister. It's almost as if he forgot how to play. He was so used to being the good one, the able one, that when Mary came home and functioned as a capable, responsible family member, Charlie acted lost and uncomfortable. Leonard and Melissa were tempted to try to fix him, but only briefly. They have learned that lesson well. Now they are waiting to see if Charlie will decide that there is room for two lovable and capable kids in the family.[9] Leonard and Melissa hope so.

They have also learned to visualize. They envision Mary healthy and lovable, a competent accountant with a job she likes, moving easily in a new social sphere and making lots of friends and not having to please any of them.

They visualize Charlie lovable and competent. They picture Charlie becoming the future Charlie who spends much less time taking care of them and much more time doing what Charlie wants to do. They imagine him rid of his anger about Mary's drug abuse. They see him comfortable about being equal with Mary and having her be as supportive and sociable as he is.

Not everyone believes in "responsibilizing." Melissa's mother thinks that Melissa and Leonard have abdicated their responsibility as parents, and she calls Melissa regularly and says, "You really must take better care of that child. She needs you. She isn't out of the woods yet. After all, you are her mother."

After her calls Melissa and Leonard visualize themselves completely committed to "responsibilizing" and "winnerizing." They congratulate themselves on having learned to take care of themselves and Mary and Charlie in ways that are healthy for all of them.

Leonard is allowing himself to feel his feelings more often—even though sometimes they are not pleasant. Melissa is dealing with the newness of having Leonard feel his feelings and the strangeness of not feeling for him. Melissa is continuing to examine and update the messages in her stroke buffet basket. Leonard and Melissa have a stronger, more loving relationship than they did before this whole painful journey.

Last night as Mary hurried through the hallway, she caught a glimpse of her father sitting motionless in his favorite chair, facing the TV screen. The set was not on. Mary skidded back and called, "Pop, whatcha doing in there?"

Melissa popped her head up over Leonard's shoulder, winked at Mary, and said, "Watching the news, dear, watching the news."

Notes

1. Words which have a special definition as presented in this book are set in boldface the first time they are used in this chapter. The definition of these words is given in the Glossary.

2. See the Redefinition worksheet on page 237.

3. Thanks to the foster parents of PATH (Professional Association of Treatment Homes) for their participation in the development of this exercise.

4. See the Four Ways of Parenting exercises on pages 231-232.

5. Thanks to Sheila Hartmann for help in developing and testing the stroke buffet.

6. For further information on how children decide, see Ken Ernst, *Pre-Scription: A TA Look at Child Development* (Millbrae, Calif.: Celestial Arts, 1976) and Claude Steiner, *Scripts People Live* (New York: Bantam, 1975).

7. See the Early Messages I Chose to Hear worksheets on pages 235-236.

8. See Sheldon B. Kopp, *If You Meet the Buddha on the Road, Kill Him!* (Toronto, Canada: Bantam, 1976).

9. See the What You Stroke is What You Get worksheet on page 233 for examples of ways the Martinsons are encouraging Charlie to be responsible for his own needs to play, to think, and to express his feelings. On the worksheet on page 234, write strokes that you can give to a specific person to encourage that person to be well balanced.

Four Ways of Parenting*

For any situation that requires parenting—advising and supporting—there are four possible ways of responding. Nurturing and structuring and protecting ways encourage positive self-esteem. Marshmallowing and criticizing ways tear down self-esteem. Below are situations. Each situation has a response given by a nurturing, a structuring and protecting, a marshmallowing, and a criticizing parent.

Read each of the four responses to each situation. Allow yourself to hear the positive and the negative implications of each. Rewrite each answer to fit your own value system where needed.

Parent Messages

Nurturing

This message is gentle, supportive, caring. It invites the person to get his or her needs met. It offers to help. It gives permission to succeed and affirms.

Marshmallowing

This message sounds supportive, but it invites dependence, suggests person will fail, and negates.

Structuring and Protecting

This message sets limits, protects, asserts, demands, advocates ethics and traditions. It tells ways to succeed and affirms.

Criticizing

This message ridicules, tears down, tells ways to fail, and negates.

Situation: Parent says, "I'm alarmed about the drug scene at my daughter's high school."

Nurturing

It's scary, but let her know that you love her, that you care about what she does, and that she can talk with you.

Marshmallowing

Well, there is nothing you can do about it, so have another martini.

Structuring and Protecting

It may be scary for her too. You can find ways to talk with her and support her and let her know that you trust her to figure out ways to take care of herself. You can get the information and help you need to take care of yourself. Do it!

Criticizing

If your daughter tries drugs, it will be because you've failed her as a mother. You know that, don't you? It'll be all your fault.

*See Glossary, pages 269-270, for further information.

Situation: Fourteen year old says, "My friends want me to take drugs."

Nurturing

You are important. Take care of your body and mind. Trust your feelings to help you know what to do.

Structuring and Protecting

Get information about the effects of drugs on your body and mind. Don't do anything to your body or mind that you know is harmful. Find friends who don't push you to do something you don't want to do.

Marshmallowing

That's really hard. Just ignore those kids, and it won't be a problem for you.

Criticizing

Don't you ever let me catch you "on" anything, or it will be the last time!

Situation: Parent says, "My mother-in-law is not feeding the baby the way the doctor said and the way I want him fed. I feel terrible."

Nurturing

I love you, and I love the baby. You can figure out what to do.

Structuring and Protecting

Your child deserves the best care you know how to give. Listen to your doctor, decide what you believe to be best, and then insist that other people follow your feeding directions.

Marshmallowing

You don't want to cause a family fight It's better to let your mother-in-law decide

Criticizing

Don't contradict your mother-in-law. After all, she raised four children. How can you expect to do it as well as she did?

Situation: Two year old is having a tantrum.

Nurturing

You certainly are angry. I'm here if you need me.

Structuring and Protecting

I insist that you stay over in that corner of the room where I can see you until you think what to do.

Marshmallowing

What's the matter? When you get that mad it scares me! Let me help. You can't think when you're that mad!

Criticizing

You have a terrible temper, just like your Uncle Ben—the one who couldn't hold a job. Go to your room. Don't come out until you stop being mad.

What You Stroke Is What You Get

name ___Charlie___ age __16 years__ time __Fri. eve.__

To encourage people to become whole and well balanced, compliment all aspects of their personalities.

Encourage nurturing, structuring and protecting, having and using morals and ethics, and doing things for self and others.

What are you planning to do this weekend for fun?

Encourage dealing with current reality, gathering facts, estimating probability, and solving problems.

Charlie, the weather report is for clear weather — think of four ways we could spend tomorrow enjoying the outdoors together.

Encourage feeling and acting naturally and adaptively. *

Hey, Charlie, I'm glad to see you expressing your resentment.

*See page 51 for more examples of what to stroke and how to stroke.

What You Stroke Is What You Get

name —————————————— **age** ————— **time** —————

To encourage people to become whole and well balanced, compliment all aspects of their personalities.

Encourage nurturing, structuring and protecting, having and using morals and ethics, and doing things for self and others.

Encourage dealing with current reality, gathering facts, estimating probability, and solving problems.

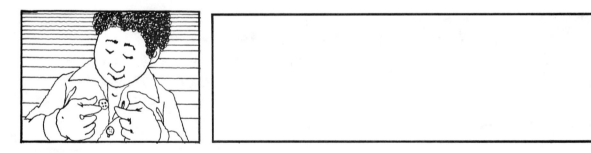

Encourage feeling and acting naturally and adaptively . *

*See page 51 for more examples of what to stroke and how to stroke.

Early Messages I Chose to Hear

This exercise is designed to help you discover early messages of yours that are helpful to you and to rewrite any early messages that are not helpful. Directions for the stroke buffet:

1. Copy some of the suggested messages listed on this page and the following page on squares of paper.
2. Spread them out on a table or on the floor.
3. Walk quietly around or among them. Look at them and allow yourself to remember which messages were important to you when you were a child.
4. Pick up messages that you felt or heard clearly.
5. If you recall any messages that are not included, write them on other squares of paper.
6. Read the messages.
7. Celebrate the ones that you use to help you in your life. If there are any messages that are not positive forces in your life tear up those squares and write new, helpful messages to replace them.

I like to hug you.
Think.
You are beautiful.
I like watching you put your puzzle together.
It's okay to go exploring. I'll still be here.
Don't brag.
You have a big mouth.
You're trying out your spoon. I'm excited watching you try new things.
Why can't you be like your brother?
She needs help.
I feel good that you can tell when you're feeling angry at me.
You're so wild.
You can succeed.
I wish you hadn't been born.
It's OK to feel mad, but you are not to hit yourself or anyone else.
You're so smart.
Oh, you picked up the block. I'm so glad!
Try, try, *try* again.
You're just like me.
Always be a happy little girl.
You are a good little girl.

You don't have to act sick to get taken care of.
You're messy.
Drop dead.
How are you?
I like your hugs.
I hate you.
I wish you had been born some other time.
She does pretty well considering her family.
You are a busy baby.
Are you still here?
You never learn.
Make me look good.
Goofed again.
Anything worthwhile is worth suffering for.
She is our slow one.
You're huggable.
I wish she were in someone else's care.
Hi, I'm glad you're here.
Why did she have to come here?
You're stupid.
You dummy.
You're ugly.
I love you.
You klutz!

Marry wealthy.
You are OK if you take care of me.
She's a problem.
She's busy all the time.
My day is better when I see you.
I'm glad you're growing up.
I'm glad you're a girl.
I wish you were a girl.
I need you to help take care of _____.
I like to hold you even when you aren't
    scared.
Why don't you get sick tomorrow so I can
    have some peace?
I like to hold you.
Anger and unpleasantness are not allowed.
Work hard, or I won't like you.
You can't do anything right.
Behave properly because if you don't that
    makes us bad parents.
Work smarter, not harder.
Try harder.
I'm not afraid of your anger at me.
I'm afraid of your anger.
Poor little thing, her parents are terrible
    drinkers.
I'm glad you're a boy.
I wish you weren't a boy.
I wish you weren't here, so I could have
    some fun today.
She's our feisty one.
If you have a problem, fix it.
Don't have fun.
What will the neighbors think?
Don't have fun, work.
Think the way I tell you to think.
Please other people.
Be successful.
Hurry and grow up.
Your needs aren't important. Don't expect
    others to take care of you.
Work hard.
You don't have to wave bye-bye in order for
    me to love you.
You can be in control of yourself and still
    have needs.

If something goes wrong, it must be your
    fault.
You can trust yourself to know what you
    need.
I knew you could do it.
You don't have to hurry and grow up.
You can think even when you feel scared.
There's no excuse for a bad mood.
You're so slow!
Mind your own business.
You're crazy.
When I can, I'll get a good job and let some-
    one else take care of these brats.
You drive me to drink.
You keep on like that and you'll end up in
    prison.
I enjoy you.
You're smart.
(And others
 not listed here.)

Redefinition

To sharpen your ability to recognize redefinitions, indicate the switches in each of the following pairs by identifying whether the how, what, where, when, who, or why are switched to another category or whether one who is switched to another who, one how to another how, and so on.*

1. _____ How much money do you need?
   _____ I don't need it until later.

2. _____ Did people smoke marijuana at the party tonight?
   _____ Why do you ask?

3. _____ How did you get the hole in your shirt?
   _____ I'm going to wear another shirt today.

4. _____ What does my coming into your room have to do with your problem?
   _____ I was thinking about that this morning.

5. _____ Do you like my new coat?
   _____ Where did you get it?

6. _____ I like you.
   _____ Oh. (Looks out the window.)

7. _____ I'm so angry at you!
   _____ Have you let the dog out?

8. _____ I hear you did a great job. How did you get started?
   _____ I always do a great job.

9. _____ Let's get pizza.
   _____ I ate a lot at the movies.

10. _____ When is it convenient for you to come?
    _____ When is it OK with you?

11. _____ What kind of dance do you like to do best?
    _____ Whatever pleases people.

If you wish to work with another person, have one person read the question, and one person read the answer. Pursue the original question or statement until you get a straight, meaningful answer. Compare the feelings you had when you got straight answers to the feelings you had when you were redefined. If you don't have another person, carry on the conversation in your head.

*Thanks to Marge Reddington for identifying these switches.

9

The Care and Feeding of Support Groups, or If You Haven't Got a Good One, Start Building

*Support groups come in different sizes and ages and varieties and colors. What support groups have in common the world around is that they are the places where people get the **strokes** [1] they need to stay alive. Support groups don't have to look any certain way, they just have to work.*

For each one of us, the breadth and quality of the group of people who care for us and about us and whom we care about and for is a crucial factor in our health, well-being, and happiness.

People can improve the quality and extent of their support in many ways. They can do it by making new friends, joining ready-made groups, finding new sources of nurturing and enjoyment in their own family groups, improving the quality of the relationship with old friends, and improving the way they treat themselves.

Some People Go Out and Find Support Groups

Sonia Poduska does not have a permanent support group, but she knows how to make new friends. She and her husband Robert decided that he would keep his job in sales, knowing that for ten years they would be living in no one place longer than two years. They agreed that Sonia would not seek paid work outside of the home during these nomad years. She would handle the moves and do whatever volunteer work she wanted to do.

The first three moves came within nineteen months. Sonia soon discovered that her husband's credentials moved with him and that he could find new support groups rather quickly. The three boys found friends at school, in sports, and in clubs. Sonia's kids made friends fastest in the swimming pool. She said she didn't know if water helped all kids slide into friendships or if her kids were more sociable wet than dry.

The person that had the hardest time finding an immediate support group was Sonia. She discovered that her volunteer credentials didn't transfer like her husband's work credentials. Each time they moved, Robert was promoted and Sonia went back to "Go." Most of the clubs and church and civic groups Sonia joined expected her to apprentice for a year as a committee person before she was given a position of responsibility. Before the first year was out, Sonia had moved.

After the first three years, Sonia was bored. The prospect of seven more years repeating beginning-committee-assignments reminded her of the prospect of repeating Anthropology I ten times before she would be allowed to enroll for Anthropology II.

Sonia devised a set of moving rules. No matter what time of the year they moved, Sonia made sure the children had goodbye parties for their friends and said their goodbyes to the place they were leaving.

If at all possible, the family did not move after school was out. The children found their support groups more quickly if school was in session. If they had to move during the summer, Sonia preferred moving the last week before school closed for the summer. One week was such a short time that the teachers didn't expect the boys to 'catch up' with their classmates. That left the kids free to spend their energy making friends, psyching out what clubs to join in the fall, and learning the kids' names before they met on the beach and the ball field.

While the boys were in school, Sonia and her four-year-old daughter, Lexie, were on the move, putting the third rule—meet lots of people—into action. When new neighbors or colleagues of her husband's said, "What can I do to help you move in?" Sonia had her list ready. "Will you recommend a grocery store, a dry cleaner, and a hairdresser? Will you tell me which church in the area is friendliest to newcomers? And will you tell me any place that I can go during this coming week to make friends?"

Sonia reports that, when people are asked this list of specific questions, they often reply, "I would be glad to. Come to a political party meeting with me" or "I have a friend who would love to take you to a League of Women Voters meeting" or "My church circle meets on Tuesdays" or "Come to the Art Center with me and see if you would like to join" or "There is a Sports and Health Club that has an active program for women and your children can swim there" or "Be on my PTA committee."

Sonia's next question is "Is there a social or civic group just starting in this area?" Sonia has discovered that brand new groups need people with organization skills immediately, and new groups don't have the time to put everyone through the beginning-committee-work sequence. Sonia accepts each invitation and pursues every lead until she has met six people that she thinks are willing to see her again. She also looks for two or three organizations in which she thinks she will be comfortable. This usually takes Sonia about six days. Then, and only then, does she unpack the pile of boxes in the center of the living room floor. Before that time, her family lives out of suitcases and with a minimum of household equipment. Sonia says if they were living in a motel no one would expect to have everything unpacked. She long ago discovered that finding a support base in the new community is more important for her and the family's welfare and happiness than washing out all of the cupboards and unpacking the books.

Sonia recognizes that for her having a support group means finding one. There is no ready-made group waiting for her when she moves to a new community.

Other People Come Home and Nurture Support Groups

Marita, in contrast to Sonia, has a stable support group and moves out from it. I flew into a small town on the Range to do a workshop, and Marita met my early morning plane. Breakfast with Marita is coffee, rolls, and a living travelogue. Marita taught school for years and traveled every summer for as many years. Any place I can think of in Europe, Africa, or South America, Marita has visited. Before each trip she studies the people and the land she will be visiting, and her assessment of cultural differences is fascinating.

"What brings you to the Range, Marita?" I enquire.

"This is home. I've retired here. I still travel a lot, but I've taught here for years and these are my people. Some say the people who live on the Range are 'different.' I say they are 'mine.' Sure the winters are hard, and sure we have some tough times during strikes, but I wouldn't consider living any place else. I still travel, but I plan my trips so that I'm home on holidays and for big weddings and things like that. I have some people I see often and others that I only see once or twice a year, but they're all important to me. For example, I wouldn't miss Thanksgiving weekend for anything. I fix the turkey and take it to my brother's house and see all of the family. The Friday and Saturday after Thanksgiving I go to several houses that I only visit that time of year. I take a loaf of my special bread, and they look forward to seeing me. People like to visit after a big holiday dinner. The Range is my home. I love its beauty, and the people are my people."

Marita travels around the world and keeps her support group alive and healthy in one place.

Ready-Made Groups

Sometimes people do find ready-made support groups. Certain religious communities are careful to integrate new members into their groups. There are jobs that provide ongoing support systems. For example, George and Meredith are career Air Force people. They move often and find an established social group at each new base.

Some people belong to clubs or fraternal organizations that have a state or nation wide support system. People who have specific support needs can find or organize groups to meet their needs.

Roy has Lupus. Not many people understand the special needs of people who have that disease. Sometimes Roy needs to talk with someone who understands exactly how he feels. He writes a letter or calls another member of his chapter of the Lupus Foundation and they encourage and support each other and exchange survival ideas.

Alcoholics Anonymous, Alanon groups, and the various other Anonymous groups, such as the Emotions Anonymous and Over-eaters Anonymous groups, give support to people with specific needs.

There's No Place like Home

People can improve their support system by improving the quality of support they get within their own immediate families.

Peyton has been married for years and he and Karen have a comfortable marriage, but there are several areas in which he would like more support from his family.

Peyton asks his family to listen seriously to his request. He explains, "You know that I think that we have a great family. I'm going to ask you to do something for me that I've not asked before. I realize that sometimes I don't ask for what I want and need from you; so you have no way of knowing that I want something. I'm going to start asking for what I want. When I say, 'Will you do this for me or with me?' I realize that you may say yes or no. If you say no, I won't get what I want from you, but I often don't now because I don't ask."

Peyton's daughter Katrine asks, "Hey, Daddy, are you sick or something? I've never heard you talk like this before!"

Peyton chuckles, "Maybe I've never talked like this, Katrine, but sick I'm not. Perhaps I've never been healthier."

Peyton's son Grant says, "OK, Dad, but in this family it'll never work. We don't do stuff like that."

Peyton replies thoughtfully, "Maybe we haven't, Grant, but I intend to do my part by asking for what I want, appreciating help if you give it, and not being resentful if you don't."

Peyton's wife Karen is hesitant. "Well, it sounds like a good idea for you. Will you ask for a lot? Will there be a lot more work?"

Peyton grins at her, "We might have more fun instead of more work. Then, too, Karen, you might decide to ask more often for what you want."

"What sort of things are you planning to ask for, Peyton?" Karen questions.

"Well, first of all, I would like three hours during each weekend entirely to myself. I think I am too much with people, and I need some time alone with Peyton. I am willing to negotiate the time, but I don't want to take any phone calls or be interrupted by anyone."

Grant says, "Gee, Dad, that's not even hard. What else do you want?"

"Well," Peyton says much more hesitantly, "I think the rest of you are all more social than I am. But I like good times too, and I wonder if you are willing to plan a small party for me to celebrate that I've passed the forty-year mark and am making some changes."

Katrine squeals, "Gee, Daddy, you must be kidding—I thought you would ask for something hard. What kind of party do you want?"

"Just something small and simple," Peyton replies hesitantly.

Katrine continues, "Daddy, I don't know what has gotten into you, but I like it. Can we plan it right now, or do you want a surprise?"

"Suit yourself," Peyton says with relief.

Peyton risked asking his family to do things he had never asked of them before and improved the quality of interactions between himself and his family members. People who do not live with other family members can also find ways to help each other.

If You Care Enough to Send the Very Best, Write a Letter

Sally and her son Tom have decided to improve the quality of support they give each other. Tom is away at school, so they do not see each other regularly. They are exploring new ways to give support through distance.

Last week Sally visited her older son's home and held her new grandson, Jason. As she looked at him she remembered when Tom was a baby. While she held Jason, Sally wrote Tom a letter, telling him about her love for him. If Tom, at age nineteen, has not registered some of the **affirmations** his mother gave to him, he has a chance to hear them now. If he's not ready now, he can put the letter away and read it again later. If he has a child of his own, Tom can hold his infant and reread the letter then. The letter may help Tom **recycle** his own early **being** decisions.

Dear Tom,

I have so many things I want to tell you. Most important of all is that I sure do love you. I remember before you were born, I cried when I menstruated because I wanted to be pregnant. Then we got pregnant, and you were born. I looked at you, touched you, and held you, and I was so happy that you were a boy! When I was pregnant with you, John, Diane, and Jane were already here. Friends would say "Wouldn't you like another little girl?" or "A boy would make it even." I thought about what they said and decided that your sex was not what was important. What I knew is that whatever sex you were, I wanted you. When you were a baby, I took good care of you. Your needs were OK with me. I knew the first six months of your life were very important and that you needed a lot of care, and I liked taking care of you. You did not have to hurry and grow up. You and I used to take each day as it came. We enjoyed what we had.

It seemed like all of a sudden you were a year old and I watched you do new things—sit up, scoot around (you didn't crawl, you scooted), and stand up. We had a slinky toy that Diane would put on the top of the stairs, and you watched it come down. You were so curious about that toy! You would watch it slither down, yell at it, and Diane would take it back upstairs and let it slither down again for you to watch. I'm glad you were curious. I hope you never give up being curious. You were getting braver at trying new things. Once you crawled inside a low kitchen cupboard. You went in head first and then did not know how to get out. You yelled something to me, and I yelled back that your being there was OK. I went to you and put my hands on your back and you backed right out. What you wanted was a little moral support, and you got that. You can always do things and get support at the same time. Playing Peek-A-Boo with you was fun, and we both had a good time doing that. You didn't have to play Peek-A-Boo to get my approval, though. You are a special person because you are you, not because of the things you do.

244

I liked watching you grow up. Summer came, and you learned to walk. You loved the mobility and walked everywhere in the house, the yard, and into the neighbor's yard. We did have some problems with you going to the neighbor's yard. You went next door one day on your own. I saw you and went over there and brought you home. You were really mad at me for bringing you home! I was not afraid of your anger. When you were angry at me, you yelled at me. Then you figured out that you could have feelings and think at the same time. You stopped yelling, took my hand, and we both went over to the neighbors. A lot of people never realize that they can think about what they feel and then act on those feelings or not act. Too bad, isn't it?

One area I had to work on was letting you do things for yourself and not for me. You were seventeen before I was aware of you taking care of me. Your dad had died, and you started doing the household jobs that he did when he was alive. You and I sat down and talked about how we would get the household tasks done. I'm pleased with the way we worked out who would take care of whom and how.

When you were little you were sure about what you needed. I seldom had to remind you of your bedtime. When you got sleepy, you went to sleep. Sometimes you didn't get to your room. You went to sleep in the middle of the floor.

I remember when I started taking communication classes, way back when, and I would come home and practice the techniques with you kids. That was when you and I learned to express our feelings straight. That's when we learned that I didn't have to act sick and you didn't have to act sad to be noticed and cared for. You were a powerful person and you told me what you wanted and needed. I'm proud of you for not ignoring your needs.

I loved to watch you grow. I remember the first time you disagreed with me and how surprised you were to find out it was OK to disagree. Being OK with doing things your own way is a necessary step in maturing and accepting responsibility for your own actions. You used to check out what you were feeling to help you know what was going on with you. Once you told me you had a strange feeling inside of you and you didn't know what was going on. We talked about it, and you told me you were having a lot of verbal fights with your friends and you didn't like some of the things your friends were doing, like stealing tomatoes and throwing them. You did trust your feelings to help you know something was wrong and when you talked to me about how you wanted friends but didn't want to do what they were doing, you did think before you made a rule of your own. You never were one to suffer to get what you needed. Some people struggle and work sooooo hard. You work but you do not make it hard work. That is very smart of you.

When you were in high school many kids your age drank, smoked pot and tobacco, and used other drugs. I saw you thinking about that and making up your own mind about how much drinking and smoking you wanted to do, if any. I know you talked to a counselor about that, and I am glad you asked for advice and found someone you trusted to ask. You can trust your own feelings to let you know what is best for you. You know better than anyone else what is good for you and that decision can be different on different days. Some of your friends might tease you or make fun of you when you don't follow them and that is the way people are. You can listen to them and disagree. Be your own person.

Now you are nineteen, and I see you wondering who and what you are. It's OK to know who you are today. You might be the same person tomorrow, or you might change. That is OK too. I don't know anybody who is the same person all his life. One thing I do know about young adults is that you can be a sexual person and still have needs. Your sexuality adds another dimension to your being and is part of the sorting out I see you doing. Sometimes I feel like you and I are on a yoyo, coming and going. I heard a riddle the other day. It was "Who is it that comes in the house with a pack over his back saying Ho Ho Ho?" Santa Claus, you say?—wrong. "It is your child home from college with dirty laundry." I'm delighted to see you come home with dirty laundry or come home because you want to come home. You are welcome to come home again.

I sure do love you. I sure am glad you are my son.

Mom[2]

This Group Is My Group—I Chose It

Infants cannot choose their support groups, but as soon as children get into school they have the opportunity to choose friends.

Marvin went to high school in a small college town where for years the ruling clique of kids had been made up exclusively of children of college professors. It was a closed group. Either your Dad or Mom taught at the college, or they didn't, and if they didn't, you were not one of the "Hill Kids." Marvin looked longingly at this prestigious group, tried to make friends with some of the members, and spent all of his high school years without the support of a peer group because he could not find a way to enter "the" group.

Gisela went to the same school. She took a look at the situation and went home and asked her folks, "What are the chances of either one of you teaching at Clabber College?"

Her father laughed and said, "If they need a course in how to run a clothing store, I guess I could teach it, but generally a liberal arts college doesn't list courses like that."

246

Her mother looked thoughtful and said, "Gisela, it would probably take me most of the time you are in high school to get the necessary academic degrees to teach at Clabber. And then I couldn't be sure that they would hire me."

Gisela inquired, "Do you think there is a chance we will be moving during the next four years?"

Her dad laughed again, "Anything is possible, Gisela, but I certainly *hope* we don't move. Do you want to move?"

Gisela said, "Well, no, not exactly. I was just checking." Gisela found a group of friends with whom she laughed and partied and did school activities and had long conversations about love, abortion, communism, religion, sex, teachers, clothes, and what to do after graduation. Her group of kids did not have top billing on the school's status list, but it had top billing in her life and through the group she expanded her capacity to belong, to take care of other people, to ask them to take care of her, to resolve problems about competition, sex, drugs, and loyalty, to make friends with boys, and to have special boy friends.

Same high school—Marvin stayed on the outside looking in; Gisela created a support group to meet her special teenage social needs.

I Think I Will; I Think I Won't

> *Sometimes you can't find the support where you are, and you have to make a choice.*

Tim has just entered Alliwitch College. Alliwitch was an all-white college until a few years ago. The first Black, Raymond, was an outgoing, friendly athlete. He went through four years at Alliwitch as something of a celebrity, football hero, and super student. He was invited to be on every committee and in every club.

Now there are several Black men at Alliwitch and none of them is another Raymond. Tim is quiet, not well coordinated, a good student, and doesn't have Raymond's easy way with people. Also, Tim doesn't have a woman back home as Raymond did.

Tim looks around. Most of the Black men hang around together. When they date white women, the couples are hassled by the white men. One Black man, Jack, repeatedly attempts to make friends with white students. A few of them respond, the rest set him up for ridicule, and he is no longer welcome in the Black group.

The school administration and faculty that Tim talk with think it would be nice if he gets along well. Tim assesses his choices. "I don't want to do what Jack is doing. And I don't really want tc be limited to the small group. I could stay and be a loner. That might be OK academically, but it wouldn't be good for me as a person. I could become an activist and try to change the school. I don't really have the personality for it, but I could learn. I could look for ways to find friends and support off campus, or I could look for another school."

Tim can make his choice in any of these directions—but he is making a choice—he is not sitting back and letting life happen to him. He is not **discounting** *his problems or pretending that his own needs are not important.*

Bernice needs a special kind of support group. Bernice is a pioneer. She is chief-of-police in a town that has never had a woman in that office before. Besides the usual pressure focused on law-enforcement people, Bernice experiences the special pressures of a populace that has not yet grown accustomed to this example of changing sex roles. She needs extra support from her family and friends to weather this period of stress. She can decide whether she can find the necessary support or if she should look for a new job.

I Can Do Some of This All by Myself!

Lorrie improved the quality of support in her own life by improving the way she treated herself. She was in the habit of getting positive strokes from other people by pleasing them and taking care of them first, with the result that she was always putting herself second. Then she ended up resenting what she did for other people. When Lorrie first decided to take care of herself as well as other people, she felt very strange and found it difficult to do. Eventually she discovered the technique of writing her own name on her appointment calendar one day a week. On that day she did something nice for Lorrie. The first few times, her enjoyment was mixed with apprehension. She was afraid her friends wouldn't like her if she stopped taking care of them. But she didn't stop taking care of them, she only took care of them a bit less, and they liked her better. When she took better care of herself, she lost the edge of resentment that used to creep into her voice periodically.

Lorrie even moved to the point of sometimes saying no to her friends' requests. She discovered that they didn't cease to be friends. Lorrie says that the neatest thing about improving her support system by improving the way she treats herself is that she carries that support system with her all the time.

Selma watched Lorrie's success and determined to try it for herself. Selma had rigid rules in her head that it was vain to think or say anything nice about herself. Whenever she thought about being nicer to herself, she got scared or sick. Selma joined a therapy group and sorted out her confusion between vanity and **self-esteem**. She got some new messages about it being OK for her to be lovable, even to herself! Selma improved the way she treated herself and also improved the way in which she took care of other people.

How to Create Your Own Support Group

> *Sometimes people create their own support systems for very specific kinds of support.*

David and Harry and Kevin were each making changes in the ways they communicated with their families. David was fitting affirmations into his daily family life. Harry decided to stay out of hassles between his sons and their mother, and Kevin was replacing reminding and nagging with positive remarks about jobs well done.

Since even in families where members want change, some resistance to change often occurs, David, Harry, and Kevin decided to get support outside of their families while they were going through the first stages of change. They met weekly for one hour to report their successes and get ideas from each other about better ways to do things. That was eighteen months ago. As each of them integrated the new ways of behaving into their lives, the new ways became habit patterns. The three continued to meet because they enjoyed weekly reinforcement that they did not have to earn from each other.

> *One of the functions of Harry, David, and Kevin's group was to provide reinforcement for new behavior. Deciding how to change one's behavior is the first step in new ways of living. Doing the new behavior and repeating it often enough to allow it to become habitual can take time and energy. If the forces that invite one back into old behavior are strong in this particular area of one's life, a support group is especially important.*

> *Another function of a support group is to provide a place where people can depend on getting **positive strokes for being**. Still another reason to maintain support groups outside of one's immediate family is to avoid placing too much responsibility on a few people. It is a way of avoiding having all of one's eggs in one basket.*

Three things that people often want to know about creating a specific support group are how to start one, how to keep it going, and what to expect from it.

How to start one is to start it. Take the initiative. Ask some people to join you. Keep asking until you find people who are willing to join you and who want to improve the quality of support in their lives also.

How to keep a support group going is to keep it open and even. Open means people ask for what they really want and are willing to accept yes or no for an answer. Even means it does not always focus on the same person.

What you can expect from it is good strokes, good friends, help in ways that you may not have experienced before, that it will change, that people will come into the group, enjoy it for awhile, and then leave when it no longer fits their needs.

Some of the ways to help support groups stay support groups and not become just another social group are the following:
1. Have regular meetings for designated lengths of time.
2. Alternate responsibility for finding meeting places.
3. Alternate responsibility for activities, for making sure that each person's needs are met, that everyone's **stroke level** *is high when they leave. Careful sharing of this role prevents one person from becoming mother or father to the group.*
*4. Adhere strictly to a no-blame, no-***negations*** rule. No member is allowed to blame another person—"Let me tell you what my wife did . . ."—and no person is allowed to blame himself. He may say, "The next time I get into this situation I am going to . . ." but he is not allowed to say, 'Let me tell you the dumb thing I did." Following the no-blame, no-negation rule protects the group from becoming a gossip group and prevents individuals from using it for a personal guilt trip.*
5. Insist that people must ask for what they need. No secrets. If Mac comes into the group and says "I'm fine" when in fact he has been in the hospital, he is breaking the support group contract. The group must insist that he ask for what he needs. It is OK for him not to tell why he is needy; he can say, "I'm hurt and I want you to comfort me" or "I'm blue and I don't want to talk about it" or simply "I just want to be here with you today, no questions please."
6. Do a quarterly review; compare people's expectations to the way the group is functioning. Decide to continue, discontinue, or redirect the group.

Cindy belongs to such a support group. They meet as a group for two hours, twice a month, and sometimes get together for fun or call each other to talk in between. They all understand and use the **affirmations**.

Cindy felt blue so she stopped at Bernadine's house. Bernadine answered the door and said, "You look depressed! What's your **stroke bank** level?"

Cindy looked at the floor and said, "About 21."

Bernadine gave her a hug and said, "I'm on my way out. I can't stay to comfort you, but you can use my phone to call someone else."

"No," Cindy complained, "I don't trust anyone else as much as I trust you. They might turn me down."

Bernadine insisted, "Here is the list of names and phone numbers of people in our group. Will you call until you find two different people who will give you good strokes today?"

Cindy protested, "What will I say?"

'Tell them you are stuck in blue glue and you need encouragement," Bernadine tossed over her shoulder as she dashed out the door.

Cindy glanced down the list of names: Shann, Adelaide, Kay, Marianne, Carol, Gwen, Val, Trice, Irene, Judy, and Jan. Cindy felt terrified. What if they turned her down? They have the right to.

Cindy dialed Trice. Busy. Cindy dialed Irene's number. No answer. Cindy's spirits dropped even lower. She dialed the next number and heard Judy's voice. "Hello."

Cindy didn't speak.

Judy's greeting was a question—"Hello?"

In a very soft voice Cindy said, "Judy, this is Cindy. My feet are stuck in blue glue. I need a few minutes of nurturing."

Judy said, "Do you want to tell me about it?"

"No," Cindy said emphatically.

Judy replied, "OK. I wish you were right here with me so we could talk. But you're not, so I'll talk and you listen. I like you. You are important. I admire you. I admire how you have grown and changed and that's important for the rest of us who are watching you. You are a good thinker. Are you scared about all the changes in your life?"

Cindy said, "I don't want to talk, I want to listen."

Judy repeated, "I like you, I like being with you."

Cindy's "Thank you" sounded tentative.

Judy reassured her, "I'm glad you called."

Cindy felt relaxed and proud. She thought, "It really is OK to ask. I'm not too good at asking, but nothing horrible happened. I don't know Judy really well, but I don't have to worry about how she is feeling."

Cindy dialed Trice again and said, "Trice, I'm stuck, I want some nurturing, will you give me some for about three minutes?"

Trice responded willingly. "Yes. Do you have any certain things you want?"

Cindy sighed, "No certain ones; I want them all; I want to listen; I want to just let them in."

Trice said, "OK, I can do that. I like you. It's important that you are you. I like being with you. You don't have to do anything right now. When you decide to do things, you do them well. You are smart. You can decide what has to be taken care of right now. Do that. Let the rest go for now. You are creative. You can trust yourself to know what you need and to get that. You are important and caring and warm. I want you to let the little girl in you play."

Cindy's voice sounded brighter, "Ya, I'm going to do that."

Trice continued. "I want you to be vibrant and beautiful."

Cindy was silent. She felt resentful and she thought, "Don't tell me to please you!"

Trice asked, "Is there something more you want me to say?"

"No," Cindy said, "I heard loudest that it's OK for me to be and I can decide what I have to do. Thank you for being home and talking to me."

Trice said, "I like you and care about you."

252

Cindy felt comforted, but she was also angry at Trice's expectations and realized that she had been angry at another person's earlier. The awareness diffused her anger. Cindy's energy was up; she felt better, but everything still wasn't OK. But it was better than two years ago when she would have stayed in a four-day funk.

Cindy thought, "Guess I'll get some more help." She called Jan, "Can you go with me to the meeting I have tonight? I need company."

Jan replied, "No, I'm busy, let me tell you all that is going on. . . ."

Cindy interrupted and said, "No, I wanted to know if you could go with me. I'll call you another day." Cindy kept her good feelings, wrote Bernadine a note, and let herself out of Bernadine's house thinking, "Sure beats being blue for four days! And I'll return the favor to someone else on another day."

Cindy had asked for what she needed, gotten reassurance that she was a worthwhile person, was going off to resolve the clash in expectations, and had recaptured the confidence that she was lovable and capable.

> *These are a few of the many ways that people improve their support bases. The broader our support bases are, the better chance we have of getting what we need and of being able to meet the needs of other people in our lives. Children who are taught by their adults how to extend their own support bases and are expected to do so are lucky indeed.*
>
> *Go ahead.*
>
> *You can do it.*
>
> *And you can be creative about it.*
>
> *You deserve to feel lovable and you are capable.*

Notes

1. Words which have a special definition as presented in this book are set in boldface the first time they are used in this chapter. The definition of these words is given in the Glossary.

2. Thanks to Sally Dierks for permission to include this letter.

Four Ways of Parenting*

For any situation that requires parenting—advising and supporting—there are four possible ways of responding. Nurturing and structuring and protecting ways encourage positive self-esteem. Marshmallowing and criticizing ways tear down self-esteem. Below are situations. Each situation has a response given by a nurturing, a structuring and protecting, a marshmallowing, and a criticizing parent

Read each of the four responses to each situation. Allow yourself to hear the positive and the negative implications of each. Rewrite each answer to fit your own value system where needed.

Parent Messages

Nurturing

This message is gentle, supportive, caring. It invites the person to get his or her needs met. It offers to help. It gives permission to succeed and affirms.

Marshmallowing

This message sounds supportive, but it invites dependence, suggests person will fail, and negates.

Structuring and Protecting

This message sets limits, protects, asserts, demands, advocates ethics and traditions. It tells ways to succeed and affirms.

Criticizing

This message ridicules, tears down, tells ways to fail, and negates.

Situation: Parent says, "I don't want my fifteen month old to grow up so fast! She doesn't have the time to cuddle anymore, and I still want to hold her."

Nurturing

You need cuddling, and your daughter needs to explore. Both of your needs are important.

Marshmallowing

Bribe her with cookies. Or, you could get pregnant again.

Structuring and Protecting

Allow her to explore at her own speed. Get yourself a puppy to cuddle.

Criticizing

You only care about yourself. You will probably want to go to school with her.

*See Glossary, pages 269-270, for further information.

Situation: Parent says, "My four year old tells lies."

Nurturing

You are a competent, caring mother, and you can solve this problem.

Structuring and Protecting

You are important, and you can help this four year old sort out what is real and what is imaginary.

Marshmallowing

It's awful the way kids lie, and I know there isn't anything you can do about it.

Criticizing

Kids! You can't trust them for a minute. Better give him a good spanking. That's what he really needs. Come down hard on him, or he'll lie the rest of his life.

Situation: Thirteen year old says, "I got a B in Math instead of the usual C or D."

Nurturing

You must be proud of yourself. I knew you could do it.

Structuring and Protecting

Super! What did you do that was different? You can do that again. Keep up the good work.

Marshmallowing

I'm glad I helped you so much. I'll be glad to help you again.

Criticizing

With your brains, you should have gotten an A. Your older sister did. You never quite make it, do you?

Situation: Mother says, "When I'm gone for the night, my fifteen-year-old daughter and my husband sleep in the same bed."

Nurturing

You are a strong, protective mother. You can solve this. Get help if you need it.

Structuring and Protecting

A fifteen-year-old girl needs open, loving acceptance *and* protection from incestuous invitations. Take immediate action.

Marshmallowing

Well, nothing really happened.

Criticizing

Mothers are supposed to stay out of the relationship between a daughter and a father.

Postface—How Not to Use This Book

This book is about self-esteem for people. It is not meant to be used by one person at the expense of other people. The thesis of this book is that we are all responsible for ourselves. We are also responsible for giving and receiving nurturing and protecting, for thinking clearly alone and with other people, and for having fun alone and with others.

Some people have interpreted "You are responsible for yourself" to mean that they have no responsibility to others and that it is OK to intimidate, exploit, and manipulate. For example: some people say, "It's OK for me to use as many drugs as I want. It's my body and what I do with it is nobody else's business." Do not misuse the affirmations in this book in such a way. That would be anti-self-esteem.

Following is a list of ways the affirmations should be used and ways they should not be used whether they are being offered the first time around or used for recycling.

Recycling is the process of reexperiencing earlier developmental stages in more sophisticated ways at later ages. Teenagers recycle earlier development. Adults can recycle in a rhythmic way based on age or in response to the stimulus of external events. Adults are often activated to recycle the stages their children are going through. Each recycle gives adults a chance to resolve uncompleted tasks.

Affirmations for Being—Deciding to Live: Birth to Six Months

You Have Every Right to Be Here

Recycling *You have every right to be here* does not imply that you have the privilege of being any place at any time. This affirmation does not give permission to crash a party or interrupt a private conversation. Instead, it means that you have the right to exist, to take your space on this planet, to grow, to become the lovable and accomplished person you are capable of becoming.

Your Needs Are OK

The mother who is recycling *Your needs are OK with me* will not throw out the baby and say, "I need to get out of the house and go dancing today!" Instead, she will be aware of her own needs and express them openly. She will not pretend that she has no needs. On a day when she feels trapped, she will recognize, "I need time away from the baby today." If this occurs on a day when she does not have a loving, competent adult to leave the baby with, she will get some time away with a phone call, a fantasy trip, or an escape novel while the baby is sleeping.

I'm Glad You're a Girl/Boy

I'm glad that you're a girl does not imply that boys are not as good as girls. It does mean that before a girl can fully appreciate and enjoy boys, she must love and appreciate herself and her femaleness. *I'm glad you are a boy* says to a boy, "I'm glad you are you." There is no implication that being a boy is superior to being a girl. Recycling the important task of accepting and enjoying one's maleness or femaleness does not imply that one may use the affirmation to defend displays of female-degrading machismo or male-blaming feminism.

You Don't Have to Hurry

Recycling *You don't have to hurry* doesn't mean that the parent of an infant will never do anything in a hurry. It does mean that if the parent decided to hurry and grow up too fast when he was little or if he decided to take too much responsibility too early, he will now have the chance to watch his baby grow at her own pace and will allow himself to get in touch with his own natural space and rhythm. He can also reassess his present responsibilities and give up those responsibilities that he has chosen that burden him and/or invite other people to stay dependent on him.

I Like to Hold You

I like to hold you does not give the person recycling birth- to six-month messages license to hold anybody, anyplace, anytime. It does mean that you are a lovable person, who deserves to be held, touched, hugged. You deserve to be touched as much as you want and need to be. If you have a "don't touch" or a "don't get close" message in your head that gets in the way of getting touched, you deserve to rewrite that message. It is important to separate sexual touching from nurturing or affectional touching and not use a "touching-is-sexual" rule to prevent yourself from being touched.

Affirmations for Doing—Starting to Do Things on Our Own: Six to Eighteen Months

You Don't Have to Do Tricks to Get Approval

Recycling doesn't mean that the adult who has been using tricks to get approval will stop being pleasing or entertaining or competent. It means that he will watch his youngster explore and will reclaim his own wonder and delight. He will claim his right to be loved for being, and he will give up believing that he has to earn every stroke.

It's OK to Do Things and Get Support at the Same Time

It's OK to do things and get support at the same time does not mean that the person recycling this affirmation is to allow herself any dependency that she chooses. It does mean that she doesn't have to do things alone. It's OK to ask for and accept help. It also doesn't imply that the supporting person is expected to give support forever. When three-year-old Kyra first used the big slide in the park, Sheila stood behind the steps while Kyra climbed up. Then Sheila ran to the front of the slide to make sure Kyra had a safe landing. *It's OK to do things and get support at the same time* does not mean that Sheila should continue to monitor both ends of the slide after Kyra has learned to use it safely. It's marshmallow parenting to continue support beyond the learning period, for one's self or one's children.

Affirmations for Thinking—Deciding It's OK to Think: Eighteen Months to Three Years

I'm Glad You Are Growing Up

For adults to recycle *I'm glad you are growing up* doesn't mean that they have to hurry, grow up, and get perfect at everything at once. And it most assuredly does not suggest that they can rush their child and urge him to grow up fast so they can be rid of him. It means to stop any "I liked you better when you were in the crib" messages. It is the extension of the birth-to six-month affirmation *You don't have to hurry*, and it offers both the child and the recycling adult the opportunity to feel their own rhythms and move at their own pace.

I'm Not Afraid of Your Anger

Recycling this affirmation does not mean that the parents of a two year old will behave like two year olds. It means that parents who were not allowed to express anger openly as two year olds will reexperience the old frustrations that they had buried and will learn to express anger openly in a constructive way. They can say "I don't want to do that" and not do it, instead of doing it and then saying, "You made me do that and I didn't want to!" They can express anger at the time the maddening incident occurs and not store the anger in rigid muscles or pile up small angers to let out in a volcanic outburst.

You Can Think About What You Feel

You can think about what you feel is permission to think and feel at the same time, or feel and think at the same time. It means the recycling adult can give up old rules like "I was too scared to think" and install "I think fast and clearly when I am scared." It does not give permission for the person to say, "Yes, I thought about how mad I was, and then I spanked her anyway." It implies responsibility to feel and think at the same time. The statement "I suddenly found myself feeling angry" reveals that I was angry and not feeling the anger. The affirmation does not mean to substitute thinking for feeling or feeling for thinking. This affirmation says, "I can feel all of my feelings all of the time, and I can think about them while I am feeling them."

You Don't Have to Take Care of Me by Thinking for Me

This doesn't mean that the woman who is recycling *You don't have to take care of me by thinking for me* will stop doing things for her husband. It means that she will stop guessing what he wants and doing what she thinks he wants. Instead she will ask him what he does want. Another way this affirmation could be manipulated is by saying, "OK, I will never again do anything for you that you don't ask me to do." *You don't have to take care of me by thinking for me* is not permission to stop practicing social manners or thoughtfulness.

You Can Be Sure About What You Need and Want and Think

You can be sure about what you need and want and think does not mean that a fourteen year old recycling two can declare that he needs to listen to 100 decibel rock music in his room. He may want to listen to loud music. But for his health and safety, he needs to protect his hearing. He can be sure about the difference between needing and wanting.

This affirmation does mean that the recycling adult can review his own responses to the adamant no's of the two year old or the intermittent outbursts of the fourteen year old vehemently defending her space or style. He can think if there are times when he means no and says yes, or vice versa. If he is manipulating his own needs and wants and thinking according to out-of-date rules, he can examine and update those rules and let his feelings help him know what he really wants and needs and thinks.

Affirmations for Identity—Learning Who We Are: Three to Six Years

You Can Be Powerful and Still Have Needs

You can be powerful and still have needs does not mean that a recycling sixteen year old is to say, "I am a powerful good driver so I need a Mustang II with a sunroof, Dad." What it does mean is that every experience of power, whether internal or external, involves related needs so don't get trapped by a "I'm too big and strong to need anybody" rule in your head.

This affirmation means that no matter how big, competent, accomplished, and titled a person is, he still needs support and care. He still needs the opportunity to be dependent at times.

You Don't Have to Act Scary or Sick or Mad or Sad to Get Taken Care of

You don't have to act scary or sick or mad or sad to get taken care of is the follow-up to the eighteen-months- to three-years affirmation *You can be sure about what you need and want and think*. Sixteen-year-old Jerelyn used to get sick to be taken care of. That was how she could get Mom's attention. She misinterpreted the affirmation to mean that she was not to get sick, so she substituted the trick of always being pleasant to get people to notice her. This affirmation means "Ask straight for what you need." Say, "Will you spend some time with me?" instead of acting sad to get attention.

You Can Express Your Feelings Straight

The adult who has survived by being manipulative and who is recycling *You can express your feelings straight* is not to take this as permission to act upon anger in a hurtful way. "Express" means tell, not hit or hurt. *You can express your feelings straight* means that when you are scared, you say you are scared and do not pretend that you are mad; when you are upset, you don't say "I'm fine; nothing is wrong." When you express a feeling, take responsibility for the feeling. Own it. Other people can't make you feel any certain way. If you feel sad, say "I feel sad," not "You make me sad." Then, if you want comforting, say so. Don't expect the other person to guess whether you want to be left alone or whether you want to be comforted.

Affirmations for Structure—Learning to Do Things Our Own Way: Six to Twelve Years

You Can Think Before You Make That Rule Your Own

You can think before you make that rule your own does not give the recycling seventeen year old permission to drive on the wrong side of the street. It means she can consider a rule and decide if she agrees with it. If she doesn't, she may obey it anyway, for a variety of reasons. Knowing that it's not her rule, she may work at changing the rule to make it better for herself and others.

You Can Trust Your Feelings to Help You Know

You can trust your feelings to help you know means letting your physical reactions and emotions help you know what is going on. It means feeling the tight throat, the rigid shoulders, the abdominal pain, or the wiggling foot and listening to the message. It means that a person trusts his feelings (tight throat) to help him know he is scared instead of listening to the old rule in his head that says "Don't admit fear." He knows that he is afraid and does whatever he needs to do to protect himself.

You Can Do It Your Way

Recycling *You can do it your way* does not mean that a person can go to work and tell her boss, "I don't have to do things your way anymore!" It means that she can claim a new freedom to use her creativity and feelings to let her find more personally satisfactory ways of doing things rather than being bound by out-of-date rules she has had in her head since childhood.

It's OK to Disagree

The adult recycling six to twelve years is not to use this affirmation as permission to say glibly to the arresting policeman, "I disagree with your speedometer. I think I was going thirty." It means that it is OK to examine, to question any rule—even your spouse's rules, your parents' rules, or your children's rules. And it is OK to agree to disagree about any issue that does not violate your or other people's rights.

You Don't Have to Suffer to Get What You Need

You don't have to suffer to get what you need is not to be twisted to read "I never have to do anything that is hard." It does give people permission to ask for help before they get tired. Examples: Get your eyes checked before you get headaches. Get a pap smear before you observe cancer symptoms. Ask for a party before you are too old to dance. Work easy!

Affirmations for Sexuality—Working Through Old Problems with Sexuality Added and Separating from Parents: Thirteen to Nineteen Years

You Can Be a Sexual Person and Still Have Needs

You can be a sexual person and still have needs is not a license to engage in irresponsible sexual acts. It means that people have interdependency needs all of their lives. It's important to separate sex and nurturing and to continue to get nurturing all our lives. Sexual people can feel little and dependent sometimes. Adults can need support and get it.

't's OK to Know Who You Are

This affirmation is not to be misinterpreted by the person who says "This is the way I am, I can't change" as permission to remain stuck. What it means is "Know who you are at every age. Don't settle for letting someone else define you."

You're Welcome to Come Home Again

You're welcome to come home again does not mean that the teenager who breaks family rules can expect to return home and continue to break those rules. Nor does it give people permission to remain dependent. It does not suggest that parents should allow other capable adults to return home as dependents. It means people are welcome to come home as separated adults. For recycling adults, it means that they will create new homes to which they can return after their adventures.

I Love You

If *I love you* has a rider it is misused! Throw away "because," forget "when," and ignore "if." *I love you* must stand alone—whole, complete, and unconditional.

Glossary

Adoptive Family: one that takes permanently and legally into the family a person not originally born to that family.

Affirmations: powerful, positive messages—verbal or nonverbal—which define who we are and how we expect to be treated. They can be given to us by other people and by ourselves.

> Example: "I am a worthwhile, competent person." (See Chapter 2, page 34.)

We tell people how we expect them to behave and feel about themselves by what we say to them and about them.

The following sets of affirmations are messages that invite human beings to become whole people who are capable and who care about themselves and others. Each set has an approximate age designation, indicating the ages at which that particular set of affirmations should start. These affirmations are based on developmental theory and are taken from Pam Levin's book *Becoming the Way We Are.* (See Bibliography.) The sets build up each other. Adults need the entire series.

Affirmations for Being—Deciding to Live: Birth to Six Months
You have every right to be here.
Your needs are OK with me.
I'm glad you're a (boy, girl).
You don't have to hurry.
I like to hold you.
(I'm glad you're here.)

These affirmations for being are particularly important from birth to six months, for early teenagers, for people who are ill or tired or hurt or vulnerable, and for everyone else.

Affirmations for Doing—Starting to Do Things on Our Own: Six to Eighteen Months
You don't have to do tricks to get approval.
It's OK to do things and get support at the same time.
(Try things, initiate things, be curious, be intuitive.)
(I'm glad you're here, and I see you are doing things.)

The affirmations for doing are particularly important for six- to eighteen-month-old children, for thirteen- and fourteen-year-old children, for people starting a new job or a new relationship, for people starting to learn any new skill, and for everyone else.

Affirmations for Thinking—Deciding It's OK to Think: Eighteen Months to Three Years

I'm glad you're growing up.
I'm not afraid of your anger.
You can think about what you feel.
You don't have to take care of me by thinking for me.
You can be sure about what you need and want and think.
I'm glad you're here, I see you are doing things, and I expect you to start learning about cause-and-effect thinking.

These affirmations for thinking are of special importance to children who are eighteen months to three years old, to young people in the middle teens, and to everyone else.

Affirmations for Identity—Learning Who We Are: Three to Six Years

You can be powerful and still have needs.
You don't have to act scary (or sick or sad or mad) to get taken care of.
You can express your feelings straight.
I'm glad you're here, I see you are doing things, and I expect you to continue learning about cause and effect. I expect you to start differentiating feelings and actions and to ask for your needs to be met straight.

These affirmations for learning who we are have special importance for children who are three to six years old, for middle teenagers, for people who are owning their power to be who they are and to ask straight for what they need, for people who are giving up old and inadequate ways of dealing with life or who are giving up crutches and are incorporating healthier ways, and for everyone else.

Affirmations for Structure—Learning to Do Things Our Own Way: Six to Twelve Years

You can think before you make that rule your own.
You can trust your feelings to help you know.
You can do it your way.
It's OK to disagree.
You don't have to suffer to get what you need.
I'm glad you're here, I see you are doing things, and I expect you to continue learning about cause and effect. I expect you to differentiate between feelings and actions and to ask to get your needs met straight. I also see that you are trying out, thinking about, altering and claiming your own way of looking at things, and doing things in order to take care of yourself.

These are the structure affirmations. They are particularly important for six- to twelve-year-old children, for people in the late teens and early twenties, for people of all ages who are entering new social settings (such as organizations, businesses, recreation groups, families, and re tirement), and for everyone else.

Affirmations for Sexuality—Working Through Old Problems with Sexuality Added and Separating from Parents: Thirteen to Nineteen Years

> You can be a sexual person and still have needs.
> It's OK to know who you are.
> You're welcome to come home again.
> I love you.
> (I see that you're recycling and going over old needs and problems with an added dimension of sexuality. It's OK to work through, to separate, and to assume responsibility for your own needs, feelings, and behavior as a grown-up person in the world.)

These affirmations for sexuality are important for thirteen- to nineteen-year-old human beings, for any older persons who are making relationship separations, and for everyone else. (The letter to Tom in Chapter 9, pages 244-246, incorporates all the affirmations. See also worksheets on pages 48-49, 82-83, 110-111, 142-143, 171-172, and 206-207.)

Affirmation Blocks:[1] three-inch colored cardboard cubes with affirmations printed on each surface. Holding a block, looking at the affirmations, and reading them aloud provide a kinesthetic, visual, and auditory way of presenting the affirmations.

Affirmation Cymbals:[2] colored circles with affirmations printed on them. They can be read, stacked, arranged.

Blended Family: a family unit consisting of a father and a mother and their children, one or more of whom was born to a previous mate and either of the parents. (See Chapter 7.)

Communal or Voluntary Family: a group of people who live together, who may or may not have biological or legal connections but who function as a family unit psychologically and financially.

Converting a Stroke: the process of accepting a stroke (see *Stroke* in this Glossary) from someone else and then changing it from the form in which it was sent to a form that is consistent with the expectation of the person receiving it.

> Example: Earl knows that he is not good-looking. That is his frame of reference. He expects to have that reinforced. Mabel thinks Earl is

good-looking. She sends a sincere message, "Earl, you look handsome today."

Earl puts that message through his "I'm not good-looking" filter and converts it into an insincere message and chooses one of the following responses: She thinks I'm good-looking; she must need glasses. . . . She's not sincere. I wonder what she wants. . . . She's making fun of me. . . . She says I look great today; does that mean I looked even worse yesterday? . . . She lies; I won't trust her anymore. . . . She said I look horrid today.

Strokes can be converted in any direction. Fred said, "Al, you look good for a guy who needs a hair transplant," and Al chose to internalize, "Fred says I look good." (See Chapter 8, page 217.)

Criticizing Parent: (See *Four Ways of Parenting Description* in this Glossary.)

Discounting:[3] the process of not taking into account some aspect of reality. One can discount, reduce, alter, or minimize a situation, one's self, or other people. One can discount or deny that a problem exists, that a problem is serious, that a solution is possible, or that one can use one's own ability to solve the problem. (See Chapter 5, pages 116-117 and 123.)

"Don't Be" Messages: messages which imply that a person should not have been born or should cease to exist. They are unconditional *negative strokes*. (See italicized words in this Glossary. Examples are listed on page 270. See also Chapter 1, page 21, and Chapter 2, page 33.)

Extended Family: a family nucleus with several relatives functioning as a support system. (See Chapter 6, page 148.)

Extended Stroke Base or Support Network: The collection of people that extends beyond the self and the immediate family and from whom one regularly receives strokes. This base (see *Stroke Base* in this Glossary) can include colleagues, regular social contacts, and deliberately acquired support groups. It can be the extended biological family, an extended group of friends of the family, support groups, sports groups, friends, fellow bird watchers, or any other individuals one receives strokes from. (See Chapter 6, page 149; Chapter 7, pages 196-200; and all of Chapter 9.)

Family: one or more persons living as a social unit with economic and emotional commitment to each other and/or self. They may be biologically and/or legally connected.

For the purpose of this book a family of one is a person living alone who functions as a family in society, using an extended support base for interpersonal commitments and strokes. A single person living in an institution, boarding house, or the like is not considered a family.

A United States Census Bureau report, "Household and Family Characteristics," compiled in 1976, reports that 20.6 percent of all the country's seventy-three million households consist of one person and 30.6 percent consist of two persons; sixty-five percent of the households include a married couple. Of the nine and one-half million new households added between 1970 and 1976, seventy percent consisted of persons living alone or with unrelated individuals, or of women maintaining a household with no man present.

Family of Origin: one's early childhood family.

Family Support System: a selected, willing group of people who function in addition to, or in place of, the relatives in an extended family. (See Chapter 2.)

Foster Family: a family that takes in a child under eighteen years of age from another family for a set amount of time. Foster families are licensed and paid by a private or government agency. (See Chapter 5.)

Four Ways of Parenting Description: for any situation that requires parenting—advising and supporting—there are four possible ways of responding. Nurturing ways and structuring and protecting ways encourage positive self-esteem. Marshmallowing and criticizing ways tear down self-esteem. The four ways are described below.

Nurturing Parent: a parent or adult who gives love and gives permission to love, to be loved, to change, and to be a winner. This person uses a gentle voice and gives *positive strokes for being* and *positive strokes for doing* well and gives *negative strokes about doing* poorly in a soft way. (See Italicized words in Glossary.)

> Example: Being—"You're important to me." Doing well—"I'm pleased with your careful driving." Doing poorly—"I want you to slow down on County Road 6. It's under construction, and road conditions change suddenly."

The nurturing-parent message invites a person to get his or her needs met. It offers to help. It gives permission to do things well. It affirms!

The nurturing parent recognizes and validates the personhood of the other as being important, having strength(s), having the capacity to grow, practicing self-control, being self-determined, having goals, not being intentionally hurtful or destructive, and as being loving and lovable.

The nurturing parent gives "I" messages about personal reactions to the other's behavior and uses touch to say "I'm glad you're here. . . . I care about you. . . . I'm with you."

The nurturing parent is *gentle, caring,* and *supportive.*

Structuring and Protecting Parent: a parent or adult who protects, tells how to do things well, how to change, and how to win. This person offers options, sets limits, uses a firm voice, gives *positive strokes for being and for doing* well, and gives firm *negative strokes about doing* poorly.

> Example: "I'm proud of you for passing your driving test on the first try. There is something I want you to consider. I've noticed that some kids drive carefully for a few weeks, and then as they get more confident, they get careless. Don't do that. If you feel yourself wanting to do that, remember your good defensive driving skills."

The structuring-parent message affirms and supports the other person as a growing person who is capable and is building on strengths by offering choices, exploring alternatives and consequences, advocating traditions and ethics, demanding that preferred behavior be substituted for undesired behavior, setting up conditions so others can be successful, removing obstacles, offering appropriate incentives, telling or showing ways to build skills, providing for practice and feedback, and negotiating contracts and goals.

The structuring parent asks people to state what they want or need in a problem situation.

The structuring and protecting parent is *assertive, sets limits, demands performance,* and *offers tools.*

Marshmallowing Parent: a parent or adult who gives permission to fail and is grandiose. This parent gives *plastic strokes* and *positive strokes for being and for doing* well. He gives *negatives* about doing poorly with a rider that implies "I don't think you can ever make it by yourself." The marshmallowing parent discourages responsibility and encourages people to feel inadequate. (See italicized words in this Glossary.)

> Examples: "I know you are a careful driver, dear. I had the brakes checked, and I filled the gas tank because you're so important to me that I didn't want to take a chance that you'd forget to do that. I guess I'll ride along to be sure you find your way."

The marshmallowing-parent message sounds supportive, but it invites dependency, gives permission to fail, and negates. The marshmallowing parent judges the other as weak and inadequate—lacking strengths, lacking the ability to grow and learn, lacking self-control, and lacking self-determination.

A marshmallowing parent blames other people, situations, or fate. This parent uses "You" messages, such as "You poor thing. . . . I'll do it for you. . . . You must have had a lucky/bad break. . . . There's nothing you can do." This type of parenting enables self-destructive behavior and leads a person to wish for magic. This parent carries the other person's burden or invites a person to be responsible for other people's feelings.

The marshmallowing parent is *sticky, patronizing,* and *seductive.*

Criticizing Parent: a parent or adult who tells how to fail. This person compares, blames, uses global words, such as *always* and *never,* gives *negatives about doing* poorly, gives *"don't be" messages,* and gives information and suggestions about how to fail.

> Examples: "You dummy, you'll never learn to drive! You should have noticed that car behind you. I bet you never look in the rearview mirror! And furthermore, I suppose you'll start to drink, and then I'll have to worry about your driving while you're drunk."

A criticizing-parent message ridicules, tears down, shows or tells how to fail, and negates. It judges the other person as unacceptable by blaming and faultfinding, comparing the person with others, labeling or name-calling, using "why" questions to accuse or trap the other, and offering no solutions.

The criticizing-parent message encourages a person to do poorly or to do self-destructive acts, assumes a person is responsible for other people's feelings, uses touch in hurtful or punishing ways, and uses caustic, sarcastic, or cruel humor.

The criticizing parent is *harsh, hurtful, blaming, shaming,* and *discouraging.*

Four Ways of Parenting Exercise:[1] a method of differentiating parenting styles. The person who is using the four ways of parenting can improve his parenting skills and sharpen his ability to separate helpful and destructive parenting messages. The positive responses are *nurturing* messages and *structuring and protecting* messages, while the destructive ones are the *marshmallowing* and *criticizing* messages. (See italicized terms in this Glossary.)

The exercise can be read or can be role played. In the role play, one person sits on a chair and says the problem situation he wants to hear four messages about (a nurturing, a structuring and protecting, a marshmallowing, and a criticizing message). He listens while four people stand behind him and give the four messages. If the problem is stated by an adult (for example: "I want to. . . ."), the parenting messages are given as he might say them to himself or as another adult might say them to him. If the problem is stated as coming from a child (for example: "I am six years old and I want to. . . ."), the parenting messages are given as an adult might say them to a child of this age. (See examples of Four Ways of Parenting exercises on pages 15-16, 46-47, 72-73, 104-105, 138-139, 169-170, 204-205, 231-232, and 254-255.)

Frame of Reference:[5] the picture frame of past experience through which one looks at life.

>Example: Chinese children whose jackets button up the back have a different frame of reference about helping and being helped than American children who are given zippered jackets and urged to become independent dressers at an early age. (See Chapter 5, page 119; Chapter 6, page 151; and Chapter 8, page 217.)

Good Mothers or Good Fathers List: a collection of early messages that people carry in their heads about what "good mothers" and "good fathers" do and are. The messages can have powerful impact on the way adults relate to children. It is the responsibility of adults to be aware of their "good mothers" and "good fathers" lists and to update messages that are no longer functional. (See A Good Mother list and A Good Father list on pages 24-27.)

Healthy Hassling: the art of challenging the values, ideas, observations, expectations, and intentions of another person by asking questions, making observations, and offering suggestions in a probing, persistent, challenging, loving way. Healthy hassling is a nurturing activity. It is especially important to challenge six- to twelve-year-old children in this way because their developmental task is to incorporate their own value system. (See Chapter 6, pages 155-159 and 167.)

"I" Message:[6] states how I feel, what I will do or not do, what I want, and what I see. These messages do not include blaming statements or commands, such as "I think you should shape up" and "Take out the garbage," or "You" statements, such as "You sure are angry."

Marasmus:[7] a condition of apathy and loss of physical strength caused by lack of touching. It is usually found in infants. (See Chapter 2, page 32.)

Marshmallowing Parent: (See *Four Ways of Parenting Description* in this Glossary.)

Negations: powerful, negative messages—verbal or nonverbal—which define who we are and how we expect to be treated.

>Example: "I'm not a worthwhile person, and there is nothing I can do about that. I don't deserve to live."

These negative messages can be given to us by other people and by ourselves. (For further examples, see *"don't be" messages*, page 266, and Chapter 2, page 33.)

Negative Strokes for Being: negative units of recognition that the receiver has done nothing to earn. They are *"don't be" messages*. (For further examples, see "Don't Be" Messages worksheet, page 21.)

Negative Strokes for Doing: negative units of recognition that the receiver earned by doing something poorly. (For further examples, see Messages About Doing Poorly worksheet, page 19. See also Chapter 1, page 7; Chapter 5, page 132; and Chapter 6, page 155.)

Nuclear Family: a social unit composed of a mother, a father, and their children, all of whom are living together. (See Chapter 2, page 38.)

Nurturing Parent: (See *Four Ways of Parenting Description* in this Glossary.)

Plastic Strokes or Messages: units of recognition that have both a positive and a negative quality. They may start out sounding positive and feeling good and end with a sting, a question, or a rider that implies they aren't wholly true. (For further examples, see Plastics worksheet, page 20. See also Chapter 1, pages 7, 8, and 9.)

Positive Offerings for Being Capable: messages that tell people what and how they have done well or how they are able to do well. (See *Positive Strokes for Doing* and *Positive Rewards for Doing Well* in this Glossary. See also Chapter 1, page 6.)

Positive Rewards for Being: positive strokes for existing. They may be verbal ("Hello, Auntie Maude") or nonverbal (a hug and a smile). They are unconditional; they do not have to be earned. (See Chapter 1, page 7, and Chapter 2, page 33.)

Positive Rewards for Doing Well: compliments, gifts, certificates, hugs — any message that tells people they are behaving in a capable manner. (See *Positive Offerings for Being Capable* and *Positive Strokes for Doing* in this Glossary. See also Chapter 1, page 6, and Chapter 6, page 151.)

Positive Strokes for Being: positive units of recognition that don't have to be earned. They are positive rewards for existing. (For further examples, see Positive Rewards for Being worksheet, page 17. See also Chapter 1, page 6, and Chapter 2, page 33.)

Positive Strokes for Doing: positive units of recognition that the receiver earned or achieved by demonstrating capability in some way. (For further examples, see Positive Rewards for Doing worksheet, page 18. See also Chapter 1, page 5 and 6.)

Recycling: the process by which people reexperience earlier developmental stages in a more sophisticated manner at later ages. (Recycling is described by Pam Levin in *Becoming the Way We Are.*[8]) Teenagers reexplore each step of early development. Adults can recycle any earlier stage at any time. Recycling specific stages can be triggered by grief, loss, moving, or any kind of stress. Adults may recycle on a rhythm based on age. Parents are triggered to reexperience their own early stages of growth as they watch their children go through each growing stage. Each recycling is a new opportunity to resolve any developmental tasks unsuccessfully completed earlier. (See Chapter 6, page 153; Chapter 7, pages 184-191; and Chapter 8, page 219.)

Redefinition:[9] a specific process of altering stimuli to fit a preconceived frame of reference. The stimuli can be strokes, information, or general observations.

> Examples: Margaret admires Mike's curly hair. Margaret says, "I like your curls!" Mike does not like his hair, so Mike responds, "It needs to be cut." Redefining can also be done internally. For example, Mike can say "Thanks" and think "I wonder what she wants."

> Or, Alice can believe that she's not supposed to enjoy life. So, when Joe says, "Alice, the weather is perfect today, and the trees and leaves are beautifully green," Alice will reply, "Yes, but it's the third of July, and soon August will be here. And things will already be turning brown." (See Chapter 8, pages 217-219 and 237.)

Self-Esteem: one's assessment of the extent to which one is lovable and capable. Self-esteem is nourished by recognizing one's own lovableness and capabilities and by being recognized as lovable and capable by other people. It is the responsibility of adults to model self-esteem for children by keeping their own (the adults') self-esteem high, to offer positive self-esteem messages to children, and to teach children how to be responsible for their own self-esteem. (See Chapter 1, pages 3, 4, and 10-11, and Chapter 9, pages 248-253.)

Separating Sex and Nurturing Contract:[10] an agreement to nurture another person for a given amount of time without any sexual overtones.
> Example: One person says, "For twenty minutes I'll nurture you in any way that you want me to. I'll hold you, rub your back, or do whatever you want." The other person responds, "All right, today I want you to make me cocoa and cinnamon toast, pay attention just to me for the whole twenty minutes, and not answer the telephone or the door bell. Another day I may want you to hold me, but today it's cocoa and cinnamon toast."

Some people don't succeed at this the first few times they try it but say that it was worth persevering when they succeed in getting what they want and need. It is important for people to take turns, so they don't end up with one person nourished and one depleted. (See Chapter 2, page 39, and Chapter 6, pages 161-162.)

Single-Parent Family: a family unit consisting of children living with one parent. The other parent may be dead or living elsewhere. Although there are a growing number of single-parent families headed by men, the majority of single-parent families in the United States are headed by women.

According to the United States Census Bureau Report, "Household and Family Characteristics," in 1976 there were seven and one-third million families headed by women with no man present. This figure shows an increase of one-third over the previous decade. (See Chapter 3.)

Stroke: a unit of recognition or human interaction. It can be positive, negative, or both. It can be verbal or nonverbal, sincere or insincere. Strokes—like air, food, water, and shelter—are necessary for health. (See Chapter 2, pages 32-33 and 39.)

> Examples: a smile, a wink, a hello, a kick in the shins, a telegram, a letter, a gift, a hug, a telephone call, a dirty look, an insult, an "I love you."

(See also *Negations, Affirmations, Positive Strokes for Being, Positive Strokes for Doing, Negative Strokes for Doing, Negative Strokes for Being*, and *Plastic Strokes* in this Glossary.)

Stroke Bank Theory:[11] an analogy that compares the amount of strokes one seeks out and records internally to a bank balance. (See Chapter 4, pages 95-97 and 108-109.)

> Example: Consider Jim's stroke bank. It is the size that will hold an optimum amount of strokes for him. (People's banks may be different sizes—two bushels, a ton, four kilograms. No matter, each person's bank will hold the amount that person needs.) If Jim's bank were empty, Jim would be dead. If Jim's bank is zero to twenty percent filled, his stroke level is dangerously low! People whose stroke banks are that low are usually institutionalized, and Jim would be in a hospital or prison.
>
> When Jim's bank is twenty to sixty-six and two-thirds percent full, Jim is just living, getting along, surviving another day. "Thank goodness it's Friday" or "Oh, yuk, Monday again!" is his attitude. Jim needs strokes and will grab almost any stroke that is offered. Plastics and negatives are better than none. (See *Plastics* and *Negatives* in this Glossary.)
>
> If Jim's level is between sixty-six and two-thirds to eighty-seven and one-half percent, Jim is experiencing good living and feels really great. He looks for positive strokes and rejects negatives.
>
> When Jim's bank is eighty-seven and one-half to one hundred

percent full, Jim's stroke level is in the safety-deposit box area. His stroke bank is so full that he can put some strokes away for arid times. He actively seeks positive strokes; his well-being and vitality attract them, and he is comfortable rejecting negative strokes. Adults are responsible for keeping their own stroke bank levels high. They use stroke rules to help them keep their strokes at certain levels.

(For further examples, see *Stroke Rules* in this Glossary.)

Stroke Base: the group of people from whom strokes are regularly received. It might include only self and immediate family but could also include extended family, colleagues, and regular social contacts. (See *Extended Stroke Base* and *Strokes* in this Glossary.)

Stroke Buffet: the total collection of positive and negative messages and experiences that a family offers a child and from which the child selects significant early messages. Adults are responsible for putting positive, healthy messages on the buffet. Children are responsible for choosing and deciding what to do with the messages. And later, they are responsible for updating them. Adults are responsible for challenging the child to think about and be responsible for the messages she/he has chosen. (See Chapter 8, pages 222-225 and 235-236.)

Stroke Drain: any situation or internal rule that pulls down energy and self-esteem. Examples of situations include fatigue, grief, illness, or injuries. Example of an internal rule: "If too many good things happen to you, you'll have to pay (or suffer)." (See Chapter 2, page 38.)

Stroke Economy: the total of the ways one receives, gives, denies, seeks, accepts, rejects, asks for, discards, takes, and redefines recognition or strokes and the feelings one has about these strokes. Stroke economy includes one's rules for controlling feelings about different kinds of strokes and the flow of strokes. It is also the way one stores, remembers, and recycles strokes. The establishment and maintenance of one's stroke economy is a major factor in the way one structures time, chooses relationships, and chooses motivations. (See Chapter 7, pages 196-201.)

Stroke Level: the number that indicates to what percent one's stroke bank is filled. (For further information, see *Stroke Bank Theory*, Chapter 4, page 95. See also Chapter 4, pages 108-109.)

Stroke Quotient Decision Theory: suggests that people decide what proportion of positive and negative messages they deserve and that they then seek out those responses, possibly without realizing that is what they are doing.

The stroke quotient theory hypothesizes one way that young children make sense of their world. They decide that the number of positive and negative strokes they get is somehow correct for them. Because this is a very early and primitive decision, people go through their lives setting themselves up, outside of their conscious awareness perhaps, to continue to get the same proportion of positive and negative strokes they got as a young child. The theory explains some choices of peers and spouses and some people's conversion of positive strokes into negative ones and vice versa. It also explains why, once individuals become aware that each person decides what his/her stroke quotient is, they can change that decision and behavior and improve their stroke economy dramatically. (See Chapter 3, pages 57-58.)

Stroke Rules: indicate what strokes we should give, take, ask for, believe, or discount. Everyone of us needs strokes every day. Stroke rules can protect us and help us fill our stroke banks, or they can encourage us to discount strokes. Discounting strokes is reducing the number and quality of strokes that we collect. Our rules are offered to us by our culture, by our families, schools, churches, peer groups, and by ourselves. They can be used to help us make our stroke quotient decisions come true. They are our responsibility. If they aren't working for us, it's our job to update them. (For further examples, see Stroke Rules worksheet, pages 76-79; Thoughts About Changing Stroke Rules worksheet, page 80; and Chapter 7, pages 199-200.)

Structuring Parent: (See *Four Ways of Parenting Description* in this Glossary.)

Visualizing: the process of deciding how you want to see yourself or another person and of then creating that image in your mind's eye. It is a way of focusing energy for positive, supportive attitudes and behavior.

> Example: Thirteen-month-old Andrea climbs, shakes, pokes, pushes, and tastes her environment with the energy of a frisky puppy. Her mother, Deborah, feels tired and impatient and recognizes her wish to inhibit the child. Deborah pauses, stands straight, plants both feet firmly on the ground, balances her weight between them, breathes deeply, closes her eyes, and imagines her child older, in school, listening as the teacher says, "You can figure this out on your own." Deborah sees Andrea as alert, interested, confident of her ability to discover the data and understand the connections and implications of her findings. Or, Deborah centers herself, takes a deep breath, and visualizes herself as rested, calm, capable, and enjoying watching her important, energetic thirteen-month-old Andrea learning to trust herself in her environment, testing her senses, and claiming her creativity and ability to discover and enjoy life.

(See Chapter 2, page 37.)

What You Stroke Is What You Get: the belief that rewarding behavior in either a positive or a negative way encourages that behavior. For example, complaining to a child "You're so noisy!" tells the child that you expect her to be noisy. Noticing when she is quiet, even for a moment, and saying "Thank you for being quiet" encourages the child to be quiet.

It is easy to stroke what people already do well. Jim is a good thinker so it is easy to tell him how smart he is, which encourages him to focus more on thinking well. Stroking him equally for his thinking, for his nurturing, and for his structuring and protecting abilities and stroking him for such qualities as spontaneity, creativity, willingness to compromise, and other positive adaptations will encourage him to grow in all areas. (See worksheets on pages 51-53, 74-75, 106-107, 140-141, 174-175, 210-211, and 233-234.)

Notes

1. For information on *affirmation blocks*, see page 154.

2. For information on *affirmation cymbals*, see page 154.

3. For further reading, see Jacqui Lee Schiff, *Cathexis Reader* (New York: Harper & Row, 1975), Chapter 2.

4. Thanks to Sheila Hartmann and Sally Dierks for helping to conceptualize and develop this exercise.

5. Schiff, op. cit., Chapter 5.

6. For further reading on "I" messages, see Thomas Gordon, *P.E.T., Parent Effectiveness Training: The Tested New Way to Raise Responsible Children* (New York: Peter H. Wyden, 1970; New York: New American Library, 1975).

7. For further reading on marasmus, see Ashley Montagu, *Touching: The Human Significance of Skin* (New York: Harper & Row, 1971).

8. For further reading, see Pam Levin, *Becoming the Way We Are: A Transactional Guide to Personal Development* (Berkeley, Calif.: Transactional Publications, 1974), p. 50.

9. For further reading, see Jacqui Lee Schiff, op. cit., Chapter 2.

10. Thanks to Jerry and Terri White for suggesting this idea.

11. For a description of the Stroke Survival Quotient, which Hedges Capers later called the Stroke Bank Theory, see Hedges Capers and Glen Holland, "Stroke Survival Quotient or Stroke Grading," *Transactional Analysis Journal* 1, no. 3 (July 1971):40.

Bibliography

Babcock, Dorothy E., and Keepers, Terry D. *Raising Kids O.K.: Transactional Analysis in Human Growth and Development.* New York: Avon Books, 1977. History, tasks, and needs of families and the people in them; psychological development of infants to adolescents; and how to deal with problems in child rearing.

Briggs, Dorothy Corkille. *Your Child's Self-Esteem: The Key to Life.* New York: Doubleday, Dolphin Books, 1975. Briggs discusses mirroring, self-image, safety, journeys of self, handling feelings and discipline.

Dusay, John. *Egograms.* New York: Harper & Row, 1977. Readable explanation of personality and how to strengthen the various parts.

Ernst, Ken. *Pre-Scription: A TA Look at Child Development.* Millbrae, Calif.: Celestial Arts, 1976. An introduction to the concept of scripts (plans for living one's life)—how children attempt to make sense of the messages they receive and how those messages and decisions can produce winners or losers.

Fraiberg, Selma H. *The Magic Years: Understanding and Handling the Problems of Early Childhood.* New York: Scribner, 1968. Gives a detailed and interesting description of how children mature from birth to six years and of the problems associated with each stage of development.

James, Muriel, and Jongeward, Dorothy. *Born to Win: Transactional Analysis with Gestalt Experiments.* Reading, Mass.: Addison-Wesley, 1971. Explains TA theory and how to use it for yourself and with others.

James, Muriel, and Jongeward, Dorothy. *Transactional Analysis for Moms and Dads: What Do You Do with Them Now That You've Got Them.* Reading, Mass.: Addison-Wesley, 1974. How parents can use TA in their families to deal with feelings and with family crises.

LeShan, Eda. *What Makes Me Feel This Way: Growing Up with Human Emotions.* New York: Macmillan, Collier Books, 1974. Describes human emotions in a way that children can understand. Helpful for grown-ups, too.

Levin, Pam. *Becoming the Way We Are: A Transactional Guide to Personal Development.* Berkeley, Calif.: Transactional Publications, 1974. Transactional Analysis from a developmental point of view, including the "permissions" that are the base of the affirmation exercises in *Self-Esteem: A Family Affair.*

Levin Landheer, Pamela. *The Fuzzy Frequency.* San Francisco, Calif.: Transactional Publications, 1978. A delightful, eye-catching story for people of all ages that tells the what, how to, and why of warm fuzzies.

Reid, Clyde. *Celebrate the Temporary.* New York: Harper & Row, 1972. An invitation to experience today, fully, with delight.

Satir, Virginia. *Peoplemaking.* Palo Alto, Calif.: Science and Behavior Books, 1972. A warm book about family process and how the people who make up the families can build self-worth and improve communications.

Steiner, Claude. *The Original Warm Fuzzy Tale.* Berkeley, Calif.: Transactional Publications, 1977. A story about warm fuzzies and cold pricklies by the man who originated the concept.

Acknowledgments

Thanks to Dick, Marc, Jennifer, and Wade Clarke for being and for growing with me.

Thanks to all the families from whom I have learned and with whom I have enjoyed.

Special thanks to Pam Levin Landheer for providing the affirmations and the theory of recycling and for your encouragement and your careful editing of the manuscript.

Thanks to Joanne Moses, my advisor in Transactional Analysis, for encouraging me to write and to become.

Thanks to Hedges and Betty Capers for encouraging me to grow and to know.

Thanks to Marie Fielder for describing the family in Chapter 4, to Judee Soucek for the scenario of the family misusing chemicals in Chapter 8, to Sally Dierks for your contributions to the sections on grief, and to Sheila Hartmann for identifying the issues in Chapter 5.

Thanks to Adelaide von Alven, Jean Koski, Laura Thorpe, Deane Gradous, Ellen Walton, Claudia Freund, Jim Hartmann, Marjorie Marquis, Lorrie Casselton, and Diane England for your thoughtful reading and helpful insights.

Thanks to all of the facilitators of the classes in Mothers, Fathers, and Others Who Care About Children for your energy, support, ideas, confrontations, and love.

Thanks to Sandy Stoltz and Sonia Rada for pushing me to claim my creativity.

Special thanks to Sally Dierks and Sheila Hartmann for your friendship and nurturing, continuous challenges, creative support, and contagious laughter, and to Sheila for your willing typing.

Jean Illsley Clarke, author of Self-Esteem: A Family Affair, *founded the family-care workshops "Mothers, Fathers, and Others Who Care About Children." Besides acting as a consultant for the University of Minnesota, Ms. Clarke also teaches Transactional Analysis to university management personnel. Active in adult education for over twenty years, she has worked extensively with children from nursery school through adolescence. Ms. Clarke holds a master's degree in human development from St. Mary's College in Winona. Sne is married and has three children.*

Ms. Clarke conducts workshops for people who want to facilitate a group learning experience based on Self-Esteem: A Family Affair. *In addition, she has developed a leader guide which provides a systematic approach to the use of this book in eight group sessions.* Self-Esteem: A Family Affair Leader Guide *is available from Winston Press, 430 Oak Grove, Minneapolis, Minnesota 55403. Inquiries about the leader guide and other ideas in the program may be directed to Ms. Clarke, care of Winston Press.*

Thoughts on Ending. . . .

I hope you have used this book to help you find ways to value yourself and other people more. I had a whole bunch of fun writing it. Thank you for joining me.

Jean Illsley Clarke